FAITH AND THE OTHER

A Relational Theology

PAUL R. SPONHEIM

FORTRESS PRESS   MINNEAPOLIS

FAITH AND THE OTHER
A Relational Theology

Scripture quotations unless otherwise noted are from the New Revised Standard
Version Bible, copyright © 1989 by the Division of Christian Education of the
National Council of the Churches of Christ in the United States.

Cover design: Terry W. Bentley
Cover illustration: "Western Sky," tapestry by Julia Schloss, Bar Harbor, Maine.
Other credits appear on page 248.

Library of Congress Cataloging-in-Publication Data
Sponheim, Paul R.
    Faith and the other : a relational theology / Paul R. Sponheim.
      p.   cm.
    Includes bibliographical references and index.
    ISBN 0-8006-2658-3 :
    1. Theology—Methodology. 2. Theology—20th century. 3. Faith. 4. Christianity
and other religions. I. Title. II. Title: The other. III. Title: Relational theology.
BR118.S686   1993
291.2—dc20   92-35718
                                                              CIP

The paper used in this publication meets the minimum requirements of American
National Standard for Information Sciences—Permanence of Paper for Printed
Library Materials, ANSI Z329.48-1984.   ∞™

Manufactured in the U.S.A.   AF 1-2658

97   96   95   94   93   1   2   3   4   5   6   7   8   9   10

CONTENTS

Preface   v

1. The Critical Massing of the Many   1
   Qualitative Change in Worldview   5
   Where in the World Is God?   16

PART ONE: EXCAVATING LIFE IN RELATION TO THE OTHER

2. Life within the Other   25
   Life within the Spacetime Continuum   25
   Life with Nature within the Spacetime Continuum   33
   Life within the Body with Nature within
        the Spacetime Continuum   40

3. Life with the Other   51
   The Givenness of the Other   51
   The Gift and Task of Self and Other   57
   The Claim of Self and Other   67

4. Life "before" the Other   75
   The Categorical Difference:
        We Turn to One Who Is First   75
   The Transcendent Commitment:
        The One Who Is First Is for Us   87
   Consequences in Life and Thought:
        We Live "before" the Other   101

PART TWO: EXPLORING FAITH AND OTHERNESS

5. To Become Other in Faith   111
        Faith's Direction   111
        Faith's Resources   124
        Faith's Telos   135

6. To Be with the Others in Faith   147
        Discerning the Difference of Other Faiths   148
        Claiming the Connection of Unfaith   159
        Living Faithfully and Fruitfully   166

Notes   177

Index   238

Credits   248

PREFACE

This book seeks to help the person of faith find and face the one who or that which is other. It would speak of some one or something meeting us truly from outside—outside our skin, our thinking, our believing, our world.

I offer here, then, a relational theology: the book is about relationships with the other. The argument seeks to deepen awareness of the other and to guide the person of faith in a living and believing that responds to that awareness.

Thus the book begins with the nearly undeniable fact of our human experience of otherness. Increasingly, the other is "given" for us as we see faces and hear names that are truly new for us. And as I meet the other(s), I become anxiously aware that my sense of reality, my world, is no longer available to me as a secure possession. Were it not so visually obstructive, I would regularly place the words *other* and *otherness* in quotation marks to indicate precisely this loss of a comfortable worldview in which the subject/object distinction reigns supreme. This may seem a perilous time. It is not strange that in such a time people might respond by "cleansings." To be pure one must act—so runs the logic of anxiety. In fact, we hear reports of certain decisive actions that are painful reminders of ethnic holocausts and religious wars thought to be safely interred in some dark past. This is indeed an anxious age. But the first chapter closes with the conviction that informs the whole book: Christian faith is well suited for travel across boundaries once thought firm but now seen to be eroding.

The longer part of the book then places the contemporary dramatic experience of human otherness in the deep context provided when we realize that our very life is constituted by relationship: we live in, with, and "before" the other. Such relationship is not optional. To speak of the other is to speak of spacetime, of our bodies, of that other human being whom I may have mistakenly assumed is just like me. And it is to speak of God.

In these several speakings one makes more fully the point Elizabeth A. Johnson stresses in her fine new book *She Who Is: The Mystery of God in Feminist Theological Discourse* regarding the import of Trinitarian speech about God, that "relatedness rather than the solitary ego is the heart of all reality."[1] I regret that Johnson's important study had not yet appeared when this book was being written. Sadly, the timing involved in publication schedules also prevented consideration of Catherine Mowry LaCugna's significant work *God for Us: The Trinity and Christian Life.* In joining Johnson in stressing the ontological priority of relatedness LaCugna not only includes the several "others" that concern me, but boldly derives this emphasis from her understanding of trinitarian faith in God: "The living God is the God who is alive in relationship, alive in communion with the creature, alive with desire for union with every creature. God is so thoroughly involved in every last detail of creation that if we could truly grasp this it would altogether change how we approach every moment of our lives. For everything that exists—insect, agate, galaxy—manifests the mystery of the living God."[2]

Relationships are not optional, but in this given relatedness crucial choices face anyone who seeks to believe and live as a Christian. We need to face the other who is given; we need to find the other in the given. Part Two takes up these challenges by considering how the Christian is called to become other within continuing Christian existence (chap. 5) and to live faithfully and fruitfully with those whose faith is truly other than Christian (chap. 6).

This book is a relational theology in a second sense. I seek to write about relationships and *to do so relationally*. The subject of otherness is not faith's private property. While I have written as a Christian, the structure of the discussion is not one dictated by Christian considerations. The discussion does not come tidily to rest within traditional dogmatic loci. In this sense the conversation here may be what Ted Peters has called ecumenic (as distinguished from ecumenical): "It points to the window of faith that opens out toward the world beyond. It opens out to the universe that lies beyond the church."[3]

Peters is emphatic that ecumenic courage calls for the Christian to recognize that "no field of knowledge is off limits." I agree. Moreover, the very discussion of the other cannot be controlled by the structure that Christian dogmatic self-understanding comfortably provides. One can read this book as taking up the theme of otherness, as given to Christian *and human* existence, as that theme cuts across several doctrines: God, creation, anthropology, cosmology, person and work of Christ, the church, last things. But I have not written with such a systematic list controlling the discussion.

This departure from systematic order may be confusing. Furthermore, difference marks not only the structure for the conversation but also the voices to be heard in it. My hope is that any confusion the book occasions in the reader will derive only from the reality of the living situation I seek to describe. Particularly in describing in Part One the deep rhythm of relationship constituting life, I draw on many sources, though I am painfully aware that I lack the range and depth needed to treat the topic truly adequately. And the diversity in this book is not only one of sources of information; it is a diversity of *voice*. The composition is fugal, fitting the complexity of life. The voices are many; one may not be able to discern a familiar melody line. But I do not seek to worship cacophony. Thus the book closes with comment on how one may hear the voice of the other, discerning difference and claiming connection in faithful and fruitful ways. (In trying to hear voices from the past, I have been persuaded to avoid sprinkling *sic* throughout the many quotations where noninclusive language exists. Perhaps the fact that we have relatively recently recognized the importance of this matter is both discouraging and encouraging.)

I believe the Christian is called to find and face such difference and diversity in conversation. Simply as a human being, the Christian is placed in such a position by the collapsing of the Enlightenment's dominion over all rules for rational thinking. And as a Christian the believer is called to such recognition by what Patrick Keifert has written of in other terms as the biblical call to "welcome the stranger."[4] I am a white male North American Christian, but I need to listen to other voices. There are many voices that need to be heard, voices within and outside the church. To find and face such diversity entails risk. We need to proceed with considerable care. We will need to make distinctions, but we will also need to beware of making distinctions—as between description and prescription, between an inner pluralism and an outer one—too early, too cleanly, too finally. That is how it is with the other. There is necessary risk, but in the risk there is promise as well. After all, a relational theology is about difference and *connection*. The book surely makes clear that we do live together. I hope it shows as well that we can speak together.

So this book is an outline and an invitation. The skeletal structure of relationship is exposed for faith's attention and a proposal is made for how a person of faith may live and believe in recognition of that structure. I hope that others—yes, *others*—will respond to the invitation and join the conversation for the good of faith and the other.

I have had help from many already in the issuing of the invitation. I wish to thank the board of Luther Northwestern Theological Seminary and its president, Dr. David Tiede, for granting me sabbatical study time and for continuing support in this effort. Many colleagues have assisted me in this work. Those who read the entire manuscript were Terence Fretheim, Mary Knutsen, Paul V. Martinson, Kirsten Mickelson, Linda Nelson, Ron Olson, Lee Snook, Don Sponheim, and Curtis Thompson. I am grateful to the student assistants who over the years have helped me in the preparation of this manuscript: Neal Halvorson, Mary Lowe, Mary Wallum, and Jan Wiersma. Dianne Jelle and Paula Murphy provided exceptionally competent secretarial service. Timothy G. Staveteig and others at Fortress Press have worked hard at trying to make the discussion no more confusing than it need be.

Finally, I dedicate this book to my companions in the conversation. I think first of my companion for nearly forty years, my wife, Nell. She has tried to help me understand and live the wise words of Alfred North Whitehead: "Seek simplicity and distrust it!" Her task has not been an easy one, and she deserves a thank-you. I complete this preface as I begin my thirty-second year of teaching. Particular student faces come emphatically into my mind, evoking a strong sense of gratitude. I say thank you to these companions in the conversation, even as I make bold to invite others to join us.

1

THE CRITICAL MASSING
OF THE MANY

Like many millions of people, I am a bastard child of history. Perhaps we all are, black and brown and white, leaking into one another, as a character of mine once said, like flavours when you cook. (Salman Rushdie)[1]

DIFFERENCE QUALITATIVE AND UNDENIABLE

Many of us living in the West would agree with Rushdie that our lives cannot be lived alone—in undisturbed continuity, self-contained or even self-directed, as it were. Indeed, the word "leaking" may understate the tempo of change. Terms like "coursing" or "cascading" might come closer to catching the character of our life with "the other." It is not a quiet time. That a new millennium soon dawns may seem a somewhat melodramatic but essentially fitting accompaniment to what is sounding in our lives. Something is happening, something having to do with the other. The current of change in which we are caught may be marked in dramatic events or it may flow more quietly, "leaking" beneath the superficially solid surfaces of the faces we present to the world and to ourselves. But, one way or another, willingly or not, we are increasingly having to do with the other. There may be promise in this—or risk. But that the one who or that which is different will make a difference for us, that much is becoming increasingly clear to us. In the meal that history is making, the flavors do come together. To turn the metaphor another way, the meal does not seem to come out of a melting pot; at least things taste rather strange.

Who and/or what is the other? I will use this category to remark concerning our relationships with a wide range of realities, including our own bodies, spacetime, and God. But it is likely that what we are most immediately and dramatically aware of in this connection is that we human beings are other to each other. Moreover, while any two human beings will suffice to demonstrate otherness, certain differences strike us with special forcefulness—notably those associated with race, gender and class. Such otherness seems hard to ignore. Yet the dominant group or culture can deal with even such dramatic difference without truly engaging it. Consider the field of art. In the past the dominant artistic culture may have recognized different voices by absorbing them. Or it could marginalize the blacker, the more Spanish, Indian Asian, feminist or gay as exotic titillation.[2] Such a strategy will face difficult going in the time that is ahead. Already in the 1980s the rate of increase in the minority population was nearly twice as fast as in the 1970s, which led demographers to speak of "the dawning of the first universal nation."[3] At some point such massing of difference becomes critical. For example, recent events in the world of art suggest a challenge that is qualitative. As the 1980s ended and the 1990s began, the art sections of the newspapers were dominated by debates concerning the boundaries of "good taste."[4]

THE NATURE OF BOUNDARIES
That word, "boundary," figures prominently in our lives. Therapists call on us to draw the boundaries in our interpersonal relationships and to observe them. But where are the boundaries to be drawn? We face this question as individuals and we do so as a people. It is not only at Stanford that people puzzle about which books belong in humankind's "core curriculum." How permanently can boundaries be drawn? After the tumultuous events of the last few years one cannot doubt that political boundaries are essentially subject to change. Walls once set in concrete stand no longer. What of other boundaries?

What *are* boundaries, in any case? Granted that they can change, when they are in effect how firm are they? On the one hand we sense that definite boundaries are essential to human identity. Wasn't Spinoza right that all meaning is by negation? If the other doesn't stay on the other side of the boundary (and I on mine), can we know or even be ourselves? The Oxford English Dictionary says that a boundary "indicates or fixes a limit." That sounds quite firm and may appeal to us as we sense the burgeoning reality of "the other." When we come to a boundary, we do know that on "the other side" lies that which is not our own. Yet realities meet at boundaries. At the boundary I sense not only difference but connectedness as well. Are boundaries perhaps not only malleable but permeable as well? Is that one reason why we sense promise and risk in the reality of the other? What looms for the self's identity at any particular boundary: erosion, destruction, expansion, enhancement?

FAITH'S STATE AND STAKE

I will respond to these questions in this book and will do so with particular attention to faith. People of faith share the experience of and interest in otherness and boundaries. In the last section of this chapter, I will argue that religious faith assigns special importance to the other. Moreover, the Christian—to take the example I claim as my own—senses a new urgency in the quest to live faithfully and fruitfully on the boundary with other faiths. Of course Christians have long manifested an interest in the other world religions and in their adherents. But this interest was referred to a specialized realm; most often, it was a concern to be handled under "foreign" missions. It is no longer so. Today, when the midwestern mainline Christian hears a daughter announce that she intends to marry the Buddhist boy she met at the university, that Christian knows that things will not be the same in the family. In 1986, Lutherans might rightly have concluded that things were changing when the Lutheran Council in the U.S.A. issued a report "for study and discussion" in which guidelines were given for participation in joint services of worship.[5] These Lutherans were not talking about praying with Presbyterians or Eucharist with Episcopalians! They were responding to the fact that it is now clear in the schools and streets of our heartland that Muslims, Hindus, and representatives of the other world faiths exist not only overseas or, say, on the East and West coasts.

If that were not enough, there is the dizzying expanse of the new religions. There is the "new age," which flows from the stereos and bookstores into the congregations and families of the faithful. Subjected to such a current, many of the boundaries we once thought firm do seem to erode: Creator/creation, body/mind, past/present/future, life/death, male/female, good/evil, religion/science.[6] In such a listing I am not proposing some pattern of parallelism. There are mixed cases here, but such a miscellany serves to suggest that boundaries once thought firm seem softer in many of the newer religious currents. A similar erosion may be at hand through more socially respectable routes, such as the remarkably influential work of Joseph Campbell as received through public television interviews with Bill Moyers. Under Campbell's evocation of *"the power of myth,"* "facts" softened, and the viewer could come to feel the call of the Hindu suggestion that the stories of the gods are really about us.[7] Campbell has been rather sharply criticized by some feminist writers for what they held to be a male-centered and patriarchal interpretation. But in some strands of feminist thought the same boundary of Creator/creature seems to be under stress. Here is Starhawk's way of putting the matter:

> The image of the Goddess inspires women to see ourselves as divine, our bodies as sacred, the changing phases of our lives as holy, our aggression as healthy, our anger as purifying and our power to nurture and create, but also to limit and destroy when necessary, as the very force which sustains all life. Through the Goddess, we can discover our strength, enlighten our bodies and celebrate our emotions. We can move beyond narrow constricting roles and become whole.[8]

Even the boundary with what might be supposed to be faith's clear opposite, *unfaith*, has come to seem less clear. There is a certain convenience for Christians to be able to define themselves over against the angry and unambiguous village atheist. But what are we to do when what stares at us is the softer face of someone like the physicist I. I. Rabi:

> So we reached a sort of *modus vivendi* where at home I conformed to everything. I didn't try to persuade them of anything else. They would have really suffered from that. They didn't ask very much what I did outside. So I was a good son in that respect. I have a great respect and a great feeling for those things. It's part of a culture, a way of life, an outlook. Sometimes I feel I shouldn't have dropped it so completely—I'm talking about the way of life. There's no question that basically, somewhere way down, I'm an orthodox Jew. In fact, to this day, if you ask for my religion, I say "Orthodox Hebrew"—in the sense that the church I'm not attending is that one. If I were to go to a church, that's the one I would go to. It doesn't mean I'm something else.[9]

"The church I'm not attending is that one"! Perhaps such troubled ambivalence may be most dramatically evident in the strongly familial reality of Judaism, but one wonders what diverse Christian parallels may exist.

THREAT AND PROMISE

Thus something is happening at boundaries—for faith as well. Such phenomena having to do with the meeting of the faiths and of faith and unfaith may be alarming. Alarms do get our attention. When we hear an alarm, we cannot block out what we are hearing. There is indeed something here that requires our attention. But must the power at work in the other simply threaten? Perhaps not. In 1987 the Association of Theological Schools issued a special journal supplement devoted to "Theological Education in a Religiously Diverse World." Margaret Miles of Harvard Divinity School well characterized the seriousness of the occasion by asking:

> Where do we go from the realization that our differences are irreducible, our beliefs and even our feelings are the products of our different perspectives? . . . Where do we go from the unsettling recognition that there is no value-free interpretation of each other or of our texts?[10]

That the other is truly other still seems here to carry the tone of threat. That the one who is different will make a difference for me is not seen as promise. But must it be so? In the same issue of *Theological Education,* Gayraud Wilmore could write that "diversity, for all the exasperating tensions and problems it creates, is an asset—no less a gift of God, to be treasured, rather than deplored."[11]

Perhaps. But does not diversity also threaten? Wilmore sought to distinguish between different kinds of diversity, including the diversity represented by "non-Christian faith communities." But his overarching affirmation of dialogue raises once again the questions concerning the nature of boundaries. That our experience of difference is itself dizzyingly diverse only intensifies our questions about the permanence and permeability of boundaries. As our experience of difference reaches critical mass, what insights may be claimed for and from faith?

QUALITATIVE CHANGE IN WORLDVIEW

It is clear, then, that I meet in the other what is truly different from, and yet genuinely connected with, me. So it is that we do bear upon each other in our connectedness, and yet our difference seems to hinder genuine understanding and appreciation. I will suggest that such experience with the other is to be found in our relationships with other-than-human realities—with nature, with God. But even in the experience of difference among human beings it is clear that as the number of encounters increases, so do the questions about boundaries. Those questions become personal. We can no longer assign them to "foreign" missionaries (with regard to faith differences) or to specialists in cross-cultural matters.

THE MODERN SELF/WORLD DISTINCTION UNDONE

The change we sense in our time has a subtler and more pervasive aspect to it as well. Our basic sense of reality is at risk. We seem to be undergoing a qualitative change in our worldview—a change so radical that we may hardly speak any longer of a "worldview." Such a change will materially affect our particular experiences—how we have them and what we make of them—including our experience of human difference. The change that I will seek to describe may have been caused in part by a general increase in contacts with the others. In turn it intensifies those experiences, as the other meets us in the open, outside the comfortable structure of an understanding that we had supposed was a universal home for humankind.

I am thinking of the apparent dismantling or erosion of that understanding we in the West have thought of as the "modern" world. Stephen Toulmin points out that "the chief girder in this framework of Modernity . . . was the Cartesian dichotomy."[12] René Descartes could not doubt his own existence as a doubting self, but he needed an appeal to a nondeceiving God to assure himself of the existence of the world.[13] It is not surprising, then, that if certainty is to be sought, it will be in the "clear and distinct" ideas of the human consciousness. Toulmin points out that Descartes was also interested in the empirical study of the world but that there too it was the clarity and distinctness of basic ideas that held the promise of "self-guaranteeing" certainty.[14]

Thus Descartes introduces us to the self/world distinction by which (we?) moderns understand reality. By virtue of our reason we human beings are other than nature, but we can confidently move to understand and act upon nature. The "two" in this dualism are not created equal. Descartes's reliance upon the self and its consciousness represents one form of inequality. In a strange way in the matter of assigning differing values to self and world the empiricist side of the Enlightenment parallels the Cartesian rationalism to which in a sense it is an alternative. David Hume is very clear that trustworthy knowing must begin with raw sense data which the subject passively receives and actively orders. Elsewhere Hume does write of a subject not so easily constructed out of the bits of color, taste, and smell—as when he writes of the self's moral sentiment.[15] But the dominant strain in the legacy of Hume seems to have been a view of reality by which what can be truly trusted is what can be seen, touched, tasted, and felt.

One encounters ambiguity in ascertaining the legacy of the Enlighten-ment, related perhaps to an inner volatility in the very structure of the self/world polarity. Polarities easily fall prey to polarization. Polarization can take the form of withdrawal or domination. Thus the distinction seems to offer a strong separation, even or perhaps especially in the tendency of self or world to monopolize being and knowing. At one level such mo-nopolies depend upon and in turn enhance the definiteness of the entities involved. The distinction between self and world is firm. Boundaries seem clear here, whether in Newton's "solid, hard, massy and impenetrable" atoms, in Leibniz's "windowless" monads making up all reality, or in the notion of the self-contained individual or nation-state.

Less clear is the boundary of the modern era itself. How long does the self/world structure hold sway? Does it still do so? Consider postclassical developments in the arts in the terms of this distinction. Here one can chart what might well be called an "emancipation of dissonance," the chaotic otherness of that which is not human.[16] John Cage, who died in 1992, struggled to "let sounds be themselves rather than vehicles for man-made theories or expressions of human sentiment," as he experimented with randomness, silence, and exotic rhythms.[17] Earlier, Cage's teacher, Arnold Schoenberg, had written music in which the tonal system was suspended. Using the twelve tone row without a tonal center, Schoenberg gave each note its own value and resisted the developmental unfolding of classical compositions. Something is different here, but just what is hard to assess. In such artists are we witnessing an attack on the reign of the self/world distinction and/or an expression of that distinction in objectivist terms?[18]

A similar question about the controlling subject can be charted in other developments concerning the arts. Hegel had spoken of primal art as a first ("primitive," as we say) stage in which the spiritual subject fails to find genuine representation. Thus he classified Chinese, Indian, and Egyp-tian art as immature in sensitivity, "formless or of a bad and false defi-niteness of form."[19] That would not be the judgment represented in Igor Stravinsky's *Rite of Spring* in which listeners are to be transported "to the foot of a sacred hill, in a lush plain, where Slavic tribes are gathered to celebrate the spring rites."[20] Such transport was available in Gauguin's version of Persia, the Far East, and ancient Europe. Here the viewer or hearer is at the very least moved to meet a subjectivity that is thought to be truly other. Yet one can ask, Is primitivism perhaps the mirror image of rationalism?[21]

Is the sovereignty of the subject still intact? In someone like Jackson Pollock the ordering subject is faced with an artist whose drippings broke with "traditional hand and wrist inflection" as they covered from all sides without regard to top and bottom those oversized canvases that defied the traditional illustrative "picture."[22] Here one can feel again a desire to break free of the objectifying control of the human subject. These developments speak for that which was ordered under the "object" in the accepted traditions of the arts. Pollock spoke of his art as "very representational some of the time and a little all of the time," and Stravinsky said of his octet that it "was not an 'emotive' work but a musical composition based on objective elements," such as form, movement, and volume.[23]

AMBIGUITY IN THE ENLIGHTENMENT HERITAGE

It is difficult to know how to evaluate this Enlightenment legacy. Does one not want to defend the Cartesian emphasis on the individual self and on the importance of clarity and precision in thought? Would one want to jettison the advances in medical technology made possible through a tradition of empirical research? But do not other developments—for example in nuclear energy—support Langdon Gilkey's judgment that "the human intellectual creativity represented by the Enlightenment has revealed itself not only as ambiguous but also as potentially lethal"?[24] Jürgen Habermas may point the way for us in seeking to distinguish in modernity an intersubjective, community-based "communicative rationality" from an instrumental subject/object rationality.[25] Thus it would be only the second, or subject/object, rationality that would justify Richard Falk's criticism, when he speaks of the failure of the modern world as "associated with false and constraining boundaries":

> The problems of modernity would be less severe if the separateness could be consistently sustained, but it cannot. It is the interdependence of the modern circumstance conjoined to the fierce sense of specific identity that makes the world so dangerous and frightening.[26]

Falk is particularly interested in the boundary of the nation-state and of how, in that context, nuclear weapons as instruments by part against part doom the whole. But he also refers to boundaries of race, class, religion, ideology, gender, language, age, and civilization.

Evaluation aside, things are clearly changing. This has been becoming clear for some time. In 1982 the physicist Fritjof Capra could write of a turning point in these terms:

> The transformation we are experiencing now may well be more dramatic than any of the preceding ones, because the rate of change in our age is faster than ever before, because the changes are more extensive, involving the entire globe, and because several major transitions are coinciding. The rhythmic recurrences and patterns of rise and decline that seem to dominate human cultural evolution have somehow conspired to reach their points of reversal at the same time. The decline of patriarchy, the end of the fossil-fuel age, and the paradigm shift occurring in the twilight of the sensate culture are all contributing to the same global process. The current crisis, therefore, is not just a crisis of individuals, governments or social institutions; it is a transition of planetary dimensions. As individuals, as a society, as a civilization, and as a planetary ecosystem, we are reaching the turning point.[27]

A SENSE OF ENDING

Not everyone sees what Capra believes he sees. But he is not alone in speaking of a qualitative change. This is a time when one hears people speak of the end—of history, or of nature, or of Europe.[28]

For example, consider science. The 1989 Nobel Conference at Gustavus Adolphus College (St. Peter, Minnesota) took as its focus the theme "The End of Science." Such titling may reflect principally the apocalyptic mood of the time, but clearly scientists and philosophers of science no longer write as they once did. Gone is Descartes's vision of a natural world yielding its laws to a mind mastering Euclidean geometry and Newtonian mechanics. And what of the empiricist side of the Enlightenment? Many of us who are laypersons in relation to the sciences might have supposed that what was going on in the laboratories was precisely the hard labor of induction under the regimen of "the scientific method." The story of what has happened is not written or read identically by all concerned, but it is clear that we have come a long way from a Humean appeal to hard-sense data. In such a story there needs to be a chapter that discusses the diverse efforts (by such people as Karl Popper and Imre Lakotos) to rescue a reliable

principle of falsification and a chapter on the approach represented by Paul
Feyerabend's *Against Method*'s evocation of "anything goes" as over
against something supposed to be "the scientific method."

   Probably the most influential statement in this story was Thomas Kuhn's
The Structure of Scientific Revolutions, published in 1962. Ironically, this
book appeared as an annex to the *Encyclopedia of Unified Science*, a project
to base science on formal logic. Toulmin aptly terms the publication a
Trojan horse.[29] Certainly the efficacy pouring from this structure did not
bolster any effort to see science as reading a world corresponding to the
clear and distinct ideas of a Cartesian consciousness. But the assault on
rationalism did not clear the ground for science to offer us the foundation
of an alternative real world. The emphasis is, rather, on the controlling
role of the scientist's highly historically conditioned choice of a particular
"paradigm" or research program. This emphasis prevails now, three decades later. One of the more influential philosophers of science at this time
is Mary Hesse, who writes in Cambridge, England, with its tradition of
Nobel prizes in biochemistry. She notes that when scientists are invited to
announce the real world, they decline to accept. Instead, they tell us that
data cannot be detached from theory, "for what count as data are determined
in the light of some theoretical interpretation." She speaks of science as
"metaphorical and inexact," as "imaginative," and concludes that "meanings in natural science are determined by theory; they are understood by
theoretical coherence rather than by correspondence with facts."[30]

POSTMODERN DIFFERENCE
Such qualitative change in the self-understanding of scientists is paralleled
by other changes in the way we live and think. Peter Hodgson has distinguished five areas in which there is a crisis or fundamental shift: the
cognitive, the political, the historical, the socioeconomic, and the religious.[31] These changes fuel the discussions about the emergence of the
"postmodern." There are complex questions to be asked and—eventually—
answered about the relationship of the postmodern to modernity.[32] But such
a term can well serve to suggest how the modernity of the Enlightenment
vision and the traditional verities challenged in that vision *both* come under
attack in the changes that are now upon us. It is instructive to contrast
what we are hearing and saying in the last decade of this century to precisely
those modern voices which one might regard as genuinely representing a

"rhetoric of suspicion." Modern liberators such as Marx and Freud called upon us to look beneath the solid surface of our construction of reality to find class conflict and erotic desire. But they did not leave us comfortless, as Mark Edmundson has pointed out:

> The problem with this modern tendency to disenchant the world was that it turned the old religious drive upside down. The traditional man of faith seeks transcendence. He wants contact with God, the One, Truth. The modern thinker, inspired by Marx and Freud, found truth in repressed or hidden impulses, but he found truth nonetheless. Similarly, modern artists and critics found organic cohesion, autonomy—a form of truth, perhaps—in the grand works, works like Joyce's *Ulysses* or Eliot's *The Waste Land*.[33]

Edmundson goes on to make the point that the postmodern voices are urging us to "accept no substitutes for God"—not scientific truth, the self, or the destiny of America, for example.

That certainly seems to be the message of other currents. Ludwig Wittgenstein cautioned us about the "disease of language," and the later Heidegger set about the dismantling of Western metaphysics. But the French deconstructionists are particularly radical in challenging the conventional order. We are called to recognize the way in which we are inextricably formed by language. Indeed, we learn that what must be questioned is our very sense that our speaking refers to what is other than itself. In such learning, the foundation for true knowing and acting, shaken but rebuilt in modernity, is simply shattered. Jacques Derrida speaks of "the ruse of reference" being manufactured out of the primordial human longing for a return to paradise. Just so: all efforts to ground or found our lives represent an attempt to escape from history. This assertion does seem to represent a qualitative change from Enlightenment thinking. Toulmin perceptively points out that, despite their different "material" decisions, both rationalists and empiricists were operating with a vision of a "clean slate":

> Neither Descartes nor Locke had much doubt that the very diversity and contradictions of traditional, inherited, local ways of thought required philosophers to emancipate themselves from the constraints of those traditions. . . . Right up to the 1950s, philosophers of both empiricist and rationalist stripes assumed that an unchallengeable starting point *of some sort* was available, as the natural "scratch line" for beginning rational reflection in philosophy.[34]

Yet perhaps one can see postmodernity as representing in a one-sided way some of the currents of modernity. Lawrence Cahoone has focused on the modern notion of a personal consciousness confronting an alien world, a notion of this sort:

> The individual's true essence is *consciousness*, a non-interactive, private field of givenness taken *sui generis*, for which all encountered reality can be thematized as intentional, representational objects, for which nature, objectivity, society and culture are extrinsic factors, devoid of inherent meaning and value.[35]

Cahoone is stressing "the expansion and radicalization of subjectivism" by which "so-called transcendental capacities and features" ("God, state, monarchical authority, the unity of the self and ultimately the concept of transcendental reason") "were gradually reinterpreted as either purely subjective factors, the product of wishes, illusions, perspectival limitations, or as the effect of objective determinations of the subject, the product of environment, and conditioning, biological factors." His conclusion makes it clear that we are back to the career of the subject/object distinction:

> This gradual loss of the transcendental, the breakdown of the subjectivist-transcendental synthesis that had made subjectivism workable since the seventeenth century, initiated a profound alteration of the subjectivist categories themselves. The subject and object categories were thereby freed to be universally and radically applied, unencumbered by God or reason or any other trans-subjective factor. . . . It becomes impossible to conceive of subjectivity and objectivity as being independent existences *and yet* as being interrelated, mutually involved.[36]

HOW FINITE A FOUNDATION?

In the revolutionary rhythms of both the modern and the postmodern, one detects the tendency to celebrate at the funeral. One remembers Simone de Beauvoir's insistence against Dostoevsky that it is *only* when God is dead that ethical responsibility can be taken truly seriously. In a like spirit in his "postmodern a/theology," Mark C. Taylor writes:

> When becoming no longer needs to be validated by reference to past or future but can be valued at every moment, one has broken (with) the law. Such transgression does not breed guilt and sin. In this case, lawlessness proves to be inseparable from grace—grace that arrives only when God and self are dead and history is over. The lawless land of erring, which is forever beyond good and evil, is the liminal world of Dionysus, the Anti-Christ, who calls every wandering mark to carnival, comedy and carnality.[37]

The history that is over is the linear whole that moves to a fulfilling telos. But in another sense what we are left with in this postmodern

FAITH AND THE OTHER

13

understanding is precisely the history of "one thing after another," one linguistic framework after another. The "slate" is never "clean." We give up the effort to ground or found life or to fulfill history. In the language of William Dean's title we come to recognize simply *"history making history."*[38] Thus Michel Foucault's title, *Order of Things*, may sound rather promising to someone looking for a foundation, a worldview. But the point is to come to recognize that *"the finitude upon the basis of which we are, and think, and know, is suddenly there before us."*[39]

What kind of basis can finitude provide? It becomes difficult to tell the players without a program. In this postmodern vision one still seems to hear the self's Cartesian evocation. Taylor calls the self, such as it grittily is, to celebrate "mazing grace." The music for the occasion is provided by an understanding of philosophy in which any attempt to "mirror" nature is replaced by a call to "edification."[40] The dancing is directed by the family therapist who "cannot reveal 'the truth' about the family members' relationships with one another. He or she can only propose to make available other sets of distinctions—bringing backgammon to the attention of a group that has grown accustomed to playing checkers."[41] The novelist Milan Kundera's summary serves well: "If God is gone and man is no longer master, then who is master? The planet is moving through the void without any master. There it is, the unbearable lightness of being."[42]

Much of this seems alarming. Yet I intend no summary denunciation. The trends I have mentioned here are complex and resist even the summarizing descriptions I have offered. Perhaps the ambiguity that one encounters if one sets out to assess postmodernism is itself the mirror image of something we find in modernity, with the distortions that fun-house mirrors provide. In any case, these developments are not simply ominous. They do provide some breathing room for a person choking in a room filled with either incense or industrial fumes. Perhaps Toulmin is right in saluting a return to "the oral, the particular, the local and the timely."[43] Perhaps we can find in postmodernism a statement of the "bankruptcy of modernity" to which Douglas John Hall points.[44] Perhaps. But perhaps the very complexity of these historical changes makes a descriptive point for us. As we seek to orient ourselves, we find that vast and qualitative historical changes have deposited us in a place where our view of reality is shattered or shaken. We are not sure where we are or how we got here. Thus our grasp of reality cannot be restored by historical review. But in the meantime we find ourselves in this place where our multifarious experience of the others is intensified by the fact that we have no ordering sense of the unified reality of things that could serve as a safe structure for the mediation of these dizzying experiences.[45]

That we are without such an ordering framework is now a commonplace. Perhaps we have lived too long on the interest accrued from the intellectual capital of the likes of Darwin, Marx, Einstein, and Freud.[46] Our intellectual bankruptcy is revealed when we do seek to make normative moral claims, as Alasdair MacIntyre has shown so trenchantly:

> It is precisely because there is in our society no established way of deciding between these claims that moral argument seems to be necessarily interminable. From our rival conclusions we can argue back to our rival premises; but when we do arrive at our premises argument ceases and the invocation of one premise against another premise becomes a matter of pure assertion and counter assertion.[47]

Perhaps, then, it is not strange that what grounds our choosing is nothing more than the choosing itself. Robert Bellah is probably the best known of the commentators who have remarked about this American "habit of the heart":

> If the self is defined by its ability to choose its own values, on what grounds are those choices themselves based? For . . . many . . . there is simply no objectifiable criterion for choosing one value or course of action over another. One's own idiosyncratic preferences are their own justification, because they define the true self. . . . The right act is simply the one that yields the agent the most exciting challenge or the most good feeling about himself.[48]

Of course these privately normed choices come to coexist in a decidedly nonprivate world. Thus we are treated to the unattractive dialectic of such truly "public" matters as international economic and ecological crises going unaddressed in a climate where one does not easily look beyond the self *or* to various fundamentalisms moving in to deny the right of the other to exist.[49]

FRAGMENTATION OF THE *FIDES QUAE*

At the outset I wrote of how people of faith are affected by the increased contact with others that characterizes our time. The qualitative change I have been discussing in this section also affects them. In the next section I will seek to chart a direction for faith; here I only seek to point out a few specific aspects of the situation for faith. What, for example, is to be made of the pluralism apparent within Christian self-understanding? The first third of this century witnessed the confident reign of theological liberalism, the second the supervening sway of neo-orthodoxy. Now in the last decade of this century there seems to be no comparable controlling framework for reflection on the faith. For example, Lutherans, with their high confessional profile, may all look alike to Christians belonging to other denominations. But when six Lutherans put their theological reflections together in 1984, the editors of the volume (modestly titled *Christian Dogmatics*) had reason to note that "those who like to label theologians— 'hope,' 'process,' etc.—will by our calculations need seven or more labels for the six of us."[50] Perhaps diversity within Christian self-understanding represents promise more than risk. Certainly there are voices speaking that have too long been silenced. But one needs to ask how such pluralism is to be kept from developing into full relativism.

The challenges of the other within and without are to be distinguished, but they are related in that in both instances one seeks some kind of ordering structure to accommodate or adjudicate the differences. Moreover, the emergence of the "many" within and without reveals something about what causes—or at the very least occasions—such developments. I will argue that, in the language of faith, the Word needs (to create and/or to find) a world in which to mean. As the world collapses, it is not strange that the people of faith will argue among themselves about where God is to be heard and obeyed. In the loss of worldview the communication of the very content of the faith that we believe (the *fides quae creditur*) is at risk. Suppose the believer wants to assert that God is the Lord of history. Very well, but what if the notion of history is no longer clearly available? Or, another believer bids to confess that it is in God that the true fulfillment of the self is to be found. But what does that mean, if we have no access to agreement about what it means to speak of self?

Perhaps it is not strange, then, that a disquietude exists in the churches with regard to the question of the believer's relationship to the unbeliever. There is no agreed-upon framework in the terms of which the believer's claims (and the unbeliever's) could be heard and assessed by the other. What will happen in such a situation? The faith claims may be permitted to stand, but in a marginalized and enfeebled position where they reside safely (for the believer) and harmlessly (for the unbeliever) beyond the range of argument. This amounts in effect to reducing the claims (*fides quae*) to the claiming (*fides qua*), the passion of faith. Strangely, I am saying, believer and unbeliever can collaborate in this strategy. The unbeliever may sense the lack of a "worldly" structure needed to mount a sustained attack on faith's claims. The believer may repair to the comforting notion that the purity of the flock is reflected in its minority status. The activities of a zealous few (fiery theists and fist-shaking atheists) provide an entertainment that distracts us from attending to the quiet erosion of authentic argument taking place within our culture and within the church.

A striking illustration of these developments in and for faith may be found in the puzzlement or conflict the churches experience in trying to decide how to regard the vast array of groups (from Alcoholics Anonymous to Human Potential) that exist alongside and within the church. Is the one who acknowledges dependence on a "higher power" to be claimed as a full member of the family, as having one foot (which?) in the faith, or as a competitor—or, indeed, as "all of the above"? Without a clear sense of reality, the argument cannot be completed, or even well begun. In this book I want to offer some help toward a beginning. But first it remains to identify in a preliminary way how faith understands itself as it seeks to engage the other within and without.

WHERE IN THE WORLD IS GOD?

In meeting the other, faith asks this question: "Where in the world is God?" and, in doing so, issues an invitation. It may seem strange to find an invitation in this question. That it makes sense to do so can be indicated by noting how two words are together in the question, the words "God" and "world." In meeting the other, faith would be true to itself, it would be faithful before God. Thus, in seeking to understand the others, in trying to live faithfully and fruitfully with them in the world, the Christian asks of God.

WORLDLY QUESTIONING
The Christian knows that her or his understanding and living in relation to God will be here—in the "world." Dietrich Bonhoeffer put it well: "The reality of God discloses itself only by setting me entirely in the reality of the world."

But of course we have just been talking about the loss of worldview, of ordering perspective. Clearly, in this time—given that discussion—we cannot act as if "the world" were neatly available. Perhaps, then, it is not so strange that the invitation is through a question. But this contingent historical situation may in its chaotic character the more dramatically demonstrate what is the essentially reciprocal character of the quest we enter. After all, Bonhoeffer went on to write: "And when I encounter the reality of the world, it is always already sustained, accepted and reconciled in the reality of God."[51] And so the Christian, always but perhaps especially now, wants to ask: "Where in God is the world?" Faith seeks a world, we have said. We must also ask, "Can it help us find one?" As we face the others, we seek to understand God and world together. As we get clear about that relationship, we will know what we need to know on the boundaries of life.

HOSPITALITY, DIFFERENCE, AND DEFIANCE

In living the question(s), we have a place to start the conversation—precisely in our experience of the other(s). In this time it is clear that viable notions of God and world will not fail to have to do with otherness. The previous sections made clear that whatever world we may have today thrusts the other upon us. Christian faith has its own momentum here. Christian faith is dramatically interested in the human other, notably in that one whose otherness marks a "stranger." The Christian is called to attend to the reality of the stranger in various ways: one is not to oppress the stranger (Exod. 22:21; 23:9) but to provide for him or her (Lev. 19:9 10, Deut. 24:19-22; Luke 14:16-24). Indeed, to minister to the stranger is to minister to Christ (Matthew 25) and God's blessing comes to and through the stranger (Deut. 14:28-29; 26:10-13; Luke 4:25-27; 14:16-24).[52]

So it is that the Christian is called fundamentally to an ethic of hospitality in which the stranger, the sojourner, is received and welcomed.[53] This ethic is implicit already in the basic Christian vision of God. Christians know with Isaiah that there is only one God, beside whom "there is no other" (Isa. 45:6). The will of that one God is one will. Specifically, this one God "desires everyone to be saved and to come to the knowledge of the truth" (1 Tim. 2:4) and so acted in Jesus of Nazareth that "whosoever" believes will be saved.[54] So goes the claim.

One must not make things too easy for oneself here. Christians have not thought or acted in consistency with belief in one God with one will willing salvation for all—that I freely and sadly grant and I grant as well that it is no simple thing to know just what this belief means in the light of the "many" we meet. The inconsistencies and intricacies must be faced and I will seek to do that in Part Two. But, as we start, the faith reminds the Christian that interest in the other is not dictated by what is "politically correct" but by the fundamental logic of faith. That the invitation to the other is so rooted emphasizes both the promise and the risk involved. The Christian who hears the call to "test the spirits to see whether they are from God" (1 John 4:1) knows that "the bid is raised" for faith in this serious game with the other. To use traditional dogmatic language: As I meet the other I must ask what in *our* otherness is creaturely difference and what is sinful defiance. To ask is not yet to answer. The believer does not know what will come out of the meeting—for the stranger or for the believer. But as the Christian asks, "Where in the world is God?" the Christian has a place to start.

THE OTHER AS SHARED HUMAN GROUND

It turns out that the Christian is not alone there.

Certainly the experience of some otherness is not the private possession of Christians. Thus it should not surprise that interpretations of this broadly human experience arise outside the church and join the believer in speaking of the experience in terms of promise. Consider these witnesses:

1. The Jewish philosopher Emmanuel Levinas, noticing that it is only in relation to an other that one can have the *right* to anything or the *responsibility* for anything, nicely makes the inference that "plurality is not a mere privation of intelligible unity, but the fundamentally better situation in relation to which unity, as loss of relationship, is the privation."[55] The truly fundamental, world-forming, character of relationship here comes into view.

2. Similarly, Vico saw that to understand was to recognize the otherness.[56]

3. Or that paleontologist turned author, Loren Eiseley, could comment on a similar recognition by Francis Bacon:

   "There is no Excellent Beauty that hath not some strangeness in the Proportion," wrote Bacon in his days of insight. Anyone who has picked up shells on a strange beach can confirm his observation. But modern man, who has not contemplated his otherness, the multiplicity of other possible people who dwell or might have dwelt in him, has not realized the full terror and responsibility of existence.[57]

Eiseley's reference to terror and responsibility well marks the momentousness involved in meeting the other. I note as well that "shells on a beach" seems to broaden the vision well beyond the human stranger near at hand.

4. It was in such an expanded sense that the poet Wallace Stevens, no apologist for religious faith, could stress that literature had to mediate "for us a reality not ourselves" by revealing "something 'wholly other' by which the inexpressive loneliness of thinking is broken and enriched."[58]

5. Perhaps it is this broader sense which sounds in folk literature when special ethical significance is attributed to the outsider. Anthropologist Victor Turner points to such symbolic figures as the good Samaritan; the Jewish fiddler Rothschild in Chekhov's tale "Rothschild's Fiddle"; Mark Twain's fugitive Negro slave, Jim, in *Huckleberry Finn*; and Dostoevsky's Sonya, the prostitute who redeems the would-be Nietzschean "superman" Raskolnikov, in *Crime and Punishment*.[59]

The dizzying sweep of such human otherness seems to speak of more than the human. Thomas Ogletree, writing as a Christian, lets many expressions pile up in indicating what the other calls us to:

wonder and awe in the presence of the holy,
receptivity to unconscious impulses arising from our being as bodied selves,
openness to the unfamiliar and unexpected in our most intimate relationships,
regard to characteristic differences in the experiences of males and females,
recognition of the role social location plays in molding perceptions and value orientations,
efforts to transcend barriers generated by racial oppression.[60]

Such a listing may render this first chapter's orientation disorienting. It will hardly do simply to assume that otherness is one thing that characterizes all things and then ask, "What does this (one thing) mean?" What we propose to do in Part One is precisely to distinguish and relate the various boundaries on which we meet the other. But it is worthwhile to note at the start that we in fact have a promising place to start and that we are not alone there.

CREATION AND FALL CONTINUING

This coming together of believers and unbelievers around the reality of the other may instruct the Christian as to what, theologically considered, we are about in this project and accordingly offer perspective on how we are to proceed. We are, I have said, asking what the reality of the other suggests about the world in which we find ourselves. To seek a world is

to come upon the ground of creation talk. Of course it will not do to suppose
that all that we find comes without remainder from the creative hand of
God. Christians will not fail to speak of evil, of how God's creative intent
is resisted. Surely the experience of the other is too widespread, too fundamental, to escape the mark of radical evil. But deep within the Christian
faith lies the conviction that God's will to create abides so that, despite
the horrendous moral evil that human history bears witness to, this world
is still God's world.[61]

I am saying that this is how Christian faith understands itself in this
matter. Moreover, Christian faith does not install this conviction concerning
God's will to create as a first stage to be trumped by a more elevated
assertion under, say, the rubrics of redemption or sanctification. The Christian believes that it is the goodwill of God that we be creatures and whatever
more is to be said about our relationship to God will not overrule that
status, that invitation. Indeed, the "more" of Jesus Christ underscores the
theme of creation. Bonhoeffer was driven by the question, "What is Jesus
Christ for us today?" The "experiencing of God and the world together"
theme is not a preamble to be left behind for that christological focus:
"Whoever professes to believe in the reality of Jesus Christ as the revelation
of God, must in the same breath profess his faith in both the reality of
God and the reality of the world; for in Christ he finds God and the world
reconciled."[62]

Bonhoeffer clearly does not regard the person and work of Christ as
simply an instance of God's creative work. That is not the point. But in
trying to focus to understand the Jesus event—indeed, in understanding
it—he is driven back to the reality of God and world.

THE OTHER AS ORDER OF THE DAY
Bonhoeffer's word was "whoever." To attend to the world is not optional
if one would speak truly of Jesus Christ. Thus one may well say that for
the Christian to attend to the other—that reality which seems so much a
part of our world—is not to indulge some urge for luxury. One might
wrongly suppose that having to do with the other is for the Christian
community way out on the edge of things and so perhaps, frankly, a
peripheral matter. To the contrary, if the experience of the other is constitutive in the world we meet (even as that experience shatters some worlds
we once construed/constructed as real), it is something to which all faithful

reflection must attend, as surely as Christians claim God's living will to create. If theological thought fails to grasp the reality of creation, it cannot be supposed to illumine any other work of the Creator God. Thus there is no safe center back in mythic gospel security such that these interactions with the other could be delegated (relegated?) to some curious scouts. But in speaking adequately of the real world, the Christian will indeed speak a gospel word of God's action, as chapter 4 will make clear. Attending to the other will take different forms, of course, but it is essential for Christian reflection.

If we are to speak of boundary, we must give that speaking a temporal ring. After all, to worship God as creator is not to make some mythic effort to return to Eden, to that time (*illa tempore*),[63] but to praise the work of God in the agony and ecstasy of history. Just so: the logic of Christian theological reflection looks ahead to the future of Latin America, Africa, and Asia, not back to the Europe of fond memory. Following this temporal logic, the Christian will keep company in life and thought with those whom the poet David Ignatow described as:

> I feel along the edges of life
> for a way
> that will lead to open land.[64]

FAITH AS CO-OWNER IN THE CONVERSATION

I have been unpacking the specifically Christian orientation to the other. Christians have much to receive from their own store in this respect. But if we are trying to hear the worldly word of our Creator in the other, we will need to listen to all who speak with clarity about the strange world of otherness. The conversation cannot be limited to the circle of faith. True faith is not a requirement for being a creature, and it is not a requirement for speaking insightfully of the creaturely life. Of course the Christian will not fail to speak as a Christian in this conversation concerning the boundaries on which we live and believe.[65] The conversation will address both questions: "Where in the world is God?" and "Where in God is the world?" Thus the conversation about boundaries itself occurs on a boundary, not on privileged ground.

Conversations have a spontaneous and unpredictable character about them. They carry the chaos of that which is living. We do well not to seek to establish some universal method at the outset. We should not suppose,

for example, that from outside the circle of faith come creaturely questions
to which creational answers are made from within the faith.[66] The Christian
does not claim to be the credentialing authority for this conversation about
the other. Christians know that of the gospel itself they must say "we have
this treasure in earthen vessels" (2 Cor. 4:7, RSV). We are invited not to
forget that when we set about to think theologically about creation we do
not suddenly cease to be creatures alongside other creatures. And it is
becoming increasingly clear to Christians that the task of interpretation
cannot be completed prior to or apart from the conversation with the other.[67]

Our inquiry into the other will itself thus plunge us into the experience
of otherness. Accordingly, Christians will want to hear from more than
one perspective. The voices that have something to say to us do not need
to be wedged together in one grand plenary session. William Placher makes
this point well:

> Critical thinking would not have to begin by questioning all our previous
> beliefs at once; indeed, that seems impossible. Dialogue would not have to
> await *universally* acceptable starting points before it could begin; particular
> conversations could start with whatever their participants happened to share
> and go from there. We could admit that of course we all stand within traditions
> and can never achieve an "objective" point of view; we could try to learn
> from one another's traditions rather than casting them all aside.[68]

Placher is speaking about the conversations among varying faith perspectives. I write in the service of one such perspective, Christian faith.
In Part Two, I will try to uncover the direction, resources, and telos the
Christian may claim in life on the boundary. I will ask how the Christian
may live faithfully and fruitfully on the boundary with those who are other
with respect to faith. But already in Part One, I will turn now here, now
there, as I seek to piece together some picture of the several boundaries
on which we live. I am trying to get at those deep creational dimensions
of otherness which characterize the reality of life on the boundary to which
one makes some kind of response with respect to faith. Perhaps the founding
"world" is to be sought deep within but not beneath our dramatic experience
of difference. I do not suppose that I have transcended my own human
and religious particularity in this effort and I do not seek to speak for the
other faiths in this. But I do seek to speak in particular *of* deep boundary
realities to which the other faiths may also make some response in their
own perspectives. These boundaries are perhaps shared in greater measure

than are the faiths by which we seek to live there. At least people who claim *no* faith also speak of some of these dimensions.[69]

Thus this effort, if not privileged, is nonetheless clearly a partial one. It is finally one voice, a particular voice. I will try to hear more than the echo of my faith's passion, but hearing is not a passive act. Yet in hearing we may prepare to speak together. Surely there will be flaws and failings in the hearing and the speaking. They may seem too controlled, or—more likely, to my thinking—too chaotic. That can be borne. Salman Rushdie, following the statement with which we began this chapter, writes this: "The argument between purity and impurity, which is also the argument between primness and impropriety, between the stultifications of excessive respect and the scandals of impropriety, is an old one. I say, let it continue."[70]

That seems worth doing.

2

LIFE WITHIN
THE OTHER

Who are we human beings? In this part of the book we seek to address
this question in order to illumine the boundary zones where faith meets its
other(s). To that end, we will dig beneath the dramatic experience of
difference to ask questions—questions concerning, in effect, where, when,
and how we are. Faith will have its own word to speak of these things,
but it will also hear the word of those who do not speak for faith—the
word of people in the arts and sciences, the word of persons who simply
reflect deeply on their experience of life. If we can come to some understanding of this—of who we are simply as human beings—we will be in
a position to consider in Part Two how to live together faithfully and
fruitfully on this globe we coinhabit. There is more to such living than
understanding, but it is helpful to uncover the ground for the "more" of
the living.

LIFE WITHIN THE SPACETIME CONTINUUM

So, who are we? We are beings in relationship. We live on boundaries. If
we dig beneath the boundaries of life, we will find relationships. It is
within these relationships that the connectedness and the difference of which
we have spoken exist. I begin with the most comprehensive relationship,
that which the human being knows as part of the whole spacetime continuum. This may seem far removed from the vivid particularities with which

we began—the lively flash of difference known in other human faces. In the very nature of the case the whole does not present itself to the part with the distinctness of another part. Yet there are approximations or suggestions. Consider the youthful experience Loren Eiseley recounts:

> When I was young, in a time of boyhood marked by a world as fresh and green and utterly marvelous as the day of its creation, I found myself attracted by a huge tropical shell which lay upon my aunt's dressing table. The twentieth century was scarcely a decade old, and people did not travel as they do now. My uncle and aunt lived far inland in the central states and what wandering relative had given them the beautiful iridescent shell I do not know. It was held up to my youthful ear and I was told to listen carefully and I would hear the sea. Out of the great shell, even in that silent bedroom, I, who had never seen the ocean, heard the whispered sibilance, the sigh of waves upon the beach, the little murmurs of moving water, the confused mewing of gulls in the sun-bright air. It was my first miracle, indeed perhaps my first aware-ness of the otherness of nature, of myself outside, in a sense, and listening, as though beyond light-years, to a remote event. Perhaps, in that Victorian bedroom, with its knickknacks and curios, I had suddenly fallen out of the nature I inhabited and turned, for the first time, to survey her with surprise.[1]

OUR HUMAN HOME

It is likely that Eiseley, young or old, could hear more than most of us. But he is not alone in knowing of this relationship. Stephen Toulmin writes that "the world of nature is the place where, as members within the larger evolutionary scheme of things, human beings are 'well adapted,' and so 'at home'; where they have the power to *make* themselves 'at home,' " and he notes that when John Wheeler, the physical cosmologist and the-oretical astronomer, spoke at the Smithsonian Institution's five hundredth birthday party for Copernicus, he chose as his title "The Universe as a Home for Man."[2] Now, nearly two decades later, our sense of human diversity would lead us to phrase the title more inclusively, but we would readily join Wheeler in recognizing that relationship which includes us all: we are, indeed, at home in the spacetime continuum. To speak thus of being "at home" is not to imply satisfaction with the status quo. That things can change—that they *will* change and can change for the better— is much of the meaning of this home. Christians—like other people—look for change, and do so radically, but such hope is not an assault on time as such. It is the future to which they look for the city of God. If we are to understand who we are, we will have to understand who we are as spatiotemporal beings. This is so not merely because we are "in" space and time, accidentally or temporarily. We are there so essentially that one must say that spacetime is *in us*. Whatever else we may be, we are spatiotemporal beings.

THE ARROW OF TIME

What is being said when we speak of this relationship? While scientists hardly speak with a single voice, the experience of the "arrow of irreversibility" seems crucial. We take up our lives *in* the present with a sense of moving *from* the past *toward* the future. Yet that sense does not go unchallenged. Thus the scientific recognition of the active role of the observer can be carried to the point where irreversibility is challenged. Or Einstein's understanding of the four-dimensional continuum (the three dimensions of ordinary space and a fourth corresponding to time) is sometimes portrayed as a spatialization of time. Robert John Russell puts the question succinctly: "From the standpoint of physics, are irreversible processes at the macrolevel reducible to reversible microprocesses, or is there an irreducible physical basis for time's arrow?"[3] Can one have it both ways? One quests for a unified view. As Nobel laureate Ilya Prigogine writes (with I. Stengers): "Irreversibility is either true on all levels or on none: it cannot emerge as if out of nothing, on going from one level to another."[4]

One could try to retain our "macro" experience of time's arrow by challenging the authority of physics to speak on this matter. One might find support for such a strategy in the increasing recognition of the subjectivity involved in the physicist's craft. But that approach will backfire, if it invites reducing the quest for scientific understanding to a sharing of private fancies. To speak is not to rule. Accordingly, it seems better, albeit harder, to claim reality for our ordinary experience of irreversibility and to grant/seek such a reference as well for the chalkboards of the physicists. One need not argue for the abstract irreversibility of absolute time as a container. In classical physics every object has a definite location and time passes uniformly and universally, the same for all observers. But Einstein's work on special relativity dismantled that view. Yet we can still recognize that for any specific observer the concrete occurrences that constitute time are connected irreversibly. Ian Barbour has put the matter so:

> In relativity theory there are some events that are past for one observer and future for another observer, but for any two events that could be causally

related there is an absolute distinction of past and future for all possible
observers. There is no way in which a future event could influence the past
or present, according to relativity theory.[5]

A TIMELY FAITH

If we take as true our intuitive sense of time's irreversibility, what follows
for our understanding of ourselves as human within this spacetime continuum? What does this mean for faith? One can readily claim this understanding of time as support for each individual's sense of efficacy, of
responsibility. It matters what we do in our freedom, for we give our deeds
to the future irreversibly.[6] But is there not something more for faith to
learn/say about the whole in which these individual wills play their parts?
Certainly Christian faith has made some response to that question. The
Christian conviction is, as Kierkegaard put it, that "an historical point of
departure" is possible for an eternal consciousness.[7] That reality is such
that the relationship to God can undergo qualitative change—to speak so
is surely to speak of the whole of reality. Similarly, in support of this point,
Christian theologians have spoken consistently, if not expansively, of God
as the creator of the universe in which such "an historical point of departure" is possible. But one wonders whether something is not still being
missed here. It is helpful that reality is understood in such a way that
salvation is possible. But may not more be said in the face-to-face conversation between the student of spacetime and the believer?

At the very least it seems important to try to avoid the disjunctive
thinking suggested by "point of departure" language. What is it "to be
saved"? If the spacetime is truly in us, surely we cannot simply be saved
"out of" it, "departing" at some point, as it were. Who or what is "to
be saved"? In the next section of this chapter, I will cite Christian testimony
calling for a notion of salvation that truly includes "a new heaven and a
new *earth.*" In chapter 5, I will inquire as to how temporality can be
understood within the meaning of Christian hope, and vice versa. But here
the task is to suggest a way to speak theologically of the process itself and
of us as part of it.

Recognizing the theological significance of the creational matrix for
human life in the spacetime continuum makes a good start. Not surprisingly,
students of the Old Testament see this. Thus Odil Steck has noted that in
P's creation account it was God's will that there be lights in the firmament

of the heavens "to separate the day from the night . . . for signs and for seasons and for days and years."[8] And Claus Westermann has written wisely of a "blessing" of human life through natural processes, a gift that does not serve merely as a means to the good of "salvation."[9] Similarly, a systematic theologian such as Gustaf Wingren has helpfully driven home the point that the work of creation is itself God's *opus proprium*, the "proper work" of God, for life is a gracious gift.[10] These formulations help. But one hungers for more. What does it say *about us* theologically, that we exist as part(s) of the spacetime continuum?

Consider a statement which is not couched in specifically religious terms. Toulmin instructively contrasts two viewpoints, the "white" philosophy and "the green":

> The white philosophy has roots in psychotherapy. It encourages us, above all, to pursue self-knowledge and self-command as individuals. Our prime responsibility as human beings is to identify the points of inward frailty within our personal psyches. . . . We are then to master those frailties, by facing our inner "ghosts" and so exorcising them. In this way (it is claimed) we can make ourselves impervious to aggravation, and learn to prevent things from getting to us. . . . The green philosophy, by contrast, . . . encourages us, both as individuals and in our collective affairs, to pursue harmony with nature. Our primary responsibility is to deepen our understanding of the interdependence that binds humanity to nature. We are then to direct our lives, on both the personal and the social levels, in ways that do not interfere with the cycles and systems of the natural world but go with the grain of nature. . . . We shall achieve a command over outside events based on mutual respect rather than domination.[11]

RELATIONSHIP: THE NEW WORLD DISORDER

How shall we understand ourselves if we realize that, to take Toulmin's phrase, "the grain of nature" is *in* us? Thus far we have emphasized the arrow of irreversibility in rather bare or formal terms. But what shall we make of the material point of the second law of thermodynamics (that in every closed system there is an increase in entropy)? Somehow order and disorder need to be understood together, though there are various scientific theories as to just how to do this. The popularizing advocates of the new "chaos" science certainly stress the togetherness of order and disorder, though they may be overcome by their enthusiasm in speaking of "chaos" as this century's "third revolution," alongside relativity and quantum mechanics. A quieter witness is the reality (even in inanimate systems) of self-organization.[12] Prigogine's studies have shown how disorder at one level can be followed by order at another. A vortex appears in the turbulence of a flowing stream. In different ways a common challenge develops: a Christian view of human identity that would value order as a simple alternative to disorder faces heavy going.[13] Rather, if the thermodynamic arrow characterizes "our home," does it not seem that the "disorder" of "difference," "otherness," "heterogeneity" are somehow written into our very being? We will speak more of this in the next section in considering evolution.

We are trying to speak of the whole in which we are, which is in us. Another way of characterizing the emerging scientific understanding is to speak of relationship. This is how the thermodynamicist Jeffrey Wicken speaks:

> Granted, space consists of fields of force which exert regulative controls on material elements; but its "structure" is reciprocally regulated by those elements and their movements. The two together constitute the only "whole" of which physics can speak. If all the matter were removed from the universe, there would be no field. When the ether left, so did ontological dichotomy. Space and matter have *coevolved*, and are *relationally constituted* by each other. They have no identities apart from each other.[14]

The whole that is in us is constituted relationally. No wonder that parts of nature interrelate so intimately. Little wonder that in this universe we have learned we cannot do just one thing. That makes sense if the whole is such that physicists can realistically be at work on a supertheory in which electromagnetic, nuclear, and gravitational forces will be seen as forms of one basic force. In emphasizing connection we should not forget the element of difference essential to relationship. Thus Barbour makes the point that "relativity introduces a new form of separateness and isolation": "It takes time for connections to be effective, so we are momentarily alone in each present."[15]

THE CONSONANCE OF FAITH AND SCIENCE

How shall the Christian speak theologically about such a whole? One approach is to use scientific statements about the whole as a basis for claims about God the creator. Does the position of ascendancy that "Big Bang" cosmology has today prove (suggest?) that God created the whole out of nothing? How is one to connect God-talk with the various experiences of randomness and lawlikeness within the spacetime continuum? Does the fact that even a small change in the physical constants would have resulted in an uninhabitable universe prove (suggest?) by the "anthropic principle" that this universe is the work of an intelligent designer? I will respond to these questions in chapters 4 and 5. But it is perhaps wise to prepare for that discussion by developing the point already suggested in the first chapter that our God-talk and this (scientific) world-talk need to be connected. Ted Peters uses the term "consonance" to speak of that connection:

> Consonance in the strong sense means accord, harmony. Where we find accord or harmony between the disciplines, let us explore them further under the hypothesis that they are speaking about the same reality. In a weak sense, consonance may refer to common domains of question asking, i.e., situations where asking the question of God—whether answerable or not—is the reasonable thing to do....Whether in the strong or weak senses of the word, the concept of consonance reflects an important underlying assumption, namely, there is one God and one world so that, in the long run, science and theology are attempting to understand one and the same reality.[16]

To argue for consonance it is quite enough to contend that science and theology both seek to speak of that which is real. The real God for theology and the real universe for science are not identical (as they would be in a pantheistic view), but the frameworks for understanding the two must not contradict each other or simply lie apart in incoherence. They must not, for science and theology both claim that their frameworks definitively illumine the human, and their domains meet also in other, broader spheres. Thus Christians also engage in world-talk. In principle, one would expect such Christian theological talk about that which is not God to rhyme well with the emphasis on temporality and relationship to which we have referred here, for the Christian faith has these same themes deep within the heart of its life. Yet, sadly, there are tendencies to turn against this emphasis. Some brief critical elaboration may be helpful in trying to understand how Christian faith may find understanding in consonance with scientific views of the spacetime continuum.

FAITH AS ESCAPING FROM TIME

In chapter 1, I referred to the strong religious tendency to focus somehow on a past "Golden Age."[17] There I distinguished the Christian commitment to temporality from any such drive to revert to a primordial past. But honesty requires the Christian to acknowledge that the attempt to live in the past, to worship "that old-time religion," certainly has not been absent in Christendom. Some care is required in making this point. To refuse to deny time does not require one to level out all time so that qualitative newness disappears in the sheer indifference of "one thing after another." Thus the commitment to the givenness of an apostolic authority need not represent a betrayal of time, unless that commitment is twisted into a wooden authoritarianism that fails or even refuses to engage freshly the reality of present experience.[18]

Theological speech may fail the test of consonance in other ways, of course. The significance of human involvement in the spatiotemporal process can be denied as well by a flight to the future, when one would speak of God. The obvious form of this error will be found in those pieties which trivialize human suffering and human responsibility by denying significance to the temporal realm in the light of the ultimate future. Again, this point must be made carefully. That "the sufferings of this present time are not worth comparing with the glory about to be revealed to us" (Rom. 8:18) does not mean that we have no important choices to make here and now, for "love does no wrong to a neighbor; therefore, love is the fulfilling of the law" (Rom. 13:10).

A subtler form of this flight to the future and the resultant denial of temporality is represented by those theologians who appeal to the future as somehow already securing the outcome of what to us now seems (mistakenly, apparently) a contingent process. In such a way, the reality of irreversibility is undercut. To recognize some genuine contingency, of course, does not require one to assert that nothing is settled about the future. The specific distinctions to be made will claim our attention in chapter 4 and particularly in chapter 5. Similarly, to recognize the significance of anticipation (*present* anticipation) does not entail speaking of victory coming "from" the future.

I have critiqued the denial of temporality as that which may be found in religious formulations that trivialize the present by retreat to the past or flight to the future. But, ironically, a third "inconsonant" tendency would be precisely to isolate the present from its temporal matrix, transforming it into a nontemporal or timeless moment.[19] A theologian (or a scientist) who failed to recognize the historically "situated" character of her or his work would make that error methodologically. To recognize the distinctiveness of the present as the only temporal mode in which we live does not entail such a disjunction from the spacetime continuum. But reflection on the continuity of time and on the historical commitments of Christian faith requires one to be suspicious of ahistorical moments that tend to become eternities, whether in Christian or some other garb.

I have stressed here in particular the significance of temporality, with an emphasis on irreversibility. That has entailed other dimensions, which we seem to experience, such as the combinations of order and disorder and of necessity and chance. Another way of characterizing this emphasis would be to speak of reality as asymmetrical. Barbour offers a striking illustration:

> For every billion antiprotons in the early universe, there were one-billion-and-one protons. The billion pairs annihilated one another to produce radiation, with just one proton left over. A greater or smaller number of survivors—or no survivors at all if they had been evenly matched—would have made our kind of material world impossible. The laws of physics seem to be symmetrical between particles and antiparticles; why was there a tiny asymmetry?[20]

So then: irreversibility, difference and connection in relationship, order and disorder, the asymmetrical—these are words that characterize current scientific understanding of the world in which we are and which is in us. These themes will be caught up as well in understanding that we are in relationship to other human beings (chap. 3) and to God (chap. 4). But they come directly into clearer view when the whole offers a distinction such that we know ourselves as existing with that much larger nonhuman part of the spacetime continuum.

LIFE WITH NATURE WITHIN THE SPACETIME CONTINUUM

Within the whole a distinction appears. In the passage quoted above, Eiseley speaks of "falling out of nature" as he held the great shell to his ear and heard the "otherness" of the seas. To understand human life is, in part, to understand it in relationship to nature. This is like the part/whole relationship inasmuch as human beings are still held in the embrace or grip of nature. It is unlike it insofar as human being and becoming represent nature rising up to turn toward itself.

NATURE TURNING

Thus one speaks of humankind as evolution become conscious of itself.[21] And in that measure humankind can turn *against* nature, as surely as we cannot turn against the spatiotemporal whole. In that sense nature may seem to us to represent the most fundamental otherness, an otherness that is "singular," as Richard Wentz puts it.[22] Or it may seem so basically other as to repel the interaction of dialogue. In "The Most of It," Robert Frost depicts how nature (in the embodiment of a great buck) meets and defeats the human longing for reciprocal response:

> He thought he kept the universe alone;
> For all the voice in answer he could wake
> Was but the mocking echo of his own
> From some tree-hidden cliff across the lake.
> Some morning from the boulder-broken beach
> He would cry out on life, that what it wants
> Is not its own love back in copy speech,
> But counter-love, original response.
> And nothing ever came of what he cried
> Unless it was the embodiment that crashed
> In the cliff's talus on the other side,
> And then in the far distant water splashed,
> But after a time allowed for it to swim,
> Instead of proving human when it neared
> And someone else additional to him,
> As a great buck it powerfully appeared,
> Pushing the crumpled water up ahead,
> And landed pouring like a waterfall,
> And stumbled through the rocks with horny tread,
> And forced the underbrush—and that was all.[23]

The human heart here does not receive "counter-love." Yet nature is not simply outside, "across the lake." If we are to understand what it is to be human, we must grasp the sense in which human being is, as Philip Hefner says, "two-natured." Or in the language of Eiseley, again, we must ponder that "strangeness in the proportion" by which in the human being "by contrast with the animal, two streams of evolution have met and merged: the biological and the cultural."[24]

To do this we must speak of evolution. That the strangeness that is human uniqueness came about through evolution quietly limits that very uniqueness. Life is the product of history, and so, in turn, is human life.

Thus any attempt to separate human beings as historical from the world of nature is defeated and we are led to speak rather of the "history of nature."[25] Within the temporality of nature we recognize the continuity of evolution. Arthur Peacocke notes that those who seek gaps face the disappointing tendency of the gaps to be filled.[26]

To recognize such continuity is not to opt for the reductive "spurious homogeneity" in which qualitative difference could not arise.[27] But it is to recognize that the boundary that marks the distinction between the natural and the human also marks a connection. We human beings may have "fallen" or "risen" out of nature, but we fall or rise naturally, and in that sense we are still in nature and nature is still in us. This section is devoted to marking this boundary at which human beings rise up out of nature, while remaining related to it. In the next section we will focus on how our connection with and difference from the natural function *within* us.

Perhaps our tendency to fail to recognize our connectedness with nature is related to what we spoke about in chapter 1 as the self/world distinction understood in the terms of a firm boundary marking absolute difference. Jürgen Moltmann nicely expresses how our current understanding requires such subject/object thinking to be radically recast:

> In human societies, "nature" has found a relative concentration and a relative centralization, if by nature we mean all those sectors which for human societies make up the ecosystem "earth." But this means that in human knowledge of nature, nature really recognizes itself, and that in the human objectification of nature, nature itself becomes objective. According to this model, in the subject-object relationship between human beings and nature the subject is really nature itself.[28]

Lately scientists no longer claim that their subjectivity grasps a purely objective world. Such recognition of the limiting character of subjectivity is laudable, as far as it goes. But such an emphasis on scientific subjectivity may fail to reclaim connection with a new, living world. Helmut Peukert nicely points the way forward for antipositivist developments in the natural sciences:

> Even in mathematics, considerations of reflexivity, novelty, and temporality are necessary, since formal systems are never complete. Incompleteness always leaves room for reflective distance and choice; in this way, the critique of formalism initiates the turn to the thinking and acting subject behind science and mathematics.[29]

Very well, then: to speak of evolution is to speak of the continuity of life and to recognize our connectedness with nature in the spacetime continuum. But does not the second law of thermodynamics argue that as entropy increases, any movement toward greater complexity will be "against the grain"? In this section, as in the previous one, we need to ponder how order and disorder are together. Thus Peacocke speaks of disorder serving order:

> Certainly the stream as a whole moves in a certain general, overall direction which is that of increasing entropy and increasing disorder. . . . However, the movement of the stream *itself* inevitably generates, as it were, very large eddies *within* itself in which, far from there being a decrease in order, there is an increase first in complexity and then in something more subtle—functional organisation. . . . There could be no self-consciousness and human creativity without living organisation, and there could be no such living dissipative systems unless the entropic stream followed its general, irreversible course in time.[30]

In turn, Wicken has argued that "integrative or building-up processes provide a general means for the conversion of potential energy to entropy, structuring through dissipation."[31]

Here we have again connection and distinction in the emergence. The emergent human self is not without preparation in the random interactions by which elementary particles yield a world of atoms, molecules and then life.[32] Yet the emergence of the human self is not just one more tick of the entropic clock. I will turn in the next section of this chapter to the effort to specify what constitutes this human uniqueness. But clearly it includes the ability of the human emergent to turn toward and even against the womb of nature. This point can hardly be left in formal terms. Once again a difference of degree bids to constitute a difference of kind in two respects: (1) throughout the entire evolutionary process there exists an "open-endedness" and (2) new life comes about only through death. The disorder that serves the evolutionary process should not be branded evil. But now nature, at the very least as we know it, is put in great peril by a development in which evolution, conscious of itself and yet tragically blind, opens toward what has the sense of an ending.[33] Carbon dioxide-fueled global warming, the collapse of the food web from ultraviolet radiation, the garbage barge, the oil spills—even the frequency of the images does not remove their apocalyptic tone.

THE AMBIGUOUS ECOLOGICAL PROMISE

We have come face-to-face with nature imperiled without involving our-selves explicitly in the witness of faith. These developments do speak to the faith, often speaking *against* the faith. But Christian faith does itself have some things to say of the boundary we are discussing. Perhaps they are not clearly consistent things, if H. Paul Santmire is right in subtitling his *The Travail of Nature* "The *Ambiguous* Ecological Promise of Christian Theology."[34] Actually, Santmire's work is a historical survey and I would want to argue that the founding logic of Christian faith is less mixed than the record of Christendom, though I grant that this discrepancy itself in its persistence may count against the faith. My purpose and task here is not to retrieve or develop Christian ecological reflection. But both founding logic and historical record are pertinent, if we are asking who we are in the world.

Certainly what I have been calling "nature" is caught up in the biblical sweep of God's creative activity.[35] Moreover, covenant language is invoked for nature as well. In Genesis 9, God says to Noah, "I am establishing my covenant with you and your descendants after you, and *with every living creature that is with you*" (Gen. 9:9-10, emphasis mine).[36] But human life is not linked with nature only by the fact that they are both connected with God by creation and covenant. The connection entailed in the continuity of evolution is recognized: the earth creature is made, pre-cisely, of earth (Gen. 2:7).[37] Earth! This speaks not only of where we come from but of who we are. Sin has changed us, but it is not sin that has made us earthly. "By the sweat of your face you shall eat bread until you return to the ground, for out of it you were taken; you are dust, and to dust you shall return" (Gen. 3:19). We know that the ancient text is true, as we feel the swells of our being passing, like all other life.

At the same time, the creation stories convey a recognition of the distinctiveness of the human. The creative power of language marks that distinction: in Genesis 1 (cf. vv. 22 and 28-30), it is the human pair that God gives special responsibility and provision; in Genesis 2, to name the animals is a creational privilege and task, even as the power to name can become the reifying and dominating instrument of sin (as feminist theo-logians have emphasized). Perhaps Eiseley's meeting of the two streams of evolution, the biological and the cultural, is succinctly suggested in Genesis 2 in that the Lord God causes there to grow in the garden "every tree that is pleasant to the sight and good for food" (Gen. 2:9).

If we ask what nature is "good for," we come very close to the dominion theme. The imperatives "fill the earth and subdue it" and "have dominion" stand charged, if not convicted, in the light of the contemporary ecological crisis.[38] Biblical scholars do step forward as defense attorneys, of course. Here, for example, is Odil Steck's statement:

> There can be no question but that this ruling function—to dominate the animal world—is understood in a completely positive sense. For P (the Priestly writer) it is a matter of vocation, which is necessary for the successful continuance of the created world. Accordingly, it is entirely included in the divine approval of the world as a whole, which saw it as "very good" (1:31). It is a vocation that certainly does not give man the right of autonomous and autocratic disposal over the animal world for his own self-chosen purposes, detached from God. [39]

Perhaps. Perhaps the fact that it is only of human life that the texts employ "image of God" language is indeed to be understood as indicating through this titular language our special human responsibility—in Steck's terms, "to promote the permanent existence of all life." Douglas John Hall has offered a book-length argument for this perspective, stressing such themes as sacrifice, participation in preservation, and the recognition of the spiritual element in matter.[40] But one still must ask how and why we "got it wrong" so often. The founding logic and the historical record are both pertinent as Christians ask, "Who are we in the world?"

Santmire's summary adjective seems refreshingly honest: "ambiguous." Santmire does not limit his work to creation themes. He distinguishes two metaphors, ascent and fecundity, in relation to the experience of "the overwhelming mountain." A third root metaphor is that of migration to a good land. The metaphor of ascent yields "the spiritual motif" in Western theology, whereas the other two tend to cluster to become the "ecological motif."[41] Santmire's recognition of the complexity of the biblical witness is important. One may focus the ambiguity systematically by referring to the doctrine of God. It is a commonplace to stress that the biblical witness regarding creation "de-divinizes" nature. This is regularly linked with the notion that this same creation logic gives impetus to science, inasmuch as the "laws" of nature are the product of an ordering will and as such can be discerned, but only by empirical scrutiny.[42]

THE IMAGE OF GOD TRANSCENDENT

Very well, such speech has a pleasant ring to it, not the least to Christians trying to reconcile biblical faith with the burgeoning reality of modern science. But what if science's record is judged to have its own dark side in the assessment of the ecological peril we face? And, the status of science aside, has the theme of divine transcendence contributed to the devaluation of nature? If only we humans are in God's image, might it not make sense to regard nature as a dispensable instrument fashioned for the service of an essentially spiritual humanity which, it would seem, belongs thereby elsewhere with God rather than with nature? Can we avoid that conclusion, unless we can speak of a God transcendent *within* nature?[43] Unless we can formulate such a concept of God, will not "unique image of God" talk inevitably place the other-than-human natural realm in a merely instrumental position?[44]

I will respond to these questions in chapter 4 in speaking of God and, briefly, in the final section of this chapter in speaking of the image of God. But first it is necessary to indicate that the understanding of the relationship between nature and humankind presented here raises questions and offers corrections that do not challenge only the Christian faith. If the theme of human distinctiveness is stressed in a single-minded way, one could end up with acosmic conceptions of human destiny. Perhaps that acosmic character could be anticipated in religious themes that seem to detach one's particular human identity from one's concrete spatiotemporal context.[45] To the contrary, biblical understandings locate human identity so firmly in spatiotemporal-*natural* context that it is not at all surprising that the corresponding vision of salvation should say with Paul, "For from him and through him and to him are all things" (Rom. 11:36).[46]

It is precisely that dynamic sense of destiny which is crucial for the correction of the opposite danger: that of reducing the human to that which precedes and enables it in the evolutionary process. We have been speaking in this section of life with nature within the spatiotemporal process. Life with nature is *within* that process. One can deny time subtly by refusing to grant qualitative emergence within the process. Then evolution turns out not to be so open-ended after all. Perhaps the most severe proponents of sociobiology represent such a reduction, and perhaps those antivivesectionists who decline to distinguish levels of value do so as well.[47] And perhaps in a very different way those who speak of the earth as Gaia, as itself alive, are telescoping in such a way as to substitute a present process for a future hope.[48] To settle for the evolutionary past; to usurp the eschatological future—these come together to blunt time's arrow.

Once again, I am not here attempting an ecological ethic which could counter such troubling developments. My task is a preliminary one. If such tendencies are to be resisted, it will be essential to understand how that connection and distinction of which we have been speaking is present *within* the human.[49]

LIFE WITHIN THE BODY WITH NATURE WITHIN THE SPACETIME CONTINUUM

As a two-natured being, the human person lives on an inner boundary to which we refer when we speak of the "body(brain)/mind problem" or the distinction/relation of spirit and matter. It is particularly our bodies that remind us of our strong connection with nature. This connection is constitutive. It clearly will not do to speak as if the body were a sort of bridge between nature and the "real" person—mind or spirit. At least one cannot get safely across the bridge to a person on "the other side." As Alfred North Whitehead put it, "Nobody ever says: 'Here I am, and I have brought my body with me.' "[50] Perhaps the body serves whatever may be in us which is not body, but it is clear that this servant cannot be discharged.

OUR EMBODIED NATURE
Moreover, there is increasing testimony to the connectedness characterizing the relationship within us between body and spirit. The molecular geneticists are primary current witnesses for the body in the time-honored nature/nurture debate. On the genetic scale of average differences in DNA the differences between human beings and other primates are slight. But the studies bearing on the boundary *within* human life are perhaps even more startling. We are not talking merely about height and hair color. Much publicity has been given to studies claiming to link specific mental disorders to inherited genetic flaws.[51] A conventional response has been to point out that genes are, after all, only blueprints for the assembly and regulation of proteins. Each gene codes for a specific sequence of amino acids that the body assembles to form a protein. But here the line of direct causality

may be said to be broken, for "proteins interact with other physiological intermediaries, which may be other proteins, such as hormones or neurotransmitters, or may be structural properties of the nervous system."[52] With that wedge between the genes and behavior, room is opened for appeal to nurturing environmental factors and, indeed, perhaps to the elusive reality of human freedom.

Such qualifications are important in ruling out a "genes are destiny" view. But they cannot responsibly be used to dismiss the reality of the genetic contribution to behavior. That has been dramatically demonstrated by the studies of identical twins reared apart. For example: to the question "Do identical twins who were dressed alike turn out to be more similar in personality than identical twins who were not?" the results essentially answer "No."[53] Such environmental differences seem often not to make a difference. In the burgeoning field of twins studies by researchers such as Tellegen, Bouchard, Lykken and Rich at the University of Minnesota and Lindon Eaves at Virginia we find strong indication of genetic contribution not merely to "Positive Emotionality" ("well being, social potency, achievement, and social closeness"), "Negative Emotionality" ("stress reaction, alienation, and aggression"), and "Constraint" ("control, harm avoidance, and traditionalism") but also to differences in religious attitudes and behaviors.[54] These are impressive studies. But just what is their import? Do such studies return us to the sociobiological ground of accounting for altruism by appeal to the resultant increase in the fitness of the species to survive? Or can one argue that environment accounts for much of the development attributed to genes and that generalization from twins studies to the wider population is itself questionable?[55]

Ambivalence is justified. It is difficult to know precisely how to assess the bearing of such genetic studies, which are still very much incomplete. It is evident that the environment can exert influence in relationship to the tendencies given in genetic endowment. Perhaps the best-known example is phenylketonuria (PKU). This single-gene defect, which was linked with severe retardation, can be addressed by providing a diet low in phenylalanine during the child's developing years.[56] More dramatically, some studies suggest that an organism's purposive response to its environment can actually influence its gene cells.[57] The genetic researchers themselves disclaim any talk of "mean genes," but they are calling for a serious reckoning with the genetic factor in any attempt to understand what it is to be human.

That is a call faith needs to hear and heed. I reserve for later a fuller discussion of what Christian faith may well say of this inner boundary, but that it must recognize the importance of such genetic connectedness needs to be emphasized even now, for religion seems perpetually tempted to flee the earth and the body. Indeed, even the word "science" can be usurped for service in this flight. Religious voices, new and old, invite us to believe that if only we *think* aright, our problems will be solved. The mind is what matters! Such an approach can take a metaphysical form, as in the writings of Willis Harman of the Institute of Noetic Sciences in Sausalito, California:

> Individual minds are not separate (although individual brains may appear to be); they connect at some unconscious level. The physical world is to the greater mind as a dream image is to the individual mind. Ultimately reality is contacted, not through the physical senses, but through the deep intuition. Consciousness is not the end-product of material evolution, having had to await development of complex neuronal networks in the human cortex: Rather, consciousness was here first![58]

THE HUMAN "MORE"

My body weighs too much to permit me to make such flights! They do seem to sunder the relationship that underlies the boundary within our human being. But one can understand their appeal, and one needs to address the concern they voice. No account of human being can suffice that reduces our living to some mechanical movement of matter known to the senses. There is more to which we must attend. Thus the sociobiologist is challenged not by kin altruism and reciprocal altruism (merely) but by the reality of care and love directed beyond the kinship group.[59] A wise and compassionate neurologist, Oliver Sacks, can introduce for us the theme of that "more," as he ponders the vital resources available to his patients:

> I have known Jimmie now for nine years—and neuropsychologically, he has not changed in the least. He still has the severest, most devastating Korsakov's, cannot remember isolated items for more than a few seconds, and has a dense amnesia going back to 1945. But humanly, spiritually, he is at times a different man altogether—no longer fluttering, restless, bored and lost, but deeply attentive to the beauty and soul of the world, rich in all the Kierkegaardian categories—and [sic] aesthetic, the moral, the religious, the

dramatic. I had wondered, when I first met him, if he was not condemned to a sort of "Humean" froth, a meaningless fluttering on the surface of life, and whether there was any way of transcending the incoherence of his Humean disease. Empirical science told me there was not—but empirical science, empiricism, takes no account of the soul, no account of what constitutes and determines personal being. Perhaps there is a philosophical as well as a clinical lesson here: that in Korsakov's, or dementia, or in other such catastrophes, however great the organic damage and Humean dissolution, there remains the undiminished possibility of reintegration by art, by communion, by touching the human spirit: and this can be preserved in what seems at first a hopeless state of neurological devastation.[60]

Sacks makes at least a rhetorical flight himself. Is the possibility of reintegration literally "undiminished"? But what is he stretching toward? There seems to sound here an evocation of the transcendence or freedom of the human spirit. This is not a matter merely of rescuing an environmental factor from the geneticists' grasp. After all, behavioristic psychology would leave the environment equally silent, if one tried to speak of freedom. It seems better to recognize again both connection and difference in this matter. After all, our earlier discussion of the spacetime continuum should make clear that nature and so our embodiment in nature are themselves not without variety and contingency.[61] In what we know as human nature that which is given reaches a level of complexity which "turns" reflexively in such a way that difference takes the form of decision and contingency that of choice. What more may be said of this?

HUMAN COMPLEXITY:
LANGUAGE, PURPOSE, CONSCIOUSNESS, FREEDOM
A common element in efforts to identify the qualitative distinctiveness of human being is the theme of complexity. K. Denbigh has proposed the notion of *integrality,* "which is the product of the number of connections in a structure and the number of different *kinds* of parts." In citing this, Peacocke adds: "Integrality is not identical with 'information,' nor with entropy, it can increase in a closed system (e.g. when an egg develops into, say, a chick) and its total value on the earth has increased since life began."[62] The qualitative complexification of language marks this change. As the reality of symbols modifies the stimulus/response system, the human person is opened to a world that transcends the immediate environment.[63] Part of this symbolic complexity involves the ability to contemplate long-term goals. This is a difference of importance. Thus (even) animal rights

activist Peter Singer notes that "a creature who is capable of understanding that he or she lives over time and is therefore capable of planning for the future (i.e., a human) is a creature who loses more by being killed than a creature who lives only moment to moment."[64]

The complexity of which we are speaking not only stretches the human organism out into the future; it "doubles" the evolutionary project in the present, as consciousness gives rise to self-consciousness. Of this critical point many testimonies arise from persons working in the descriptive disciplines. As a biochemist specializing in thermodynamics, Jeffrey Wicken is not about to minimize the importance of the spatiotemporal evolutionary process, but he can write almost mystically of the "within":

> In point of fact we understand no more of the internal, subjective dimension of being today than did Plato, and we have no reason to expect that we ever will except in the philosophically restricted sense that brain centers and their electrochemical activities will be brought into tighter connection with subjective states as research proceeds.[65]

In the reflexive doubling that we know as human mentality we come over the threshold of human freedom. Mihaly Csikszentmihalyi speaks of such consciousness as "a clutch, a mechanism that makes it possible to disengage cause from effect."[66] Or Roger Sperry can find that his split-brain surgical studies lead him to ponder the integrative and directive force in the brain and to write "When a new entity is created the new properties of the entity, or system as a whole, thereafter overpower the causal forces of the component entities at all successively lower levels in the multinested hierarchies of the new infrastructure."[67] And—to hear only one further voice—Sacks clearly finds his work in neurology pertinent to human well-being, but he resists any claim to exhaustive scope:

> Of course, the brain *is* a machine and a computer—everything in classical neurology is correct. But our mental processes, which constitute our being and life, are not just abstract and mechanical, but personal, as well—and, as such, involve not just classifying and categorising, but continual judging and feeling also. If this is missing, we become computer-like.[68]

EMBODIED SPIRIT

The point here is not to pile up mystical passages until the walls of science's reductionist castle collapse under the sheer weight of such ecstasies. But if one takes note of what these students of the human, from their very different orientations, are saying, one finds something to which faith must attend as well. Long-range purpose, the "within" of subjectivity, feeling, judgment, "downward" causation—are these not the stuff of which, say, a Kierkegaardian self is made? Consider this classic passage from *The Sickness Unto Death*:

> A human being is spirit. But what is spirit? Spirit is the self. But what is the self? The self is a relation that relates itself to itself or is the relation's relating itself to itself or is the relation's relating itself to itself in the relation; the self is not the relation but is the relation's relating itself to itself. A human being is a synthesis of the infinite and the finite, of the temporal and the eternal, of freedom and necessity, in short a synthesis. A synthesis is a relation between two. Considered in this way, a human being is still not a self. In the relation between two, the relation is the third as a negative unity, and the two relate to the relation and in the relation to the relation. . . . If, however, the relation relates itself to itself, this relation is the positive third, and this is the self.[69]

That sounds familiar: givenness and possibility together in the self-relation that becomes freedom.

There is a great risk that in the enthusiasm of discovery one might overstate the point. The "life" I am seeking to describe does occur *within the body* and *within the spatiotemporal process*. Kierkegaard certainly seemed to have no sense for the presence of anything resembling genuine variation (not to say, individuation) within the evolutionary process preceding human emergence. Writing in the 1840s, he could hardly be expected to recognize the continuities dramatically demonstrated in the publication in 1859 of Darwin's *Origin of the Species*. But *we* cannot dismiss Darwin or the like-minded contemporary scientific challenges of, say, the twins studies to which we have already referred. Accordingly, we will need to speak of the mystery of the distinctively human precisely within larger than human wholes. And we will need particularly to guard against abstracting some spiritual essence—mind from body, spirit from matter. Within the relationship that is the human—that relationship of which Kierkegaard wrote without reference to scientific studies—there is distinction to be sure, but there is connection as well. In such a way one may speak of the neurochemical processes involved in the higher-level processes, or—as Sperry does—of "mutually reciprocal" interaction within the human.[70]

It should not be difficult for Christian faith to speak of such connectedness. It is clear that "the Hebrew did not think of the soul as having a body but as being a body which was alive."[71] The tendency of the Hebrew scriptures to link emotion with "the bowels" or the kidneys should not be dismissed as colorful artifice. The writings of the early Christian community were certainly crafted in an environment in which dualistic temptations were present, but in the main one finds here a strong affirmation of the unity of the human person. To the affirmation of the physical and material entailed in a belief in creation, there is added the recognition that in Jesus the eternal logos became precisely *sarx*, "flesh." That was necessary, if "what is not assumed cannot be saved." In Mark 13:20 (RSV), "no human being would be saved," the word for "human being" is, again, *sarx, "*flesh." In chapter 5 we will return to the natural consequence of this recognition of human unity: the transformation of the whole person entailed in the doctrine of the resurrection.

I say it should not be difficult for Christian faith to recognize the connectedness within the human person and between that person and nature. Yet spiritualizing tendencies have afflicted the Christian church throughout history. Frank Bottomley distinguishes two forms of "spiritualistic rejection":

> It could take the form of a complete and inordinate asceticism in which the body was despised and neglected and all its impulses stifled, where everything to do with the body and its reasonable care—nature, marriage, sex—is regarded as incurably evil and must be ruthlessly excised with the possible exception of a minimal area necessary to maintain life. Alternatively, if the body is already utterly evil nothing can make it worse and contempt may be expressed in complete indulgence—in the satiation of its appetites and the fulfillment of all its impulses so that the soul is freed from the demands of its unworthy vehicle. Gnosticism assailed the Church without and within.[72]

These two forms are perhaps nowhere more devastatingly present than in the troubled Christian history concerning sexuality.[73] That reality which should suggest so richly the connectedness of body and spirit seems so readily distorted also (especially?) in the lives of believers. Certainly some accounting of such a discrepancy is needed. It seems too facile to suggest that a church faced with cultural construals of body as machine or animal will flee to save the soul.[74] In chapter 3 we will consider how faith speaks of such dualistic distortion under the rubric of sin and evil.

IMAGE IN RELATIONSHIP

I have emphasized the import for faith of boundaries in human life as recognized without special appeal to faith. But faith does, of course, have something to say here as well. Central to what faith would say regarding the distinctiveness of the human is the notion of creation in the image of God. In Genesis, after all, it is only human life that is said to be created in God's image.[75] One cannot, of course, expect descriptive studies of the human to employ such a category explicitly. But it would be strange not to try to draw faith's speech about the distinctively human into some consonance with what has been said up to this point concerning human life.

Western intellectual history since Descartes has focused on the mind as the key to selfhood in a way that reflects classical Greek confidence in reason. Descartes's self as a thinking thing (*res cogitans*) that cannot doubt its doubting, Locke's emphasis on the human continuity found in the activity of memory, Kant's sense of the constitutive transcendental activities of the reasoning self—this kind of history, not surprisingly, can be paralleled in much of the Christian church's reflection about the image of God in the human. There is *that* consonance. Thus Moltmann can chronicle as follows:

> 1. According to the analogy of substance, the soul (which is the human being's reasonable and volitional nature) is the seat of human likeness to God, for it is immortal, and similar to the divine nature.
> 2. According to the analogy of form, it is the human being's upright walk, and his upright glance.
> 3. According to the analogy of proportionality, the likeness is to be found in man's lordship over the earth, since this corresponds to God's general lordship over the world.[76]

One might say in the terms we have been using that each of these focuses on the theme of separation, though they do so differently. Even the fourth theme that Moltmann considers, the community of man and woman corresponding according to the analogy of relation to the triune relationships, pries out a particular aspect or characteristic of human life as the image, separating that from the fullness of embodied human life in nature. I have been speaking of separation or distinction as an aspect of relationship. It is the theme of relationship that Claus Westermann finds central in the Genesis stories: "The creation of man in God's image is directed to something happening between God and man. The Creator created a creature that corresponds to him, to whom he can speak, and who can hear him."[77] This is the theme to which several theologians have recently turned as well. Moltmann does so, as does Philip Hefner.[78] Of course it would be possible in turn to abstract the relationship to God from the rest of our relationships. Against such a tendency Douglas John Hall claims Martin Luther and John Calvin as support for his "relational conception" whose whole intent is "not to demonstrate that this (human) creature is higher, or more complex, or worthier, but to designate a specific function of this creature—a very positive function—in relation to the others."[79] Hall's concern is that we recognize extrahuman creation as a third, but equally inseparable, focus of the love commandment. That surely well makes the point of connection.

Indeed it may *over*make the point, if we are to engage "in the same mode of contemplation, investigation, or reverie" in relation to God, our own species and trees, rocks and whales.[80] I wonder if that does not "flatten out" the conception of the image. After all, is there not a temporal dimension to the image, if Westermann is right that we are talking about something that is intended to "happen" between God and us? It is clear that the New Testament writings employ image talk in essentially future terms: we *will* bear the image of God's son (1 Cor. 15:49). Perhaps, then, to understand human life in the image of God is to speak of endowment in relationship for destiny.[81] As we think of the human within the sweep of the spatio-temporal process, it seems appropriate to recognize again distinctions within the connections that make up the complex of relationships that characterizes human life.

But Hall has very helpfully underlined what one might call the "spatial" dimension of "image of God" talk—that such talk drives outside ourselves to address those "others": the human other, God, and—yes—nature. We will turn now in successive chapters to the first two of these. And we expect to find linkages, as Hall has supposed. What shall we make, for example, of the fact that, with respect to the human other, women and people of other races have been aligned with "nature" by the dominant white male voice?[82] That assignment lies ahead, but in this chapter we have prepared for it by stressing precisely the positioning of *all* human life within the spacetime continuum. Surely this has implications for faith. One does not need to be a professional theologian to think so. Thus a psychologist such as Mihaly Csikszentmihalyi can write about humankind becoming "part of the choir" rather than the soloist in that the issue is no longer what one shall do to save one's individual soul but how to preserve life and the evolution of complexity in its ever-changing terms.[83] Or a geneticist like Lindon Eaves can close a paper stressing the need for theological attention to genetic studies with this: "'Spirit' is the name which embraces both the empirical phenomena of givenness, connectedness and openness, and the process which makes it possible to adapt to and live at peace with the fact that we are not self-generated, independent, or sure of our destiny."[84]

In Part Two we will ponder what this positioning of human life means for us as Christian faith meets its "others." In the meantime there are the other boundaries of which we must speak.

3

LIFE WITH
THE OTHER

In the coming about of human life something new, something different, happens in the spacetime continuum. I have argued that if we are to understand human life, we must take account of that difference within connection. It is a difference *within connection*, and I have stressed the importance of the ongoing relationship of the human with nature within the whole and of that which is more than or other than body with the body. But the difference abides and, accordingly, the relationships between and among human beings have their own distinctiveness. It is those relationships—human to/with human—that we seek now to understand What differences does life with the human other(s) make for faith?

THE GIVENNESS OF THE OTHER

We speak here of life "with" the other. Here we stand alongside each other as beings of the same order. This was not the case with regard to the relationships considered in chapter 2, though some measure of that shared "withness" was identified in speaking of the human place in nature. But as I turn to the human other I sense far more deeply that we correspond to each other, we are "together" in a nature that differs from us in a way we do not differ from each other. To say that we are "with" each other seems to describe a basic truth about us.[1] It may also *pre*scribe. We will consider in this chapter how the sense of the ethical comes to prominence in this relationship. The human person has some ethical responsibility *toward* nature, I have argued. But we human beings have responsibility *with* each other ethically. We are together in needing to work out—again, together—how we are to live.

THE GIVEN AS OTHER

A first step is to recognize the *givenness* of the other. I will shortly speak of the ineradicable presence of human others—that the other is "always already" there with us. Such talk is risky, for it might be taken to suggest that the human other is given to me for my use or disposition. That suggestion might be supported by what I have said of the "with." If we human beings exist "with" each other, alongside each other, together, what is to prevent one of us from taking charge of the other(s)? One might try to protest ethically, but there would not seem to be any barrier to such action in our very being. One way to "take over" would be to assume that when one meets the other, one meets something familiar and accessible— and hence readily serviceable to oneself. One need not state the risk with such dramatic darkness. Use and abuse aside, one might put "given" and "with" together to suggest that the other is essentially like oneself and is to be expected to act accordingly. No surprises are to be expected then in the thinking or feeling or acting of the other(s).

Against such a view, it is essential to say that it is precisely the human *other* that is given. That the one whom I meet is other is given. What does this mean? It means that the other's reality is neither created nor controlled by me. Not created by me, for I encounter the other already *there*—over there, sharing space with me. As Edward Farley says, "the other . . . is what I do not and cannot experience in the mode I experience myself. It is an 'I' which is not I."[2] And not controlled by me—for what human reality will come of that other life is beyond my purposing control. Even parents, when they look into the eyes of their children, know this. If we are dealing with another human life, we are facing that which is not an extension of our being. Children belong "with," not "to," their parents. We own property; we give birth to children. The French Jewish philosopher Emmanuel Levinas has written of this otherness in particularly powerful ways. Against the tendency to regard the other as simply another being *alongside* me and therefore like me in all essential respects, he writes of the "height" of the other.[3] We are not on the same plane. Or in countering the notion that the human other is readily accessible—fodder for my intellect and food for my purpose—he can evoke the sense of distance by speaking of the other as one who has "passed by."[4]

In such ways Levinas would awaken us to genuine and ineradicable difference. The other human being is, as I am, human. But this human being, precisely as human, is other; here is one I do not create and cannot control. And I should be suspicious about classifying this other. The existentialist writers have spoken of the human other in this sense as No/thing—not a thing, which is suitable for disposition by my intellect. In Levinas, these themes come together in a passage whose strangeness may derive more from content than form:

> The absolutely other is the Other. He and I do not form a number. The collectivity in which I say "you" or "we" is not a plural of the "I." I, you—these are not individuals of a common concept. Neither possession nor the unity of number nor the unity of concepts link me to the Stranger, the Stranger who disturbs the being at home with oneself. But Stranger also means the free one. Over him I have no *power*. He escapes my grasp by an essential dimension, even if I have him at my disposal. He is not wholly in my site. But I, who have no concept in common with the Stranger, am, like him, without genus. We are the same and the other. The conjunction *and* here designates neither addition nor power of one term over the other.[5]

For a culture or person inclined to deny difference such talk will indeed seem strange. It is precisely talk of the stranger, after all. But such talk should not seem odd to the Christian. That the stranger bears a special claim in the Christian view of things has already been mentioned and we will discuss this more fully in the third section of this chapter. But here the point is not that we are called to a certain course of action but that in our very being there is given existence alongside one who is truly other. It is in such a fundamental way that the Priestly writer speaks of creation of the human in God's image: male and female God created them (Gen. 1:27). Surely for the Christian there is no more important thing to say about human life than this, that we are made in God's image. And to speak of this, the creation story tells us, is to speak of being created *with another*, who is identified from the very beginning as other. The reference here is not to some specific social arrangement as the goal of life but to the givenness of life with the other. This, to be human with the other, is not some secondary word added to a defining common property. At the base, from the beginning, to be human is to be with one who is other.[6]

FACING THE OTHER

Levinas writes that this theme of human life with the human other can be suggested more succinctly by "the face." On a commonsense basis we would probably say that the human face best expresses the reality of an individual, even though some deception is possible also here. Levinas writes of the face revealing that the other is not under our power. In the "face" we meet the body of another, a body not under the control of our consciousness. He stresses the "nudity" of the face; it serves the being and will of the other. We may "look" at the other from what we suppose to be a safe distance. We may "gaze" at the other with idle curiosity or controlling intent. But what we see is the face of one who is other than we: "The face *means* differently. In it a being's infinite resistance to our power is affirmed precisely against the murderous will that it defies, because it has the meaning of itself, completely nude—and the nudity of the face is no figure of speech."[7]

I do not take Levinas to be denying that one person can kill another person, or that a human being can be manipulated and controlled. But then what we have—precisely, *what* we have—is no longer a human other. And the face will tell the difference. Is it not striking in this light to recall the biblical emphasis on the human face, once again in connection with the theme of creation in the image of God? Jürgen Moltmann does not want to link "image of God" talk with particular human phenomena, such as the reasoning process. But he writes:

> And yet, according to the biblical traditions, there is apparently one point at which God's relationship to human beings is manifested and can be recognized: the human face. It is the human face which becomes the mirror of God: "But now we all *with unveiled face* reflect the glory of the Lord" (II Cor. 3:18). . . . The whole person is known first of all in his committed attention, and his committed attention first of all in his open eyes and his attentive face. The play of emotions is reflected in the face, and a person's "heart" is best expressed in his face;[8]

Moltmann adds references to "the knowledge of the glory of God *in the face of Jesus Christ*" (2 Cor. 4:6) and to the Christian hope for a time when we will see "*face to face*" (1 Cor. 13:12).[9] Certainly in the biblical understanding the "face" reveals a great deal. What the Levinas material makes clearer is the recognition that in life, as we now know it, the "face" marks our differences from each other even in our existence with each other. In the next chapter we will consider what can be said of the "face of God" in relation to human life and then, in chapter 5, we will explore the hope the Christian can hold for "then face to face." Here we seek to understand what it means that even our present life is not "faceless."

SINGULAR AND REPRESENTATIVE: THE "THIRD"
It is clear that what has already been said applies to every other, to all the others. In that sense, relative similarities and differences among the others are not significant. We stress similarities, for example, when we speak of twins. But the anthropologist Victor Turner sounds the other note in chronicling the fact that the Ndembu people of northwestern Zambia conceptualize the duality of twins "in terms not of a pair of similars but of a pair of opposites": "The unity of such a pair is that of a tensed unity or *Gestalt*, whose tension is constituted by ineradicable forces or realities, implacably opposed, and whose nature as a unit is constituted and bounded by the very forces that contend within it."[10]

This qualitative point of otherness does need to be made, even with the contemporary twins studies in mind. Yet we face here a delicate dialectic. To recognize that every other is alike in being genuinely other, beyond our creation and control, is not to deny diverse connections among those others. Thus, as Richard Wentz has suggested, the human other is both "singular" and "representative":

> Since all existence is hyphenated, the self is always a singular other whose relationship to others is representative. That is, the other with whom we stand in meaningful personal relation is also a self among others. . . . Each singular other cannot be dealt with as an individually distinct possibility. That is impossible because that singular other exists in various modes of relationships that may be organized into recognizable clusters or sets.[11]

If we lost sight of the other's *other* connections, we could collapse the richness and complexity of our human connectedness into the romantic and yet ultimately rather monotonous collectivity of an indefinite number of dyads. Much would then be lost, for the recognition of my "neighbor's neighbor," of the "third person," of the You and not just the Thou, carries implications for understanding and action to which we will attend later in this chapter. Thus we seek to retain what Wentz refers to as the "representative": distinctions in reality are designated by reference to gender, race, culture, faith, and the like. But those realities are not solid substances, as if there were one thing called female experience or black experience.

Indeed, the cultural linguistic representations of such realities may gain their power partly by stabilizing—with whatever degree of selection and distortion—experience in the field to which the distinctions apply. Such stabilizing order may serve to distance one from the collective other, or in a reversal it may support a "hetero-realism," entailing alienation from one's own gender and one's own body.[12]

BENIGN ALIENATION AND MORAL EVIL

Those human beings with whom we live are other—that much is given, we have said. It remains to say that such life together is itself given. More specifically, in speaking of the givenness of the other, I seek to prevent a sentimental celebration of otherness that would actually yield an individualism where lip service is paid to difference but the human person is left alone, comfortably or uncomfortably. We are other than each other—that is given. But we are given to each other in our otherness—yes, for good or for ill. And surely it is a matter also of saying for good *and* ill. Even if we do not speak of human moral evil, one will need to speak of inescapable incompatibilities arising from our finitude. Farley refers to such realities as "benign alienation," and has examples ready at hand:

> Here we have the parent unable to simultaneously attend to the needs of all the children, the inability of an engaged couple to adjust their career plans to each other, and the impossibility of a firm to appoint all of its qualified people as its Chief Executive Officer.[13]

Moreover, one *does* need to speak of the violation that constitutes moral evil. But of course even such wounds in relationship require relationship in order to be. In chapter 5, I will speak of how that fundamental structure of relationship provides resources for the healing of those wounds.

THE GIVEN IN LANGUAGE

Part of the "modern" worldview to which I alluded in chapter 1 is the tendency to regard the terms of relationships, the persons involved, as essentially independent of the relationships. At an extreme this view leaves the self secure with—or stuck with—itself, free to fashion such relationships as it can and will. There is some truth to this, for we do make choices that affect the fabric of our connectedness. Take language, for example. At some point we do peer out at a world perspectively organized around and centered in our viewing eyes and organizing brain. I can report what

I see. But what we moderns failed to see was that the language we employ does not represent to us an objectively existing world, unaffected by our speaking and knowing. We create as we describe, though this is not to say that we create out of nothing. As we set about to choose—as in our speaking to describe, we are "always already" in our relationship. I am not alone in the world. The self that looks out from itself to the environing world is never a self without a given world. That world is not naked nature, but it is not simply the self either. "Worlds" are linguistically constituted and culturally mediated.[14] We can see the other, how ever so poorly, because we share some givenness with that other—a givenness that includes but does not collapse into language.

Martin Buber spoke of the meeting of I and Thou. He spoke of the meeting happening to I and Thou "at the same time."[15] Perhaps that understates the reality of difference and hence the "surprise" of the other with which time echoes.[16] But to recognize that surprise is to understand that the two do meet each other. They are given to each other. The other really enters my space and time to meet me, and I the other's.

Thus to stress the givenness of the other is not to abandon the self, for the self is, in turn, the other's other in the meeting which is the giving. In the meeting, otherness is not lost. But what is found? What may be said of life in the light of such givenness?

THE GIFT AND TASK OF SELF AND OTHER

The first dimension of the givenness of the other is, as it were, spatial. I am aware of, I confront, the other "always already" *there*—over there, sharing space with me in this present moment. But this other—not my creation, beyond my control, resisting my classification—*is* given to me. The givenness is not merely a condition of coexistence; it is an actual coming together. That is the second dimension of givenness, and it is emphatically temporal. Indeed, the "space" of coexistence as genuine agents in the present moment turns out to be an intermediate reality, a transitional mode. The gift of each to the other comes to be from a past. And it comes to be for a future, for in this gift there is also a task. Out of this reality of the gift and task of self and other there arises the sense of claim to which we must attend. But first we seek to understand how it is that self and other are "there" for each other, as gift and task.

TEMPORALITY AND FREEDOM

Who are these of whom we speak? I and the other whom I meet, we who are other for each other, we and all the other others—we are centers of freedom. That is why the other cannot be controlled *as other*, though the destruction of murder and manipulation remains possible. Here we return to the theme in chapter 2, where we spoke of how in the human person nature rises (or falls) to "double itself" in, as Kierkegaard put it, "a relation that relates itself to itself." Here arises the mysterious "within" of which thermodynamicist Jeffrey Wicken speaks, the "downward" causation of Roger Sperry's split-brain studies, the judging and feeling personal "soul" to which neurologist Oliver Sacks bears witness.[17] It was this to which Kierkegaard would testify throughout his turbulent authorship, as he gave notice in the preface of his first published work, *Either/Or*: "It has perhaps from time to time occurred to you, dear reader, to doubt a little the correctness of the celebrated philosophical thesis that the outward is the inward and the inward the outward."[18]

It does occur to us to doubt such leveling theses, whether they are the gift of a Hegelian metaphysics or a behavioristic psychology. The inner is not the outer, and there is indeed a sense in which a person has "privileged access" to that which lies within.[19] We are speaking of the inwardness of knowing and feeling when we say "stone walls do not a prison make" or when we remember that we can fake a headache but not a fever. And we are speaking of the will within us, for we know with Kierkegaard that "the inward work is the true work of freedom."[20] Reductionist theses, no matter how "celebrated," do not manage to banish the *feeling* of freedom. And doubt persists even in the face of claims that such feeling is itself determined, for we do not expect that the knowledge of freedom will somehow itself escape into the security of self-contained proof.[21]

Since "the inner is not the outer," we are indeed other than each other, despite some common participation in and possession of the outer. But, once again, we are "given" to each other as other. And so the inner and the outer interact in the dialectic that constitutes human life. How we perceive our situation, our "outer" state, is affected by our inner freedom, which, moreover, can move to effect change in what may seem solidly settled. But the converse is also true: the outer bears in upon us in our freedom, which is very much a limited freedom. We have some freedom in dealing with what is given to us, but the gift is at the same time our taskmaster. David Kolb has argued that the modern consciousness is particularly prone to forget this gift-and-task givenness of the other:

> One of our self-images is that we live at a distance from what was taken for granted by earlier ages or may still be taken for granted in some other societies in the world. . . . We have more choices, more possibilities. Along with distance comes control. . . . We identify everything around us, including ourselves, as possible objects for planning and control.[22]

THE OTHER AS "GOOD ENOUGH"

As the modern world—with its firm and clear boundaries—ages, we ask: How are self and other together as centers of freedom bearing on each other? How is it that they are so? At one level the answer may be sought in child development studies. D. W. Winnicott of the psychoanalytic movement known as object-relations theory colorfully captures the temporal sense of the givenness of the other in the phrase from T. S. Eliot which he adopts and adapts for one of his titles: "Home is where we start from."[23]

And how do we start? As the mother holds the infant, she reliably mirrors the child back to itself, creating what Winnicott calls a "potential space" between herself and the child. The "potential space" transcends the boundary between the "me" and the "not-me." In play the sense of personal presence in a world arises. Some frustration will be experienced as the infant moves from the initial experience of omnipotence. As Winnicott succinctly puts it: "It is not from being God that human beings arrive at the humility proper to individuality."[24] But Winnicott's emphasis is on the creativity and not compliance. Within that potential space the child can come to experience "integration, personalization, and realization."[25] Individuation thus does not occur through negation of "the other." Indeed, in the healthy child some continuity is maintained with the parental environment. The mother's role here is to be "good enough," worthy of trust, but not holding the child in dependency, for it is the very definition of health that "the individual can enjoy going around looking for appropriate opposition":[26]

> The need for a good environment, which is absolute at first, rapidly becomes relative. *The ordinary good mother is good enough.* If she is *good enough*

> the infant becomes able to allow for her deficiencies by mental activity. This applies to meeting not only instinctual impulses but also all the most primitive types of ego need, including the need for negative care or an alive neglect. The mental activity of the infant turns a *good-enough* environment into a perfect environment. . . . What releases the mother from her need to be near-perfect is the infant's understanding.[27]

Winnicott places particular emphasis on the physical, on the fact that "in the building up of the personality a . . . taking in and giving out is done through all the organs of the body, the eyes, the skin, the ears, the nose, etc."[28] This surely makes sense, given what was said in chapter 2 concerning the relationship of that which is more or other than body to body. This emphasis on the physical may be supplemented by recognizing the importance of "vocal gestures" in linguistic symbols, just as the crucial role of the mother is not denied in introducing the figure of the father. The development of role distance and the tolerance of ambiguity are provoked as the young child seeks to deal with diversity of expectations.[29]

EXOCENTRICITY

How is such testimony to be understood by the person seeking to think as a Christian about human identity? The Christian will discover here a clear witness asserting that we are not only created *with* the other, but God actually gives us life *through* the other. There seems to be no reason to limit the "through" to genetic endowment. The relationship with the human other is fundamental to our being and our becoming; no spiritual essence is exempted, whether in origin or development. This is powerfully and poetically indicated in Genesis 5, which unmistakably uses image and likeness language to link divine and human creativity across the span of Adam's troubled years: "When God created humankind, he made them in the likeness of God. Male and female he created them, and he blessed them and named them 'humankind' when they were created. When Adam had lived one hundred and thirty years, he became the father of a son in his likeness, according to his image, and named him Seth" (Gen. 5:1-3.) Seth is born in the image of one created in the image of God! Continuity in the coming-to-be of the human, I have said, seems unmistakable. But religious movements outside Christendom and inside it still suggest that one's relationship to God can be separated from such fleshly and worldly processes as being born and developing an ego.[30]

Just how God-talk is to be more precisely related to this understanding of human origin and development is not at all unmistakable, however. That positioning will be affected by what one takes it to be to speak of God. The next chapter takes up that theme in speaking of life "before God." But in anticipation one may appropriately ask here, not what God is doing in all of this, but how the developing human person may come to relate to God personally, if not necessarily fully consciously. Wolfhart Pannenberg has addressed that question in his sustained effort to "transform and retain," to "expand and deepen" nontheological insights. He appropriates Erik Erikson's discussion of the importance of basic trust in the development of identity in addressing this issue: "If basic trust is not to be lost, the child must . . . break its ties to the mother and to the parents generally. There must be a new direction that allows the growing child to maintain its trust in an *unlimited* security despite all the threats and adversities of life."[31]

The God of religious faith is then introduced as ensuring such unlimited security. Such an approach seems more dictated by Pannenberg's concept of God as the all-determining power than by the human development studies cited. After all, it is connection and *distinction* of which we have been speaking in these studies. If in the logic of relationship what the child needs is a "good enough" mother, does it follow that human trust in God requires "*unlimited* security"?[32] In the next chapter we will explore an understanding of God that seems to connect better with human freedom in development.

Pannenberg certainly does not deny the reality of development. Indeed, he is foremost among Christian theologians in speaking of the human person as "exocentric," as "open to the world." And he has rich empirical material to appropriate. We do, it seems, come to be through the other and *for* the other as well. Pannenberg roots human exocentricity in one of the traits distinguishing human life. In the (other) animals, perceptions release innate behavioral mechanisms in a closed functional circle. With human beings it is not so:

> Our instincts are for the most part deficient in development and at the same time blended with one another; for both reasons they operate in an uncertain way as compared with those of our animal relatives. Our perceptions do not release precise instinctual reactions. For this very reason our perceptions can develop a life of their own and turn to things without being limited by instinctual interests that guide our behavior.[33]

Language and culture are thus understood to compensate for human instinctual deficiency. Perhaps such need is not our weakness but our strength. Thus we are less keenly susceptible to impressions from the environment, since we are able to distance ourselves from it. And what follows from this?

> Yet precisely for this reason they [human beings] also have the ability to be present in a new way to what is other than themselves, that is, in such a manner that they are not absorbed into that other through being wholly at the mercy of the content of their perceptions. Human beings are present to what is other *as* other. When they attend to an object, they are conscious of its differentness, its otherness. And in one and the same act I grasp the otherness of the object not only in its difference from me but also in its distinction from other objects.[34]

Thus does the dialectic of self and other arise. There is a dimension of self-transcendence in the human capacity to turn to the other as other. Clearly the relationship to the other need not yield an impoverishment of the self. Indeed, to the contrary, Pannenberg—building on Erikson and other neo-Freudians—argues (against George Herbert Mead) that not only the self (the "me" as the summary of the picture others have of me) but the ego (the "I" as the agent of reflection) is derived from this relationship, as the ego puts itself in the place of others. Yet Pannenberg recognizes that the ego can at least in part refuse to accept the social self. He remarks that "only in the case of their own bodies must individuals make the best of things as they are."[35] The other opens the future. One is reminded of Winnicott, who writes not only of the "good-enough mother," but of being "happy enough" in marriage as well.[36] And Pannenberg goes on to discuss how we speak and play together, representing, creating, and regulating reality.[37]

Pannenberg's analysis is offered as *Anthropology in Theological Perspective*. For him, theology really is to have to do with something other than itself. Nontheological insights are richly present in Pannenberg's analysis. It is less clear to me that due weight is given to these insights once they are placed in theological perspective. In the next chapter it will be clear that I do not join Pannenberg in speaking of God as the "all-determining power." Obviously one's God concept will be at work in how one conceives of and discharges the task of viewing anthropological insights "in theological perspective." But if one finds Pannenberg's nontheological description instructive, as I do, how is one to understand such material in the light of Christian faith?

BEING AND BECOMING HUMAN

This theme, that we are created not only with and through but even *for* life with the other, surely finds resonance or consonance in how the Christian will speak faithfully of human life. Perhaps the two biblical stories of creation complement each other. Genesis 1 witnesses to the fundamental fact that we are created *with* the other: "Male and female he created them." This is good, "very good" (Gen. 1:31). But to read on in the book of Genesis is to be told that "it is not good that the man should be alone; I will make him a helper as his partner" (Gen. 2:18). If life is inherently temporal (chap. 2, above), we may expect to speak of it not only in terms of being but especially in terms of becoming (cf. chap. 5, below). Together, the creation stories help us to find the other in both our being (gift) and our becoming (task).

Thus one may appropriately speak of loneliness as a creaturely condition of our being that needs to be addressed in our becoming.[38] One catches that sense of movement in the text. The other is to be a "fit helper"; "helpers" "fit" when something is to happen. But the happening or becoming is not merely some extrinsic or functional matter, which leaves one's being unchanged. The problem is that "it is not good to *be* alone" and God's response calls forth this human word: "This at last *is* bone of my bones and flesh of my flesh" (Gen. 2:23a, emphasis mine). Clearly there is gain rather than loss in this movement within being. To speak of self and other as being "for" each other is not to diminish them. For the human creature, the culmination of creation (if not the "crown"), a "helper" is provided.[39] To need a helper is no weakness, and to be a helper is not that either, for the same term is applied elsewhere to God (e.g., Pss. 10:14; 30:10; 54:4). To speak in this relational way of God does not leave the concept of God unchanged, of course, but it is clearly to be understood as praise of God. That human beings, made in God's image, should need each other is not to be lamented.

It is worth emphasizing that all of this is creation talk. The rhythm of "from, with, and for" the other is not driven by the beat of the fall into sin. That the movement is to yield an increase in value does not depend on a fall into sin. Thus there seems to be reason to speak of creation as "good, but not perfect" and to recognize that the pertinence of such a distinction does not derive from moral evil. In this there is renewed warning against religious views that regard either the sociality or the temporality of our present existence as essentially negative and perhaps a suggestion that a faithful formulation of Christian hope for the future should take these dimensions into account. I will sketch such a formulation in chapter 5, arguing that the added urgency sin contributes does not yield in the formulation of the hope a reversal of these creational directions.

THE TASK OF THE SOFTER SELF

Within creation, then, a task is given in the gift of self and other. To be human is to be with the other and to need the help of the other. I mean to suggest that for human beings to live, the task must somehow be addressed. Coexistence is not optional, and in some sense cooperation is not either.[40] Sin itself is parasitic on this creational structure. As Edward Farley puts it: "Unless the human being is already drawn out of itself and conditioned by the other, it is incapable not only of availability (Marcel), encounter, and empathy but even of depersonalized and manipulating relations."[41] To live humanly is somehow to move toward the other, and to do that is clearly to be "for" the other at least in the general sense of coming to bear on the other. But there are radically different forms of such coming to bear on the other. To have a task in that sense, then, is not yet necessarily to be "claimed." Yet the two categories do keep company; within the human experience of task the sense of being claimed does arise. I will address the claim of self and other in the next section. But first I pause to gather these reflections in a summary statement of the nature of the human person.

If the person is inescapably given the human reality of the genuinely other(s), if self and other find themselves inevitably caught up in the rhythm of life "from, with, and for" each other, what remains of the solid and self-contained subject celebrated in some modern thinkers and assumed in much popular individualism? Not everything. We certainly cannot quietly insert the same old substantial and static self within the fabric of relatedness we have been describing. The boundaries of the self become softer, for the self in its radical temporality is permeable. This should not surprise us, if we do think of boundaries as marking relationships. It should not surprise us, but it is not so strange that we miss the clarity and simplicity of self *and* (with "and" not meaning "from, with, and for") world. The humorist Garrison Keillor writes wistfully in ridiculing "the new baseball":

> In a simpler era, a Ty Cobb came up to the plate in a mood of fierce determination, but today's players, aware of the diminishing importance of hitting the ball, are more content to *experience* at-batness. In the dugout, the athletes no longer discuss batting averages, girls, and the stock market but the swiftly changing dynamics and dialectics of the one-time "national pastime." In contemporary baseball, they agree, cause-and-effect sequentiality is giving way to simple concurrence of phenomena as the crisis in baseball's system of linear reaction brings on a new "system" of concentric and reflexive response, and the old stately inwardness of the game is losing out to, or giving in to, outwardness, or rather *away*ness; the static balance of baseball—pitcher vs. batter, base runner vs. infielder—will shortly slither into flow, and the crowd, not content to cheer the artifice of great hitters and pitchers, will rise in tribute to the natural organic unity of a scoreless game.[42]

Well, perhaps. Yet it remains true that "the inner is not the outer and the outer is not the inner." Mihaly Csikszentmihalyi writes of "flow" (Keillor's term) as "optimal experience," but he stresses as well "inner control" by way of consciously chosen goals.[43] We do not lose inwardness in the view emerging here, but we recognize that that which is outer does enter us. Perhaps our bodies and our emotions are particularly important gateways for such entering.[44]

And so we change. Catherine Keller has written poetically and profoundly of this:

> This empathic continuum may contain its own self-transforming principle of differentiation. The oceanic currents of deep assimilation, of identification and internalization, of resistance and of intimacy, may all turn out to be natural modes of gradual individuation. . . . *One becomes more and different by taking in more of what is different.*[45]

Again there is both a spatial and a temporal dimension to the softness of this self. Spatially the constitutive character of the several relationships contributing to the person's life reveals a kind of plurality to this self. If "individual" means undivided, we might well recognize the self in the simultaneity of the many relationships coming together undividedly rather than as a substance gathered over against the world.[46] In such a way James Hillman, former director of the Jung Institute in Zurich, has spoken against integrating the different parts of the psyche in order to achieve balance, presenting instead a polytheism of the psyche where segments rub up against each other and consciousness circulates among the field.[47] Jacques Lacan has drawn on his psychoanalytical work to speak of a subject split between unconscious desire and an ego protective of a unified image.[48] If the many and distinct relationships of one's life are as constitutive as I have suggested here, it does seem likely that no single story can encompass such a person's living.[49]

But "story" does have the right temporal ring in it. While it may be too much to say with Alfred North Whitehead that there is only a "becoming of continuity and no continuity of becoming," becoming—and that is to say, change—will characterize the identity of the human person. Whitehead's base disciplines were mathematics and physics. We can add the witness of other disciplines, as chapter 2 made clear. Thus Lewis Thomas indicates that, biologically speaking:

> a good case can be made for our nonexistence as entities. We are not made up, as we had always supposed, of successively enriched packets of our own parts. We are shared, rented, occupied. . . . The whole dear notion of one's own Self—marvelous old free-willed, free-enterprising, autonomous, independent, isolated island of a Self—is a myth.[50]

That myth may find some faint reflection in the "higher" reaches of evolutionary ascent, but one would be unprepared to find such human complexity devoid of relationship. In relationship human being is becoming. Perhaps personal identity is itself characterized by temporality, as in the continuity found in memory, intentionality, and a consistent pattern of personal interaction with the others.[51] As we locate this person so constitutively in a living social existence, it follows that the ordering of life, including that of which theologians speak of as the "orders of creation," will need to be understood as well as a temporal—and that is to say, mutable—matter.[52] Chapter 5 is concerned with the call of becoming that Christian faith hears.

Much is at stake in such becoming. Perhaps the interdependence of coexistence and even cooperation is a sine qua non for human life. But of course it is not inevitable that human life continue, nor that it continue well. With much at risk, the making of distinctions becomes crucial. In doing that, we need to consider the claim that arises within the gift of self and other.

THE CLAIM OF SELF AND OTHER

How does the sense of being claimed arise? To speak of claim is to move beyond talk of task, or within such talk, to make distinctions of value. We do not need to be mesmerized by modern admonitions against deriving "ought" from "is."[53] That prohibition made sense in the terms of a clear-cut subject/object distinction.[54] But the sense of claim needs thoughtful attention. For example, the laudable critique of the modern and/or post-modern subjectivizing of value can all too easily itself be usurped for an absolutizing of a particular set of choices in reading the "universal." I will argue that within the experience of life as self and other the sense of being claimed does arise and also that this sense connects with the reality of the religious for ground and goal. In that connection moral challenge and struggle receive the kind of metaphysical resolution the religions bid to supply. But the sense of being claimed arises without requiring the services of religion. Farley puts it well: "When we experience the face of the other, . . . we experience a summons, an invocation (Marcel), a claim, a call to commitment and responsibility. This primordial summons is the basis of the values in the normative culture: the normative culture is not the basis of the summons."[55]

What more can be said of this? Several elements can be introduced:

TASK AND CLAIM, "IS" AND "OUGHT"

1. The other is recognized as bearing on the self's being and well-being. Anthropologists bear this witness. Variously, actually. In chapter 1, I cited Victor Turner's gathering of folk literature's reference to the stranger who saves.[56] On the other hand, Mary Douglas has noted how that which falls outside traditional classificatory boundaries is regularly regarded as "polluting" and "dangerous."[57] Both testimonies make good sense, and the extremes so noted represent possibilities present in *every* other.

2. One could well argue that this interest of the self in the other does not get us to the sense of being claimed. May this not, after all, be merely a matter of self-interest, enlightened or otherwise? It is instructive to examine the logic of the sense of being claimed. Hannah Arendt has remarked about how a sense of self seems itself to require the claim of the other:

> Without being bound to the fulfilment of promises, we would never be able to keep our identities; we would be condemned to wander helplessly and

without direction in the darkness of each man's lonely heart, caught in its contradictions and equivocalities—a darkness which only the light shed over the public realm through the presence of others, who confirm the identity between the one who promises and the one who fulfils, can dispel.[58]

3. Is it not the case that the other is needed not merely externally to confirm the self's identity through judgment or forgiveness but intrinsically for the logic of the claim itself? Helmut Peukert suggests as much:

The demand "let us transcend our subjectivity!" is the norm that makes possible the justification of all other norms. Transsubjectivity is thus the "supernorm," and for this reason it has the status of "the moral principle as such." However, the question is whether this "act of faith" finally represents a form of "decisionism."[59]

Yes, that is the question. Does the connection with the other dissolve in the caprice of individual choice? But what if we do not have the self without the other? What if the decision to attend only, shall one say, to the self is a movement against the very structure of reality? Earlier in this chapter we stressed that the other is "always already given" for the self. We noted that self-identification does not occur without dealing with the identifications employed by others for the self. Now a fuller role for the other has emerged. We need a sense of being claimed to have our own identity (Arendt). At the center of *any* such claim *as claim* is the call to life with the other (Peukert). Does it not seem fitting to recognize that that is precisely what we do have: the other and so the claim?

4. The language of claim is the language of freedom and so of contingency. In grounding the sense of being claimed so definitely in the givenness of life with the other, one may seem to be speaking the language of necessity. But to be claimed does not—by its very logic, *cannot*—settle the matter of the response of the one claimed. Human beings can somehow reject the claim, and they do: of that faith speaks in pondering the mystery of sin. We will have more to say of this in chapter 5. But here it makes sense to ask whether the possibility and the reality of resistance and rejection may find a fitting parallel in ambiguity regarding the recognition of the claim itself. Certainly the formal reality of being claimed may still sound in formulations that represent material resistance and rejection.

5. There is wisdom represented in the view that the principle of moral action must be universalizable. I am, variously, claimed by *all* the others. In current reflection there is much emphasis on the role of community in

the constitution of moral discourse. This is fine as far as it goes, but it risks losing the sense of universal claim, as Victor Turner recognized in distinguishing "communitas" from Durkheimian "solidarity," the force of which depends upon an in group/out group contrast.[60] Appeal to the other is vulnerable to romantic distortion in which the reality of difference is compromised. Emmanuel Levinas wisely recognizes that the relationship with the other must not be isolated from "the third":

> Pardon is a possibility within the *société intime* formed by two, where there is always personal relationship with the wronged party and a chance to start fresh. But the existence of the third man—that is, the ramification of fault beyond our control, perhaps beyond intention, in any event beyond all possibility of "taking it back" and wiping the slate clean—institutes an order of evil yet more serious, because irreversible. It demands a foundation of justice rather than love.[61]

The centripetal force of the self and other dyad needs resistance as the claim is materially formulated and as the response to the claim itself calls for response. The author of Ecclesiastes recognizes this. Here it is clear that "two are better than one," for "if two lie together, they keep warm; but how can one keep warm alone?" But life in relationship requires more than such interpersonal warming: "And though one might prevail against another, two will withstand one. A threefold cord is not quickly broken" (Eccles. 4:9-12).

CLAIM AS RISK

Claims can be rejected. They can be inadequately or wrongly formulated, whether in ignorance or defiance. And it is fitting that the sheer existence of the claim is not a matter of self-evidence. These contingencies are clear, developmentally. Heinz Kohut, not an ethicist but a founder of the self psychology movement, writes of the need for the child's narcissism to be transformed. We hear the theme again: one needs the other in order to become oneself.[62] Empathy extended toward the infant and young child is crucial in the child's development of narcissistic self-regulation in such capacities as creativity, empathy, humor, and wisdom. Were one to use the dramatic language of faith, one might say that Kohut is pointing out how evil within is related to evil without, when he speaks of how increase in narcissistic pathologies could be linked with shifts in family and social life.[63]

Again the language of risk is required. As the sense of self emerges through the other, the becoming of this one may seek to jettison the empowering relation. Pannenberg puts this in a theological framework:

> It is self-consciousness that makes possible an ambiguous presence to the other and therefore also a closing off of the self to the otherness of the other in consequence of the self-constituting of the ego. For when human beings experience self-consciousness as immediate identity with themselves and therefore as constitutive of the self, they close themselves against the divine power that establishes their existence and, in consequence, against the otherness of others within the world.[64]

6. Does this warning mean that the other must be the focus of the moral claim, if we are not to go wrong? In some measure the answer to that question seems to be yes. I have already cited Levinas's powerful evocation of the face of the other in its uniquely revealing capacity as limiting the self's power to control. Steven Smith traces how Levinas finds more than that in the naked face of the other:

> The Other is a stranger whose "nudity" or absolution from form is at the same time his indigence, having nowhere to lay his head, the helplessness and need of widows and orphans. . . . The neighbor does not appear as an obstacle to my freedom; his ethical opposition to me is *prior* to my freedom and is its condition.[65]

The Christian has no difficulty echoing this Jewish philosopher in his emphasis on the priority of the neighbor. Already in chapter 1 we cited the biblical testimony to the claim of the "stranger." Christians know well the reality of sin against the other, and may even be prepared to join someone like Julia Kristeva in her critique of religion itself as the principled denial of difference.[66] But feminist writers have wisely warned against a single-minded passion at this point.[67] It is easy to confuse the "turn to the other" with turning against the self, if self and other are juxtaposed in one's mind-set. Religious folk—particularly women—have been harmfully called to the alleged ideal of self-sacrifice.

That ideal must be criticized on several grounds. Gene Outka has appropriately asked whether the consequences would not be self-frustrating, if everyone acted self-sacrificially.[68] Moreover, tactically, it seems clear that a self inattentive to its own need is ill equipped to care efficaciously for others. Third, one wonders how much actual damage has been done to persons in the call to self-sacrifice. Thomas Ogletree insightfully suggests that compliance to such demands would "more likely express self-hatred and resentment than love and justice."[69] Faith has much to ponder in this connection with respect to the central religious theme of the relationship of the human person to God. Is self-sacrifice the fundamental truth in this, or shall we speak with Kohut, here as well, of the transformation, not abandonment, of narcissism?

A MORE EXCELLENT WAY

That discussion awaits us in the next chapter. But here it must suffice to say that in the relationship of self and other the claim arises for the self from both the other and the self. There are two ditches alongside the road of human development, as cultural and situational tendencies amply illustrate.[70] This dual claim is implicit in the temporal character of fully human life. We do live from the past in the present toward the future, together. To focus simply on either the self or the other is to flatten out the dialectic which gives time genuine newness. Thus an oppressed people must claim their past and dream of a viable future. Black authors such as August Wilson have made this point with particular power.[71] The self must not deny itself or its history. But something new is "always already" possible for the self through the other; the circle of the self is opened. Eberhard Jüngel writes of the pulse of this newness known in authentic love:

> In contrast with flirtation, the I in love promises itself *nothing* or at least not *something*. But love promises it *everything*. . . . In the event of loving surrender, then, a radical self-distancing takes place *in favor* of a new nearness to oneself—a nearness, to be sure, in which the beloved Thou is closer to me than I am to myself. . . . What is desired is not one's own being, but rather the beloved Thou and only for its own sake. . . . But the beloved Thou gives me myself in that it has me, so that I have myself again, but in a completely new way.[72]

Perhaps this dialectical claim of self and other may be expressed by saying that, morally speaking, the kingdom of God is in your midst, that is, it is *between* you.[73] The reign of God has to do with potential space between mother and child, with "the third," with language, play, and culture.

In trying to understand the nature of the claim of self and other we have moved into explicitly religious talk. That does not seem strange to Christians. Within their own faith they have struggled to understand and heed the call to love the neighbor as oneself (Matt. 22:39). But how are the moral and the religious to be distinguished and related? On the one hand, the Christian will understands that the claim of the human other is grounded in the will of God the Creator. This God gives generously; one need not know the giver in order to know the gift. But with the gift is task and in the task claim. The human person trying to fathom the whence of the claim may be driven back toward the Creator God. And a person trying to fulfill the claim may be driven ahead to this God who is not only the God of beginnings. As we turn shortly to that God-talk, we pause only to consider briefly that second transition: how the challenge and crisis of the moral raises with existential urgency the question of God.

FORGIVEN, YET FRESHLY CLAIMED

One can fail in the face of the moral claim. Claims are only that—they carry no guarantee of success. One does not need the services of religion to know this. Indeed, anyone who knows the history of the century now nearing its close knows more than this. (We) human beings *do* fail in the face of the moral claim. This, I take it, is simply not disputed. There is less agreement about why we fail. There does seem to be a kind of entropy working here also; moral progress seems to lie uphill.[74] At this point I do not want to engage in such speculation reaching back behind moral failure to its causes. Whatever the cause of moral failure, what are we now to do? We look to what only the other can do. That is at least part of the answer, as Hannah Arendt makes clear: "Without being forgiven, released from the consequences of what we have done, our capacity to act would, as it were, be confined to one single deed from which we could never recover."[75] Arendt notes that in turning to the other the logic of forgiveness joins that of promising: "Both faculties, therefore, depend on plurality, on the presence and acting of others, for no one can forgive himself and no one can feel bound by a promise made only to himself; forgiving and promising enacted in solitude or isolation remain without reality and can signify no more than a role played before one's self."[76]

This is essentially right; the garment of forgiveness does have the right cut to fit and clothe the nakedness of moral failure. Yet Arendt's insight needs amplification as to the agent of forgiveness. In the first place, as surely as the circle of self is not closed, the nonisolated self may also need to forgive itself for moral failure in the face of the claim of self and other. In the second, the Christian who finds that claim to be grounded in the will of the Creator God will find all human forgiveness an insufficient remedy. To fail in the face of the claim is to fail before God. It is to need the forgiveness of this Other. Kierkegaard saw this so clearly that all other forgiveness paled in comparison:

> As sinner, man is separated from God by the most chasmal qualitative abyss. In turn, of course, God is separated from man by the same chasmal qualitative abyss when he forgives sins. If by some kind of reverse adjustment the divine could be shifted over to the human, there is one way in which man could never in all eternity come to be like God: in forgiving sins.[77]

This seems too strong, unless we stress that "sin" designates precisely human failure in the face of the claim of God. We do need to be forgiven by human others and by ourselves. But in his passion Kierkegaard saw something crucial to Christian faith: we do not forgive as God does. To clarify how that is so must fall to our later discussion of the nature of the relationship to God.

But in the distinction a note sounds that in closing this chapter places our human life together as self and other in perspective. In the next chapter, I will speak of God not merely as another other, but as qualitatively other. To speak of being related to God is not to speak of one more being (merely) but to speak of a different *kind* of being. And so, I shall argue, the difference characterizing divine forgiveness is a difference in kind, particularly with respect to the decisiveness of the will to forgive. That we need some such difference of kind may be indicated in reflecting on human life in the face of the moral claim of self and other. We may be troubled by the inevitable contingency of the words of forgiveness spoken by self and other.

But what of the moral claim itself? Surely we are not prepared to have the sweet word of forgiveness obliterate the fresh call of the moral claim upon human life. May that claim at times call upon us precisely *not* to forgive?[78] Moreover, within that claim sound the voices of innocent victims, whose wounds are not healed by words of forgiveness spoken to the perpetrators. How is their claim to be answered? Helmut Peukert points out that this question has particular force when we think of those, now gone from our midst, who suffered unjustly:

> This generation has inherited everything from the past generations and lives on what they have paid for. The exploited are no longer living among them, but are in the past, those who have gone before them. The happiness of the living exists in the expropriation of the dead. Is happiness at all conceivable

under these presuppositions? Is it not the presupposition of happiness that the unhappiness of those who went before is simply forgotten? Is amnesia, the utter loss of historical memory, the presupposition of happy consciousness?[79]

Then there is the fresh claim of the living. Their voices do lay a claim upon our present choices. But here can we be satisfied simply to be set before the task-become-claim once again? The character of moral failure leaves us dissatisfied with simply standing there. It is good to be there; we would not wish our being there away. But to be ever placed before the claim is only good, not perfect. We know this because of human moral failure; there seems to be a kind of radicality to the evil that we—self and other—do. Without speaking against the claim, we may be ready to say that we know we will fail. This is not merely a matter of the "law of large numbers" and our finitude—that sooner or later we will slip. The moral problem we are facing seems to root in our very will. We *choose* to "slip" and so "fall" into attitudes and behavior that are destructive of others and of ourselves.[80] Moreover, even our experience of what we may boldly call moral "success" confirms that our creaturely condition is only good, not perfect. Must "doing the right thing" be left in the precarious position of dependence on our choices?

In these questions we are asking a metaphysical question. Is there another *kind of being* to which we might look? In the drama that is life, the drama of life with nature within the spacetime continuum and of life with the human other, is there another boundary, another country?[81] We are asking of God.

4

LIFE "BEFORE" THE OTHER

We are seeking to understand human life "on the boundary," in its several relationships, looking for insight as we face the challenge of otherness in faith. It is also human life that we are trying to understand, when we now speak of God. The commonality does not lie merely in the subject of the sentences, that in both cases it is "we" who are trying to understand. Of course, it is the case that we speak here as human beings, even if the specific testimonies of faith in God have a greater prominence in this chapter. But that about which we speak is once again the relationship of human life to otherness. The question of the being of God simply as God need be engaged here only as the discussion of human life in relation to that God requires. Similarly, we have sought to speak of the spacetime continuum, of nature, of bodies, of humankind *not* in general but in order to understand what it is to live humanly within and with such otherness.

THE CATEGORICAL DIFFERENCE: WE TURN TO ONE WHO IS FIRST

To focus God-talk on the relationship between God and us may seem self-evident. How else could one proceed? Yet to do this does make a difference; indeed, it yields an implicit critique of some traditional formulations. At times theologians seem to have thought such a focus unnecessary. The claim here, however, is that there is a relationship between human life and

God such that human speech about God is possible, and even necessary if we are to understand our boundary existence.

TO SPEAK HUMANLY OF GOD

Of course there is controversy about this. Some who sing of religious ecstasy and some who speak against all religion stand together to say that human speech about God is not to be trusted. We do offer such speech here, hoping that both groups—and others—will find something of value in it. How can both true believer and true unbeliever join in this inquiry with integrity? Perhaps both can agree that a beginning has been made in illuminating human life on the boundary. That beginning leads into this chapter. The unbeliever is entitled to expect that the ideal of accuracy in describing the human condition vis-à-vis otherness continues to apply in the discussion of God as other. Whatever has been well—that is, accurately—said up until now cannot be jettisoned. At the same time, the believer naturally expects that this chapter's talk of the Other cannot be reduced to the boundary talk that has preceded it.

Both expectations are reasonable and in fact converge. The Christian will agree—indeed, insist—that the human person "before" God is none other than that human person who lives within the spacetime continuum and with human others. Why, then, is another chapter needed to illumine human life on the boundary? If the sentences purporting to describe the relationship with God merely decorate those relationships already explored, this chapter is superfluous. So I contend that (1) the unbeliever can well agree to hear and consider faith's testimonies about the human person before God with the understanding that such testimonies neither abandon nor reduce to the descriptions already in place in earlier chapters, and that (2) the believer can well be no less interested in these descriptive connections and accordingly can welcome the unbeliever's contribution in the assessment of that matter.

A DIFFERENT DIFFERENCE

When we turn to these testimonies of faith, believers and unbelievers who have followed along tolerably well thus far in our discussion of otherness will both say this is different. It *is* different. This chapter does not simply detail one more dimension of otherness. If we are to speak of God, our talk will be of a different kind of boundary: "My thoughts are not your thoughts, nor are your ways my ways, says the LORD" (Isa. 55:8).

When a believer speaks of this Other, the word used is *sola*—alone, only. *Soli Deo gloria*! To God alone the glory! "The Word alone," "Faith alone"—this is the language of faith. This is clear in the root religious reality of worship. Here God is to stand alone as the one to whom worship is offered. We may speak of loving and of serving both God and others, but God alone is to be worshiped. We may have been speaking all along of otherness, of difference. But it seems clear that we face here a *different* difference, one not easily characterized. Jürgen Moltmann speaks rather clumsily of "the transcendence of the transcendence and immanence of the world."[1] Charles Hartshorne has proposed the language of "categorical supremacy":

> God is a name for the uniquely good, admirable, great, worship-eliciting being. Worship, moreover, is not just an unusually high degree of respect or admiration; and the excellence of deity is not just an unusually high degree of merit. There is a difference in kind. God is "Perfect," and between the perfect and anything as little imperfect as you please is no merely finite, but an infinite step. The superiority of deity to all others cannot (in accordance with established word usage) be expressed by indefinite descriptions, such as "immensely good," "very powerful," or even "best" or "most powerful," but must be a superiority of principle, a definite conceptual divergence from every other being, actual or so much as possible. We may call this divergence "categorical supremacy."[2]

That seems right to Christians. They know that it simply will not do to speak of God as one who would be a threat, even a sure bet, to break pro football's rushing yardage record or as one who edges even Albert Einstein on the I.Q. charts. God, they know, is simply other than that. But how shall one speak of God? *Shall* one speak? Is to speak of not speaking perhaps the best one can do? Wittgenstein was likely right in remarking that "whereof one cannot speak, thereof one must be silent."[3] The *via negativa* beckons, either in the mystical silence or, less obviously, in the traditional emphasis on the "negative" attributes: unity, simplicity, immutability, infinity, immensity, eternity.[4]

A RELATIONSHIP BETWEEN UNEQUALS

There is something right in such appeals; they do testify to categorical difference. But, of course, if difference were the whole story, it would not be clear that or how there would be any experience to be silent about. If God and "that-which-is-not-God" are truly "wholly other" than each other—to take Rudolf Otto's much-quoted phrase—then it is not clear how

there can be a relationship such that the two can be talked about together
or even *be* together.[5] It seems better to recognize that in the witness to
categorical difference we somehow still bear testimony to a relationship.
Not every relationship is between equals. Thus Hartshorne's talk of superiority or supremacy assumes connection between God and humankind
in making a point about difference. While that relationship permits description, it may defy full expression in language. Thus one can make
sense of mystical testimony to the inadequacy of language to exhaust the
realities of prayer and of love:

> Language falters. . . . Language is necessarily complex. It is always moving
> from expressed meaning to unexpressed, from denotation to connotation.
> . . . We must go beyond words, confiding ourselves to God, letting God
> help us lift our hearts to him in silence and sometimes even without images.
> All of this is particularly clear to us when we reach the upper terraces of
> prayer. . . . We are well beyond words, yet not outside either thought or
> feeling. . . . Like the mystics who turn to the images of the Song of Songs,
> we frequently find that narrative of wooing and sexual union satisfactory.
> . . . And yet even its exalted measures may be too much, too complicated,
> too multifaceted and overladen with too many movements away from the
> central fact: love.[6]

The inadequacy of language makes believers understandably restless. C.
S. Lewis, who deserves to be ranked among the most skillful apologists
for Christian belief, closed his "eschatological" novel, *Till We Have Faces*,
with these words:

> I ended my first book with the words *no answer*. I know now, Lord, why
> you utter no answer. You are yourself the answer. Before your face questions
> die away. What other answer would suffice? Only words, words; to be led
> out to battle against other words. Long did I hate you, long did I fear you.
> I might—[7]

Such words of love bear an eloquent witness, as do the works of love.
But such poetry and passion in all their power would at the very least be
inadequate without the kind of propositions Lewis's prose represents. In
this century's last decade we are no less in need of clear God-talk than
Lewis was at mid-century. Indeed, if the argument of chapter 1 is accepted,
one must say that all meaningful speech is at risk in the tendency to collapse
all the self's talk into talk about the self.[8] We accept that tendency at great
cost, for language is an essential resource available to us on the boundaries
on which we live. Moreover, religions of the book should surely be able

to recognize the threat and as surely need to resist the unwitting concession involved in recourse to total silence. Our task in speaking is not to deny the categorical difference but to declare it—and to do that we seek to "locate" it within the relationship constituting one of the boundaries on which we live. This is not a task for which we have no resources. I shall argue that, at least for the Christian, faith testifies most fundamentally to the reality of a relationship and within that testimony speaks of God. And I shall suggest that at times faith hears echoes of that testimony even in the words of those who do not speak for faith.

THE OTHERNESS OF THE CREATOR GOD

Consider the theme of creation. The Book of Job testifies that when we turn to question God, we face our creator, who is truly other than we. To hear such a God speak is to be put in one's proper place:

> Where were you when I laid the foundation of the earth? Tell me, if you have understanding. Who determined its measurements—surely you know! Or who stretched the line upon it? . . . On what were its bases sunk, or who laid its cornerstone, when the morning stars sang together and all the heavenly beings shouted for joy? (Job 38:4-7)

As the divine speech continues, the sense of categorical difference builds, drawing on such themes as the binding of "the chains of the Pleiades," the loosing of the "cords of Orion," the sending forth of lightning, and the making of mighty Behemoth.

This beautiful testimony to the Creator finds parallels outside the biblical writings. The Egyptian "hymn of a thousand strophes" bears similar witness to nature's praise of God:

> All trees rise before his countenance/ They turn toward his eye/ and their leaves unfold./ The scaly creatures leap in the water/ they come out from their pools for love of him./ The sheep and the cattle skip before his presence./ The birds dance with their wings./ They all observe that he is in his good time./ They live by seeing him as their daily need./ They are in his hand, sealed with his seal./ And no god can open them but his majesty.[9]

THE WITNESS OF SCIENCE

From various orientations people of faith hold that the creation is other than the creator and that the creation bears witness to that difference. It may be that the creation's witness is not heard only by religious folk. Recent work in science, for example, seems to echo the poets of faith. Perhaps the most prominent note has been that heard in the ascendancy of the "Big

Bang" cosmology. Robert Russell notes how several models seem to point to the "discovery of an absolute beginning at $t = O$":

> They provide an integrative framework that links together the results of evolutionary biology, physical chemistry, geology, solar physics, galactic astrophysics, the relative abundances of elements in the universe and many other disparate areas of physical science into a consistent framework.[10]

What are we to make of this? Is science speaking here of God creating "out of nothing"? One should claim at most an "echo" in science's witness. Clearly no claim is being made by science to deliver the "initial singularity." Ian Barbour notes that it might be possible to set the Big Bang into an oscillating cosmos, in which the era of expansion that we observe was preceded by a period of contraction (the "Big Crunch"). Yet one may still hear an echo here, if "one would expect from the law of entropy that there could only have been a finite rather than an infinite number of oscillations." Barbour grants that the applicability of the law under such conditions is uncertain.[11] Some caution is required, then. The history of the relations between theology and science is littered with instances of theologians' clinging tenaciously to hypotheses once advanced but subsequently abandoned by scientists.[12] We should not claim to have in firm scientific grasp the beginning whose echoes we may be hearing. But it remains striking that one can say with Ernan McMullin that "if an absolute cosmic beginning *did* occur, it could look something like the horizon-event described in the Big Bang theory."[13]

A second scientific echo may be heard in reflection on the "anthropic principle": that even a small change in the physical constants would have resulted in an uninhabitable universe. Is there here testimony to the design of the Creator, if not to an absolute beginning? The data are very startling. Setting aside such matters as the formation of the elements (the "strong nuclear force" having just the right strength) and the particle/anti-particle ratio (chap. 2), consider only the delicacy of the expansion rate as Barbour describes it:

> If the early rate of expansion had been less by even one part in a thousand billion, the universe would have collapsed again before temperatures had fallen below 10,000 degrees. On the other hand, if the rate had been greater by a part in a million, the universe would have expanded too rapidly for stars and planets to form. The expansion rate itself depends on many factors, such as the initial explosive energy, the mass of the universe, and the strength of gravitational forces. The cosmos seems to be balanced on a knife-edge.[14]

Such testimonies to the "just right numbers" are very impressive, perhaps particularly for nonscientists and among them especially for religious folk looking for confirming help wherever it is to be found. But again, caution seems indicated. The witness offered here may speak more of *how* the universe works than of *that* it exists at all. And that we are some distance short of proof is indicated by speculations that Barbour summarizes about "many worlds": "If there were billions of worlds with differing constants, it would not be surprising if by chance one of them happened to have constants just right for our forms of life."[15]

Very well! Perhaps theistic interpretations of apparent design are possible, but they do not seem to be necessary.[16] But it remains a matter of no small interest for people of faith that such scientific echoes continue to be heard. Loren Eiseley may sum up well for us in what he writes of the giant wasp of the genus *Sphecius*. Perhaps these scientific speculations are saying that the world is not self-explanatory:

> I am an evolutionist. I believe my great backyard Sphexes have evolved like other creatures. But watching them in the October light as one circles my head in curiosity, I can only repeat my dictum softly: in the world there is nothing to explain the world. Nothing to explain the necessity of life, nothing to explain the hunger of the elements to become life.[17]

REASON'S OFFERING OF PROOF

Directly in religious testimony and indirectly in scientific speculation, we turn toward that which is categorically different. That we only "turn toward," but do not possess or deliver, one whom Christians confess as God is particularly evident, ironically, in other such efforts sometimes brought forward as reason's offering of proof. The ontological argument's appeal to concepts (that which needs nothing other than itself in order to be, that than which nothing greater can be thought) continues to fascinate but not convince. The moral argument that without God the moral sense we seem to have would collapse in foundationless nihilism may well raise the question of a ground for life.[18] But people of faith also know that "we have this treasure in earthen vessels" (2 Cor. 4:7, RSV). Thus, whether in humility or confidence, theologians write of the "hiddenness of God." James Gustafson can serve for a company in this:

> God is not susceptible to the same kinds of investigations that phenomena are subject to; God is not an object like the planet Saturn toward which

space vehicles can be sent, of which photographs can be taken, and from which a whole range of data can be collected. God is not an object like DNA so that he can be patterned by a double helix with a "genetic alphabet" of four nucleotides. God is not an object like a modern corporation that can be investigated to discern the structures of prestige and authority, the flow of communications, the decision-making process, the relations to other corporations, to the government, and to the public. God is not an object like the human brain, which, while still far from fully understood, yields its "secrets" to increasingly refined investigative techniques and can be therapeutically experimented upon with certain drugs even when it is not fully known why and how the drugs work.[19]

"God is not an object"—that is a traditional theological way of formulating the categorical difference. Later the truth that sounds for faith in such a formulation must be fitted together with the recognition that in the will of God we do come to have God as an object. Moreover, our earlier discussion requires us to say that it is not only God who is not *simply* object. But the point here is to recognize that the crucial theme of categorical difference may well be heard in such formulations and their echoes. Christians speak so of human knowing of God because of what they believe about the being of God. God cannot be known—I should want to add, known *simply*—as we are known, because God *is* not as we are. We turn toward God in faith; we do not possess God in proof.[20]

ONE WHO IS FIRST

But in faith we do turn toward God; we do have to do with God. Hence faith seeks to understand what can be said that is more rather than less fitting as a description of this one who is categorically different. We can make a start by saying this: we turn to One who is "first." To say that God is first sounds the theme that God is different in being from us. Theologians have tried various ways of saying this, appealing to such notions as necessity, indeterminacy and self-sufficiency.[21] Perhaps the language we have already sampled, that of God as creator, effectively makes the point of categorical difference in being and does so in a way that stays close to the primary testimonies of faith. To say that God is our Creator is to speak of a difference of kind. We may want to speak of the human person as "created co-creator," but the indispensable adjective reminds us that we are able to create only because we are created in the image of God.[22] In relation to that which is created the Creator clearly is "first." In our very being we are dependent on God in a way God is not dependent on us.

That is why theologians speak of the aseity of God, that the existence of God is *a se*, from or of itself.[23] The Latin of the theologians here rightly serves the logic of believers, who praise the God who is "first": "Lord, you have been our dwelling place in all generations. Before the mountains were brought forth, or ever you had formed the earth and the world, from everlasting to everlasting, you are God" (Ps. 90:1-2). That God is God from everlasting to everlasting is a statement made by someone who dwells in this God. The language of abstraction has its place—indeed, it does so because the being of God cannot be limited to any single place, since God is "from everlasting to everlasting." But the flight of speculation is fueled here by the passion of devotion. Once again the setting of worship makes the point. The *first* commandment recognizes the God who is "first": "You shall have no other gods before me" (Exod. 20:3).

Perhaps the early faith of Israel did not require theoretical monotheism. Some hint of monolatry may be heard in this commandment, but it is crucial that God be "first," that no other god be "before" the God that Israel is to worship and obey.[24] In due course as Israel pondered the deeds of God (Deut. 4:32ff.: "Has any people ever heard the voice of a god speaking out of a fire, as you have heard, and lived? Or has any god ever attempted to go and take a nation for himself?"), "it was shown . . . that the LORD is God; there is no other besides him" (Deut. 4:35). Any sense of monolatry may here have given way to a full-fledged monotheism. But these very deliverances of more developed faith may themselves serve to make clear that in order to be "first," God does not need to be alone. The Creator God is the only God there is, but the God who created that which is not God is thereafter not accurately described as alone in being. God is still "first," but that is known precisely through the deeds of God in the relationship given with the gift of being.

THE WILL OF GOD

Perhaps the connection between the firstness of aseity or independence of being and the firstness in relationship of the One before whom Israel is to have no other gods can be grasped by considering the will of God. Shortly we will consider how the act of creating reveals the will of God. Certainly the events that are to show Israel that beside this God there is no other are understood to issue forth from the will of God. If we would speak of how God is different in category from us, we will need to speak of the will of God. While important debates about translation will continue, something very important for the answering of Moses' question regarding the name of God is given with these words: "I will be who I will be" (Exod. 3:14).

What is to be said of the will of God and how does that convey the sense of categorical difference? The biblical writings indicate that with regard to willing God is "first" in a number of ways: (1) God wills what God wills. This clumsy circular construction seeks to express the conviction that the willing of God expresses God's independence in being, the difference of aseity. The willing of God issues forth in and from the freedom of God. Thus God wills to make covenant, but that will is not to be explained by reference to that which is other than God: "It was not because you were more numerous than any other people that the LORD set his heart on you and chose you—for you were the fewest of all peoples. It was because the LORD loved you" (Deut. 7:7-8a). God is "first" in willing, for the choice of God is not dependent on that which is not God. (2) God does what God wills. The willing of God determines the action of God. As such, the will of God is decisive.[25] Of course God's will is that God's willing is in relation to that which is not God. We shall need to consider the "repentance" of God. But that the God who makes covenant will keep covenant is not in doubt. God's name is "I will *be* who I *will* [to] be." (3) God is one in God's willing. The will of God is not threatened from within. After all, Israel had heard over the centuries that "the Lord our God is one Lord"; accordingly, the will of God is one will. The apostle Paul was a good enough Jew to know that "the faithfulness of the Lord endures forever" (cf. Ps. 33:11) and so 2 Timothy can have him saying this: "If we are faithless, he remains faithful—for he cannot deny himself" (2 Tim. 2:13).

Such a will—independent in origin, directing the action of the one who wills, unchallenged by inner instability—may safely be said to be different in kind from what we know in our willing. It is an other who wills in such wise to whom the believer turns. One may turn in fear and trembling, for the will of God makes its claim: "Woe is me! I am lost, for I am a man of unclean lips, and I live among a people of unclean lips; yet my eyes have seen the King, the LORD of hosts!" (Isa. 6:5). Or one may turn in gratitude, hearing the gospel word that nothing "will be able to separate us from the love of God in Christ Jesus our Lord" (Rom. 8:39). Paul trusts the will of a God who is one and whose willing thus has a decisiveness that is categorically different: "He who did not withhold his own Son, but gave him up for all of us, will he not with him also give us everything else?" (Rom. 8:32).

TRANSCENDENT IN RELATIONSHIP

I have let these "first order" deliverances of faith pile up precisely because, sadly, the practice of the Christian religion seems often to have had a different message to bring. Bernard Cooke, who identifies himself as a "sacramental theologian," has chronicled how ritual, law, temple, and cult have contributed to the "distancing of God," despite the fact that the logic of Christian beginnings is precisely "God made present."[26] Similarly, theologians in "second order" reflection seem often to have lost touch with that which is given in faith. Theologians have described the divine difference in ways which have at least implicitly denied the reality of the relationship between God and us.[27] But that is not the logic of Christian speech about creation and redemption. Søren Kierkegaard, who could speak powerfully of the "infinite qualitative difference" distinguishing God from all that which is not God, could write this of God's act of creation: "God, who creates out of nothing, who almightily takes from nothing and says, 'Be!,' lovingly adds, 'Be something even over against me!' Wonderful love, even his omnipotence is under the power of his love! Hence the reciprocal relationship."[28] And Karl Barth, who may not have wanted to speak with the Lutherans of the finite being "capable of the infinite" (*finitum capax infiniti*), could nonetheless write this of redemption:

> The God of the Gospel is no lonely God, self-sufficient and self-contained. He is no "absolute God" (in the original sense of absolute, i.e., being detached from everything that is not himself). To be sure, he has no equal beside himself, since an equal would no doubt limit, influence, and determine him. On the other hand, he is not imprisoned by his own majesty, as though he were bound to be no more than the personal (or impersonal) "wholly other." By definition the God of Schleiermacher cannot show mercy. The God of the gospel can and does.[29]

Kierkegaard and Barth knew that God's will is free, but they knew what Dietrich Bonhoeffer knew in writing: "God is not free *of* man, but *for* man."[30] Richard Creel speaks of God as "impassible in will."[31] He is not the first to know this. The Gethsemane prayer speaks of possibility and of commitment: "Abba, Father, for you all things are possible; remove this cup from me; yet, not what I want, but what you want" (Mark 14:36).

Christians who would follow this word will not pray to change the will of God. In their following and their praying there is a witness to One who is "first." In coming to the life of discipleship under the will of God, we have not left the central theme of this section: categorical difference. To the contrary, the language of radical difference is needed to describe this will. But clearly we have come unto ground that cannot be adequately covered simply by the language of difference. We turn toward One who is "first" and we discover that "the One who is first is for us." As we turn to that second word now, it seems useful only to indicate briefly what has surely been implicit in this section, that the theme of categorical difference can provide a principle of criticism for the life and thought of faith.

THE DENIAL OF DIFFERENCE

Obviously one can err by denying the difference directly, as in assorted forms of pantheism. This is abundantly illustrated by new religious formulations afoot in our time, as when Shirley MacLaine faces the ocean and declares:

> For me to deny that Divine Force now would be tantamount to denying that I exist. I know that I exist, therefore I AM. I know that the God-source exists. Therefore IT IS. Since I am part of that force, then I AM that I AM . . . The Dance and the Dancer are One.[32]

A subtler denial of difference may be apparent in the authoritarianism in which spokespersons for the Christian religion seem to forget that they do not possess God, that their treasure is had in earthen vessels.

Certainly this point about God must entail self-criticism on the part of the theologian. Thus Sheila Greeve Davaney faults both Barth and Hartshorne for failing adequately to take into account the "insight of historical consciousness . . . that no matter what our sources may be, whether revelation or logical analysis, anthropology or mystical experience, they are all human experiences or activities." Consistency in this is hard to come by, as Davaney grants that such a lack of historical and social consciousness is "ironic in thinkers for whom the notions of history, process, and relation are so important."[33] Similarly, feminist thinkers have had to remind us that when we speak of God, we do so as human beings. Eberhard Jüngel may point toward a more positive interpretation of this situation in arguing that the Pauline doctrine of justification challenges theology to be "*a theology of liberation*: liberation in the sense of (a) the liberation of the sinner from the power of sin (self-realization); (b) the liberation of theology from the leading strings of ecclesiastical institutions and traditions; (c) the liberation of worldly responsibility from clerical, theocratic tutelage."[34]

Ironically, people of faith can deny difference in just the opposite way. Seeking to avoid the sinful pride which violates the categorical difference, the believer may get caught in a "logic of disjunction" by which it seems that the one sure way to praise God is to curse humankind. Yet even this perhaps well intentioned piety fails the test of categorical difference, for it implicitly places God and humankind on the same level so that competition for pride of place is engendered. We still subtly control God, if we suppose that scorn for the human somehow elevates the One who is first. We can do better if we honor the categorical difference within the reality of relationship.

THE TRANSCENDENT COMMITMENT:
THE ONE WHO IS FIRST IS FOR US

We speak again here of relationship. Throughout this book we have been speaking of how distinction and connection are together in the knowing of otherness that comes with relationship. To speak of the Other whom Christians call God required us to speak of distinction so radically as to represent a difference of category. But even this difference was somehow to be understood in relationship. It became clear that to speak of God's superiority or supremacy is to describe a difference within relationship. The Creator God stands in relationship to that which is created. Without that relationship, human beings could not turn in faith to the One who is "first" and the echoes to be heard outside of faith would be ungrounded. But in the section's main emphasis the distinction characterizing relationship was probed to recognize divine freedom. The freedom of God was seen in that God's relationship was rooted in the will of God. That will, while directed to and in relationship, preserved the categorical difference in that the willing of relationship was an exercise of divine freedom, decisive and indivisible.

TRULY GOD, TRULY FOR US

The point of the previous section was to stress that in our relationship to God we turn to One who is "first," truly categorically supreme. The point here is the other side of the coin—that our relationship to God itself expresses categorical difference: the one who is first is *for us*. This relationship is rooted in the living commitment of One who is categorically different. We turn to one who is "first" and find that One turned toward us, committed to us, with a radicality that is other than anything else we know. Commitment here expresses rather than compromises transcendence. Transcendence is conventionally understood in the terms of distance or withdrawal or absence. Thus it is commonly asked whether God should be understood as transcendent *or* as immanent. By now it is apparent that I cannot accept this disjunction. The otherness that such formulations mean to express by transcendence is rather to be found precisely in the character of God's commitment to us, the commitment by which any talk of immanence comes to make sense. The psalmist ridicules the making of idols, not because the true God is removed from this realm, but because that God is at work in life in a way that plastic images cannot convey:

> Our God is in the heavens;
>   he does whatever he pleases.
> Their idols are silver and gold,
>   the work of human hands.
> They have mouths, but do not speak;
>   eyes, but do not see.
> They have ears, but do not hear;
>   noses, but do not smell.
> They have hands, but do not feel;
>   feet, but do not walk;
>   they make no sound in their throats.
> (Ps. 115:3-7; cf. Psalm 135; Jer. 10:4-5)[35]

In like manner Peter Hodgson writes vividly of freedom and love:

> Just as the divine love is a free love, so also the divine freedom is a loving freedom. It is not simply an abstract volitional freedom, the ability to choose options or actions "voluntarily," without external constraint. It is far more than that: it is a concrete presence-to-self mediated in and through presence-to-others. Thus it presupposes love's positing of distinction and completes

love's act of reunion. Love without freedom is an impossibility, and freedom without love is merely capricious choice.[36]

That is well said, and the saying is much needed, for there is still a lamentable tendency to separate, for example, God's self-relatedness and God's relatedness to us in such a way as implicitly to undercut the radicality of God's commitment. Here I wish to make clear that the ineradicable commitment already present in God's will to create is sustained and intensified in the living action of God within the relationship that creation represents. In the next section, I will suggest certain implications for understanding the attributes and actions of a God so ineradically related to us. It will fall to Part Two to discuss implications for the life of faith— in itself (chap. 5) and in relation to others with respect to faith (chap. 6) by life on this boundary.

GOD'S RELATIONSHIP GROUNDED IN GOD

Christian faith does find God's transcendent commitment expressed in God's will to create. We have already cited Kierkegaard's powerful witness that the God who creates says not only "Be!" but also "Be something even over against me!" That is, in creation God wills to be in relationship, God wills to know otherness. In this there is newness for God, so that one might speak of the "historicity" of God.[37] While Christian theologians may agree about this, there is some disagreement about how radically this newness is to be conceived. Does God know otherness apart from the act/ will to create? This can be heard as a question about the Christian doctrine of the Trinity. Eberhard Jüngel has written of the inner trinitarian relationships: "In this creative being of God the Son as the aim of God the Father, God is aiming at man. In that God the Father loves the Son, in the event of this divine self-love, God is aiming selflessly at his creation."[38]

To know otherness is to receive or take in that which is other. Robert Jenson has remarked that God knows this experience in what the early church theologians spoke of as the eternal begetting of the Son: "Nobody claimed to know exactly what 'begotten' meant in this connection, and yet a tremendous assertion is made: there is a way of being *begun*, or receiving being which is proper to Godhead itself. To be God is not only to give being, it is also to receive being."[39] What are we to make of this? What kind of or how much connection can be found spanning even the deep distinction the doctrine of creation expresses? I have spoken of God's act of creation as will. Is there preparation within God for freedom forming itself in the will to create? Paul Fiddes has helpfully gathered together Christian reflection in response to this question. Shall we speak (with Lady Julian of Norwich and Nicolas Berdyaev) of the "desire" of God, or (with Keith Ward and Karl Barth) of the "choice" of God?[40] Fiddes agonizes over the matter:

> Understanding God's will as desire indicates that there can be no "otherwise" in the love of God for mankind. Because he thirsts and longs for fellowship with his creatures it makes no sense to say that he need not do so. But if we ask why he so thirsts, we cannot get back behind the choice of God. Each aspect, will and desire, defines the other. . . . God is what he chooses to be, and as a matter of fact he chooses to be not just for himself but for us. It has then as little meaning to say that "he need not have loved us" as it has to say "he need not have been himself."[41]

Perhaps. Yet one wonders if Fiddes does not undervalue the element of freedom in the will to love. He is drawn toward a view in which God eternally knows not only triune diversity but also external otherness:

> This equation of will and desire in God also provides a strong theological foundation for the idea that the material universe coexists eternally with God. . . . Creation is *ex nihilo*, but only in the sense that it is ultimately "from nothing except" God's will and love, not in the sense that there ever "was nothing except" God. The universe then is dependent upon God as existing and being held above nothingness by his will, but God also is dependent upon the universe by his own desire.[42]

Figures as diverse as Mortimer Adler and Alfred North Whitehead have tried to formulate the primordial work of God in a way that does not posit an absolute chronological beginning for that which is not God.[43] Moreover, the rather widespread contemporary insistence that the "economic" (within the world) and "immanent" (within God) triune activity be held together has something of the same effect.[44] Such formulations still seem to compromise somewhat the freedom of God's will to create. Diversity, even otherness, within God is, I believe, not the same as external otherness for God. The radical newness and genuine risk of the other seem to be lacking, unless one softens the fundamental unity of God. The presence of the formal structure of diversity within God such that something like what we know as will can be posited is certainly a preparation of sorts for the will to create. But that for which there is this preparation, the actual will to create external otherness, comes about only through the material use of freedom.[45]

But then it *does* come about! In the will of God it is *now* true, as Jüngel says:

> God has himself only in that he gives himself away. But in giving himself away, he has himself. That is how he *is*. His self-having is the event, is the history of giving himself away and thus is the end of all mere self-having. As this *history* he is God, and in fact this *history of love* is "God himself."[46]

THE CREATION OF FREEDOM AS THE WORK OF LOVE

To speculate about what lies behind the will of God to create is fascinating, but that must not put in question the claim that God has so willed. The creation is not now nothing. If we stress the radical difference that external otherness represents for God—as I am inclined to do—then the act of creation marks a boundary the more prominently. If we speak of God's eternal creating of the world—*some* world—then we still need to take note of the fact that in this contingent world God seems to will the increase of freedom in the other. In the next section, I will discuss how in freely willing the other's freedom, God does come to be affected by the contingent reality of that which is not God.[47] Thus our life is "before" God, for it is a life in genuine relationship with God.

To speak in this way, of course, is to speak of creation as a work of a loving God. In chapter 2, I cited Gustaf Wingren's insistence that creation is itself God's *opus proprium* ("proper work"), for "the very fact of life proves that God has begun to give."[48] That is well said, and chapter 2 made the point that Christian theologians need to find ways to transcend anthropocentric bias so as to speak more clearly of how God "realizes value in every living thing."[49] But within the abundance of life God seems especially to will the freedom of the other. I recall some sentences H. Richard Niebuhr wrote concerning human love:

> Love is reverence; it keeps its distance even as it draws near; it does not seek to absorb the other in the self or want to be absorbed by it; it rejoices in the otherness of the other; it desires the beloved to be what he is and does not seek to fashion him into a replica of the self or make him a means to the self's advancement. As reverence love is and seeks knowledge of the other, not by way of curiosity nor for the sake of gaining power but in rejoicing and in wonder. In all such love there is an element of that "holy fear" which is not a form of flight but rather a deep respect for the otherness

of the beloved and the profound unwillingness to violate his integrity. Love is loyalty; it is the willingness to let the self be destroyed rather than that the other cease to be; it is the commitment of the self by self-binding will to make the other great.[50]

Niebuhr was not writing of God's love, but his sentences—with some slight editing perhaps (Is God's self "destroyed" in death on the cross?)—could serve as a statement of the "free will" defense of God the loving creator in the face of human evil. I would not want to speak of the freedom of the other as a sufficient statement of God's end in creation—as I will seek to make clear in the next chapter in speaking of Christian hope "beyond freedom." But such freedom is surely a necessary means for God's chosen end. Thus we must speak of the risk of God in creation. The clear-eyed defiance that radical evil represents surely should tell us that the universe is not under the all-determining control of a good and omnipotent God. Arthur Cohen draws on the stark reality of the Holocaust to make the point:

> The God of classical theism, in no way constituted by his creatures or affected by the trials and alarums of creation, has disappeared finally into the folds of mystery. . . . The *tremendum* forces a resolution of this conflict, not alone as an obligation placed upon reason to account for its occurrence in a universe fashioned by a presumptively omnipotent, omniscient, and providential ruler, but even more as an obligation it places upon our humanity . . . to account for the *tremendum*, to justify and redeem, if that is possible, the surpassing suffering of its victims and the unbearable guilt of its perpetrators. This is nothing more nor less than our obligation to account for the reality of God in the aftermath of the *tremendum*.[51]

TO BE AGAINST GOD

In this chapter, I am writing of that Other whom Christians call God. But to do so I must also write of sin, for the radicality of the holocausts of this century do speak of God. For many, they speak of God in that they speak against God, and so against faith in God. I am saying that they speak of God in that they bear witness to the risk and the cost of the Creator's love. It is not only the radicality of specific acts of human evil that does so. The continuity of that evil, by which evil deeds carry such efficacy as to weave a web of brokenness in which every human life is caught—that also speaks of the degree of risk and cost involved in God's will for the freedom of the other.[52] Risk and *cost*, for as surely as sin is against God and the will of God, we must speak—and will—of the pain, the suffering, the wrath of God.

The One who is first is for us. I have argued that this is clear in God's freely willing the creation and/or increase of freedom in the other. If that freedom is real, the risk and the cost are real. The world is not now nothing and human evil is something for God; it is against God. But part of the categorical difference characterizing the divine freedom had to do with the fact that the action of this Other is determined by a will independent in origin. A God sinned against is still God. The will of God is not controlled by sin. Just so, "the One who is first" acts for us—to preserve creation also in response to human sin.

To speak of God's action over against human sin is to stand on the threshold of the central Christian doctrine: the person and work of Jesus Christ. The deed of God in this man from Nazareth claims the Christian consciousness with an unrivaled prominence. But the good news that Christians hear in the word about Jesus is, of course, part of a cosmic story of God's will for creation. The babe born of Mary is the fruit of the everlasting will of the Creator God. The author of the Letter to the Ephesians writes that in Jesus God chose us "before the foundation of the world to be holy and blameless before him" (Eph. 1:4). The "second Adam" is not, then, an afterthought. Moreover, Christians need to resist the disjunctive tendency to buy their special praise of Jesus by forfeiting their investment in the ongoing work of God in relationship to the creation. I will seek to show that such special praise is praise of the Creator's will and work. But, consistently, it is important to indicate that God's care for creation does not collapse into the work of God in Jesus.

GOD'S CONTINUING CREATION

This continuing creational work—traditionally discussed under the category of providence—also bears the mark of categorical difference. The action of God proceeds from the will of God, I have said. Accordingly, God's will for creation cannot be simply vetoed by the resistance of the creature. On the other hand, all this talk of creation surely must entail that the will of God brings God into relationship with that which is not God. That is true of "original creation" and therefore is the more emphatically true of the providential work of God. The other is *of* the Creator's originating will and so is *for* the Creator's preserving will. Thus Langdon Gilkey, with an eye on the "dialectic of God's hidden work within history . . . protection and sustenance on the one hand, and . . . the creation of new possibilities out of the nemesis of the old on the other," writes:

> We experience ultimacy not as the all-powerful, extrinsic and necessitating ordainer of what we are and do, but precisely as the condition and possibility, the ground, of our contingent existence, our creativity, our eros and meaning, our intellectual judgments, our free moral decisions and our intentional actions. Thus the divine ultimacy, experienced in our historical life as providence—an ultimacy that establishes, grounds, limits, judges and rescues the present—is not "unconditional" or absolute in the sense that it determines human action and thus every last character of what is in time, any more than it determined Israel's response to the covenant and its obligations.[53]

We live with a multitude of forces impinging on us, of course. But Gilkey is making the point that the action of God for us is categorically different in that "ultimacy appears precisely *within* the exercise of our contingent being."[54]

The One who is first is for us. In relation to us, God's action remains first and thus theologians speak of the prevenience of God. But that first action is for us, and so truly in relation to us. Thus theologians speak not only of divine preservation and governance but of concurrence.[55] God acts uniquely, one may say, in the beginning and the ending of every event, but in between God acts *with* that which is not God. And so the choices issuing out of created freedom do come to make a difference for God. They do not determine the will of God, but they do affect God's working out of that will as surely as God would work with and within the creature. It is in such wise that the biblical writers speak of God "repenting." This is not a denial of categorical difference, as Terence Fretheim makes clear:

> There is no one-to-one correspondence between the way human beings and God repent. Thus, for example, there are certain matters concerning which God never needs to repent (e.g., sin). The OT expresses one aspect of the "no" of the metaphor in the phrase, "God does not repent" (cf. Num. 23:19; 1 Sam. 15:29). In these passages it is explicitly stated that God does not repent because "God is not a human being." Yet even when God does repent (e.g., Hos. 11:8-9) it is said that God does so because "God is not a human being."[56]

REDEMPTION, THE WORK OF THE CREATOR

Abraham will argue with God on behalf of the righteous in Sodom and Gomorrah, though he has not forgotten that before God he is but "dust and ashes." But, more to the point still, he remembers something else and so he can and must ask, "Will not the judge of all the earth do right?" (Genesis 18). Christian faith goes on to speak of God making things right.

The same dialectic of relationship is to be recognized with regard to the work of God for us in Jesus Christ. Continuity and discontinuity characterize both the relation of that special work to the ongoing work of the Creator God and the special work itself. The special work of God in Jesus is the work of no other God than the Creator of heaven and earth. Arland Hultgren finds it important to distinguish among New Testament soteriologies "theopractic" (God is the major actor in redemption) and "christopractic" (Christ is the major actor) views, but his summary is very clear about the unity in these views:

> Redemptive christology in the New Testament is then never expressed in such a way that Christ performs an action on behalf of humanity over against God. There is no thought, for example, of Christ's appeasing the wrath or justice of God. The apostle Paul says on one occasion that Christians will be saved by Christ from the wrath of God on the basis of justification through Christ's blood (Rom. 5:9), and yet this statement comes immediately after the assertion that God has shown his love in the death of Christ for "sinners" (5:8). There is no thought of a split between God and Christ in which Christ steps in to avert the wrath of an angry God.[57]

In this Jesus, Christians meet the one in whom "all things were created" and still "hold together" (Colossians 1).

Given this strong sense of continuity and holding that the creation was "good but not perfect," some theologians have argued that God would have acted in incarnation to complete creation even had there been no sin. This is how Herbert Richardson has put the point:

> The work of Jesus Christ cannot contradict the purpose for which God created the world. . . . The purpose of His coming, therefore, is simply that He be here. He is not here for the sake of something else. The presence of the Holy One in our midst is its own sufficient reason. Nothing exceeds this, for this gives human life its dignity, worth, and importance. Not the Martha who works, but the Mary who rests in the presence of God has chosen the "good portion." For to enjoy God forever is the chief end of man.[58]

Richardson does not intend to slight the categories of sin and redemption:

> To stress the priority of "God with us" over "God for us" is not, however, to deny that Jesus is our Redeemer, nor is it to derogate from His redeeming work. Though redemption is a subordinate purpose of His coming, it is essential to the chief end He seeks. Moreover, it was precisely for the sake of our redemption that Jesus Christ endured the cross.[59]

I shall want to stand with Richardson in arguing that the work of God for us in Jesus is more than restorative, and I will take up this theme in the next chapter in speaking of the life of faith. But in speaking of the action for us of the One who is first we surely do need to speak of God's action in the face of the discontinuity that is sin.

A GOD WHO BECOMES HUMAN TO FORGIVE

The work of Christ also in this regard, of course, depends on the person of Christ. Theologians have struggled to know how to speak of the difference from us characterizing the presence of God in this Jesus. But somehow Christians would say that the divine and the human truly come together to constitute the very person of Jesus. The divine and the human do "communicate" to form this person. It is out of such a conviction that Christians have spoken of Mary as *theotokos,* the mother of God. And in this there is newness—for us, we quickly say, but I shall want to argue for God as well. Such newness does not comport well with talk of the immutability of God.[60] But, again, this newness in the way of God's being depends on rather than denies the categorical difference. Kierkegaard saw that well in contrasting what we call the incarnation to the manipulating condescension of a king who *pretended* to be a servant boy in order to win the love of a humble maiden. With God there is no such deception:

> God's servant-form is . . . not a disguise, but is actual; and from the hour when he with the omnipotent resolve of his omnipotent love became a servant God has so to speak imprisoned himself in his resolve, and now must go on (to speak foolishly) whether he wills to or not. He cannot then betray himself; he does not have the possibility which is open to the noble king, suddenly to show that he is after all the king—which, however, is no perfection with the king (to have this possibility), but shows merely his impotence and the impotence of his resolve, that he does not actually have the power to become what he wills.[61]

In the poetry of Kierkegaard's parable we catch the glimpse of the newness *for God* constituted by the person of Christ. This newness does bring God near in a distinctive way—that is clear; but it does not deny the superiority of difference. God's will is not "impotent"; it can ineradicably bring about genuine newness for God.

This superiority of difference will characterize the *work* of God for us in Jesus as well, of course. This seems especially clear with respect to the forgiveness of sins. Perhaps this is what Kierkegaard meant when he said that "God is separated" from us "by the most chasmal qualitative abyss" in forgiving sins.[62] This does not require us to minimize the gravity of sin, to say, for example, that sin does not matter to God. Such language would fly in the face of the strong biblical testimony to the wrath of God.[63] God's grace is not cheap. It is Kierkegaard who has been leading us through the logic of categorical difference. Few would charge the melancholy Dane with being "soft" on sin. But Kierkegaard does not suppose that the enormity of sin can defeat the will to be for us of the One who is first.

Kierkegaard comments on the theme that God "forgets" sin:

> First of all, Christianity proceeds to establish sin so firmly as a position that the human understanding can never comprehend it; and then it is this same Christian teaching that again undertakes to eliminate this position in such a way that the human understanding can never comprehend it. . . . Christianity, which was the first to discover the paradoxes, is as paradoxical on this point as possible; it seems to be working against itself by establishing sin so securely as a position that now it seems to be utterly impossible to eliminate it again—and then it is this very Christianity that by means of the Atonement wants to eliminate sin as completely as if it were drowned in the sea.[64]

The formulation of the "for us" in the terms of forgiveness may be subjected to the charge of being nonrelational. Thus Rita Nakashima Brock in her challenging "feminist redemption of Christ" writes: "The reality of erotic power within connectedness means that it cannot be located in a single individual. Hence what is truly christological, that is, truly revealing of divine incarnation and salvific power in human life, must reside in connectedness and not in single individuals."[65]

To this, two responses may be made. First and formally, the forgiveness formulation fits well within the logic of relationship. The development of the notion of relationship throughout this book (in speaking, for example, of life "within" and "with" the other) has emphasized connection and *difference*. In relationship two (or more) come together, but they do not cease to be two. The superiority of God's difference in relationship (Kierkegaard's "chasmal qualitative abyss" separating God from us in forgiving sins) itself represents connection, for it is, after all, a superior (yes, different) form of the difference characterizing *all* genuine relationship. Moreover, one may say that such otherness is precisely pertinent for those being forgiven. Friedrich Mildenberger underlines this "external" (*extra nos*) character nicely:

> That which is outside me is the history of Jesus Christ, his life, suffering, and death. This is my righteousness. I can, however, never so make it part of myself that I am no longer able to distinguish it from myself. No matter how much Jesus Christ becomes my righteousness through faith, he remains the *other*, in whom faith trusts and to whom it clings.[66]

THE EFFICACY OF THE NEW

Second, in the language I have been using, the point that Mildenberger is making is that difference in relationship bears through connectedness on the other. This bearing is not a merely reflective thing. Difference and connection are both ontologically primary in relationship. Thus, materially, one must say that in forgiving sin so radically, God's will is done, but it is not finished. The bondage of sin needs to be addressed. Christian theology is, indeed, liberation theology. Moreover, the framework for understanding such transformation reaches back behind Jesus to the logos of creation. Creation is not completed in forgiveness; indeed, it groans in travail (Romans 8)—as does humankind within creation.

Sadly, Christians at times have spoken of the "newness" characterizing the movement from the first article of creation to the second article of redemption but have fallen silent as to what the third article might mean. Those spectacular pieties which would offer in effect only the third person of the Trinity hardly supply what is needed, for they seem to yield an unearthly Spirit and spirit. What is needed may be suggested by Herbert Richardson's effort to distinguish and connect God *for* us ("Father"), God *with* us ("Son"), and God *in* us ("the Holy Spirit").[67] Here is where there is point and value in the several efforts to, as it were, "extend" the incarnation in real efficacy. Thus Brock speaks of the "Christa community" and of Jesus as like "a whitecap on a wave," and Mark Kline Taylor speaks of Jesus as "leaven" of a "whole interpersonal movement."[68] Peter Hodgson states well the logic of such proposals:

> God is efficaciously present in the world, not as an individual agent performing observable acts. . . . Rather, God is present in specific shapes or patterns of praxis that have a configuring, transformative power within historical process, moving the process in a determinative direction, that of the creative unification of multiplicities of elements into new wholes, into

creative syntheses that build human solidarity, enhance freedom, break systemic oppression, heal the injured and broken, and care for the natural.[69]

That God is at work in the world to bring about actual change, change that does not begin or end in the first century with the years of Jesus of Nazareth—that surely is something Christians have reason to claim. I will make some effort to speak so in the next chapter in speaking of the life of faith. But I note a last time that the logic of relationship does not require or in fact permit the disjunction with which we are so commonly faced in this matter. I have indicated how much the superior difference of God matters to human beings in relationship with God. The other side of that same logic is to stress that the decisive "connection" of what we clumsily call incarnation matters to God. This is how Hultgren puts the point:

> From one perspective the cross is not necessary; God can forgive sin without it. But from another perspective—and here we presume to speak of the hidden heart of God—it is God's own need to bear the sin of humanity for the sake of his children which makes it necessary. The necessity of the cross flows from the character of God. God can do no other.[70]

So, there is new "newness" in Jesus—for us and for God, and this Jesus is the one who speaks of making "all things new" (Rev. 21:5). The transforming life of Jesus did not end in the first century. Before exploring (in chap. 5 and 6) that "newness" for the faith and life of Christians, I pause to consider how the theme of this section, that the One who is first is for us, might guide us in considering diverse faith expression inside and outside Christianity.

DENIALS OF THE "FOR US"

Perhaps the most potent danger cloaks itself in the garb of devotion, appearing to honor the ultimate by placing it in another realm altogether. (I say "it," for to use the language of personality threatens this movement.) The categorical difference seems to be honored when the ultimate is truly "wholly other." But the One who is first no longer seems to be truly "for us." At least the superiority of God's difference withdraws from the "for us." In Christian dress this presents itself in the tendency to isolate "God in Himself" from what we experience in our relationship with God.[71] This may seem not only honorable, but at the same time innocuous. What, after all, can one say of significance about God—to harm or to help—apart from what we know in our relationship with God? But there is a subtle undermining here of confidence in what we do know of God as related to us. There seems to be the possibility left open—even if it is not explicitly stated, that we somehow are not related to the very heart of God. Perhaps, then, God could withdraw from relationship. Over against this destructive praise of God, stands Kierkegaard's "foolish speech": God must go on, whether God wills to or not. Or in Niebuhr's language it is in God that we meet self-binding will for the other and so it is that Christians know that finally nothing "will be able to separate us from the love of God in Christ Jesus our Lord" (Rom. 8:39). Another form that the denial of the "for us" can take is to suggest that if we are to be with the ultimate, it is necessary for us to leave our ordinary world of relatedness. That denial seems dramatically present in those religious views which deny the genuine reality of the world of time and space which we know—a denial associated with certain Eastern ways of thought.[72] Such denial is more subtly present within Christendom in pieties that in identifying the relationship to God isolate the individual from all other relationships. If God has come to us in all of our "worldliness"—our relatedness—to be for us, we will not commune with that God by withdrawing from the connectedness of our existence.

Yet another denial of the "for us" is found in formulations that make the opposite error. Instead of letting the centrifugal force of difference push toward isolation, this tendency implosively drives toward identification. It is one thing to say that God, unlike all other agents, acts "within" the creature. It is quite another to say that God is the all-determining power.[73] If all actions are *in every respect* the actions of "two agents," it is not likely that God will be shortchanged in the accounting process. Indeed, God will likely be given full credit for the "dark" or "shadow" or "left-handed" side of life. But then how is it that we can still say that the One who is first is *for us*? The "intimacy of communion" would seem to have been replaced by identity.[74] There would be no need to write of *our* life of faith. But if this error is to be avoided, we need first to offer some sketch of the place of Creator and creature in the relationship we have in life "before" God.

CONSEQUENCES IN LIFE AND THOUGHT: WE LIVE "BEFORE" THE OTHER

Where does this discussion leave us? It should leave us where life finds us: "before" God. While distinction or difference characterizes all the relationships in our boundary existence, the relationship with God is marked by a "different difference." There is no one perfect way to express this. But the punctiliarity of prepositions may serve us. I have written of how we exist "within" the spacetime continuum ("with nature and within the body" in that process) and "with" the other human creature(s). But we live "before" God (*coram Deo*). In this clumsy way I hope to evoke the unique dimension of our relationship to God.

IN THE PRESENCE OF GOD

What is meant by "before" in this construction? Well, we do not "precede" God, except in the profound sense that our lives do go to the God who is the *omega* for all things. In that chronological sense a truth is told, for the dictionary aptly tells us that "before" can mean "to be judged or acted on by" (or even "at the disposal of"), as in "the case went before the court." But in lifting up the *coram Deo* of the tradition, I mean to suggest that we live "before" God in what may perhaps be termed a more spatial sense. Other indicated meanings for "before" are "in the presence of," "face-to-face," "close to."[75]

The biblical writers speak variously of the presence of God. To speak of God as everywhere present is not something theologians have grafted on to the first order testimony of faith. The prophet speaks for God: "Am I a God near by, says the LORD, and not a God far off? Who can hide in secret places so that I cannot see them? says the LORD. Do I not fill heaven and earth?" (Jer. 23:23-24). And the psalmist has his own question: "Where can I go from your spirit? Or where can I flee from your presence?" The person of faith knows the answer the psalmist must give. One cannot flee outward ("the wings of the morning," "the farthest limits of the sea") or within ("the darkness is not dark to you. . . . for it was you who formed my inward parts") (Ps. 139:7-13).

If we live at all, then, we live "before," in the presence of, God. But God's universal presence is not, as Ruth Page puts it, "stifling."[76] This God is present to be "for us," to create, to re-create, to increase freedom.

The psalmist praises the God who "knit me together in my mother's womb" (Ps. 139:13). Perhaps the One who is first is present first in the knitting together of each moment of life; in that sense we take our life moment by moment from the hand of God. Yet we do come to have our own life through God's providential care and so we also live "before" God in the sense of "facing," even "confronting," God. In that sense Page is right in pleading for the preposition "with" to express the nature of God's presence:

> God is present with us and all creation. That represents a solidarity not found in God being present *to* the world as a subject of contemplation and worship only. He is certainly that, but the preposition "with" conveys that he is on our side as we endeavour to make sense and value out of the world. . . . Yet the minimal distance preserved in presence *with*, which would be lost in presence *in*, is that distance which gives both God and us a measure of independence even in relationship.[77]

OUR KNOWING OF GOD

Our knowing of God seems to reflect this same dialectic. Biblical authors testify that all persons can know God—indeed, in some sense *do* know God (Rom. 1:19-23). Yet it seems we do not know God as we know other "others." To say this is not to deny the reality of religious experience. But such experience seems to be what one might call "prepositional": we know God "in, with, and under" that which is not God. In John Smith's phrasing, our experience of God may be direct, but it is not unmediated.[78] That surely remains true of what Christians find to be the clearest revelation of God. Kierkegaard had his eye on the figure of Jesus when he wrote: "Even the most certain of all things, a revelation, *eo ipso*, becomes dialectical whenever I attempt to appropriate it."[79]

Yet there is some strange kind of certainty here. So Christians will bear witness to the "gift" of faith, and unbelievers will ponder in their own way the "givenness" of what may be called the divine incognitos—the true, the beautiful, the good, the real.[80] To live "before" God, then, is to live in the unfailing presence of God, but it is not to possess God as an item of knowledge to be classified and filed away. In the previous chapter we spoke of how we never truly have the nondivine other in such a way either. But while to our great loss we may effectively "murder to dissect" the neighbor, God remains present as the living God whether we choose to ignore/reject that presence or to mummify it in the paralysis of particular "peak" experiences or in the catacombs of our dogmatics.

To speak so of the dialectical certainty by which we know God may appear to be special pleading. It may indeed *be* that. Yet the Christian faith is able to make sense of the distinctiveness of this knowing. *How* we claim to know God seems to rhyme rather well with *what* we say of God. If God is everywhere present, it will not be too surprising that observation by the method of difference will not function well in knowing God.[81] Nor do we expect to be able physically to point to God, whom we confess to be spirit. These limitations must not be converted into evidence; we are merely saying that the "how" fits the "what" of the knowing claimed. Or perhaps we should speak of "Who" is known. For at the heart of what I have written of God is the notion of living self-determining will. Here, then, the analogy may be more aptly drawn from inter-personal knowing than from the objectifying knowledge enshrined in the table of chemical elements. In chapter 3, I remarked concerning the elusive certainty (the "givenness of the other") of our knowledge of the human other. It is not that the other maliciously hides to test me. We simply know the other person differently. As we said in our earlier discussion, in the depth of our knowledge of the human other we know no/thing. On the Christian understanding, it is not less so with God and our knowing of God.[82]

My purpose in this chapter is to consider human life in relation to that Other whom Christians call God. It is not my purpose to probe deeply the justification of that claim to know God, though such an effort would have obvious pertinence in considering how a Christian believer may live faithfully and fruitfully in meeting the otherness of unbelief. But we must ask how the being "before" such a God bears on our human life. The focus, once again, is the understanding of human life—now in the context of this relationship. I aim to offer, then, no fulsome doctrine of God with assorted attributes tidily in place. Such an independent treatment would not serve my purpose, even if it somehow did not directly contradict it.

My question, then, is, "What difference does this God 'before' whom we exist make to us as we seek to live, to live well, to live in faith?" Perhaps what is needed is simply some application of the two claims that have been made: (1) We turn to One who is *first*, and (2) The One who is first is *for* us. If these two claims are true, we do live "before" this Other. What meaning does that have for human life?

THE ACTION OF GOD IN RECIPROCAL RELATIONSHIP

"Before" designates a relationship. To speak of the relationship between God and us is to speak of action. For the Christian it is essential somehow to speak of the action of God. God is not simply a constant presence, brooding or benevolent. How shall we speak of the action of God? Earlier we joined Ruth Page in saying that the presence of God is not "stifling"; neither is the action of God. Yet there are strains of piety and theology within Christendom that seem not to realize this. Somehow in those strains we seem still to suppose that the attribution of unqualified omnipotence—that is, of all-determining power—is a compliment to God. One wonders whether we have bothered to consider the events in the world for which we are sublimely assigning responsibility. We usually manage a saving inconsistency, by which human responsibility is recognized, at least for individual sin against God.[83] Or is the "inconsistency" a principled distinction? That is what Kathryn Tanner seems to suggest. She is concerned to speak of God's transcendence in a way that is not "competitive" with human agency—a concern that I share. Here is the way she proposes to serve that concern:

> God must be directly productive of everything that is in every aspect of its existence. . . . We can specify two . . . rules: First, . . . avoid both a simple univocal attribution of predicates to God and world and a simple contrast of divine and non-divine predicates. . . . The second rule is as follows: avoid in talk about God's creative agency all suggestions of limitation in scope or manner. The second rule prescribes talk of God's creative agency as immediate and universally extensive.[84]

I have said that God's relationship to/with us is characterized by a "different difference." This may be what Tanner is getting at by her non-contrastive transcendence. I too want to say that God is "first" as creator with respect to every moment of existence. But at another point we need somehow to recognize that in truly being "for" us God gives us the freedom to be *for God*. Kierkegaard spoke rightly of God's "omnipotence being under the power of love" so that God not only says, "Be!" but even, "Be something even over against me!" Kierkegaard added: "Thus love . . . lovingly demands something of him. Now that is the reciprocal relation."[85]

Systematic theologians exegete that reciprocal relation. Thus Keith Ward, while insisting that "God does not depend for his happiness and perfection upon any created world," can also specify reasons for God's creation of the world: (1) new subjects of value—the creatures, (2) new sorts of values (as, "the enjoyment of a tiring walk"), (3) God's experience of the value of the creatures, (4) the expression of God's creativity, and (5) a personal relationship for God with the creatures.[86]

THE DIVINE SUFFERING

So do we come to be "before" God. In this reciprocal relation, action moves both ways. Such action is involved in saying that God knows us fully. And to know us is to suffer us. "Suffer" can be understood in the older meaning of "experience" or "undergo"—that is, truly to know. There *is* joy in heaven over every sinner who repents (Luke 15:7). But there is no reason to avoid our more common meaning: our lives "before" God do bring pain into the very life of God. Christian theologians have been slow to say this openly. We have been reluctant to recognize that the relationship with God—by God's ineradicable will for us—is indeed a two-way relationship. We seem, for example, to deny that in loving us, God experiences any joy, any gain of any sort.[87] Perhaps we think that in saying this we risk becoming prideful. But, oddly, we seem even to have drawn back from the humbling recognition that our sins can bring suffering to God. Thus we have offered constructions such as that God's suffering is wholly vicarious, an imaginative response to our sin and suffering.[88] Or we have said that the suffering of God is only "economic"—having to do with the life of God in the world, apparently not tainting the higher immanent life of God. Even the implication of divine suffering flowing from the person and work of a Jesus who died on a cross has been intercepted by formulations of the two natures and other distinctions supposed to save the church from patripassianism.[89] Carl Braaten has well argued for making a different distinction:

> The distinction between the Father and the Son can be maintained without denying the Father a share in the incarnate fate of his Son Jesus Christ. If the dispassionate God of Greek metaphysics is supplanted by the compassionate God of Israel, the Father of Jesus Christ, a major barrier has been removed to a constructive interpretation of the myth of the incarnate Son of God. . . . Only a suffering God can be harmonized with the picture of Christ in the Gospels.[90]

The twin to unease in recognizing divine suffering is the tendency to speak of divine power in the terms of all-determining force. Douglas John

Hall speculates that we have learned in this from the culture in which we exist:

> The language of our religion has been so consistently informed by the spirit of might, winning, success, and related concepts that it is difficult to use any of the scriptural nomenclature of glory and triumph without conjuring up the whole ideology of empire. . . . The "theology of glory"—possibly the most crass and decadent form of the *theologia gloriae* ever to have articulated itself in a very long history of religious triumphalism—is openly displayed as normative Christianity every day of the week.[91]

Braaten speaks of the corrective that Martin Luther provided in another setting—a corrective that would seem to address the condition that Hall has well described:

> It was Martin Luther who made the most complete break with the hybrid system which the Christian tradition had developed out of Greek metaphysics and biblical faith. His theology of the cross (*theologia crucis*) meant that the philosophical idea of God would have to be radically transformed in light of the cross.[92]

One wonders why the theme of divine impassibility has such great power. Perhaps in this we would pay homage to the categorical difference of God. But much is at stake in how we do this. G. L. Prestige seems to hear such homage as a powerful note in the reflection of the early church, precisely on God's moral will for relationship:

> Just as God is supreme in power and wisdom, so is He morally supreme, incapable of being diverted or overborne by forces and passions such as commonly hold sway in the creation and among mankind. . . . Impassibility then implies perfect moral freedom, and is a supernatural endowment belonging to God alone.[93]

I wish to join such a hymn of praise to the "impassible will" of the One who is truly first. But the conventional statements of impassibility— in both formal dogmatic treatments and in popular piety—often seem to go beyond that praise and in fact do so in a way that actually ends up turning against that very will of God: that we be in actual relationship with God. Is Plato's reach so long that we believe that "change implies a defect of being"?[94] To this, Jürgen Moltmann has surely made the right response:

> God cannot suffer like creatures who are exposed to illness, pain and death. But must God therefore be thought of as being incapable of suffering in any respect? . . . Granted, the theology of the early church knew of only one

alternative to suffering and that was being incapable of suffering (*apatheia*), not-suffering. But there are other forms of suffering between unwilling suffering as a result of an alien cause and being essentially unable to suffer, namely active suffering, the suffering of love, in which one voluntarily opens himself to the possibility of being affected by another. There is unwilling suffering, there is accepted suffering and there is the suffering of love. . . . The justifiable denial that God is capable of suffering because of a deficiency in his being may not lead to a denial that he is incapable of suffering out of the fullness of his being, i.e., his love.[95]

To the clarity of this long passage I would add only this: the denial that God suffers because of a deficiency *must* not lead to the failure to recognize the suffering of a God transcendent in relationship! The categorical difference is realized in the relationship: God does not stop being first in being "for" us. Indeed, the superiority in being which characterizes God is known in One who is not "impotent" (as was the king in Kierkegaard's parable). God can "become what he wills" in relationship to the creatures of the divine will who exist "before" God and so come to bear on God. To that extent we are (*pace* Tanner) in a univocal continuum of action.

THEOLOGICAL TEMPTATIONS

Where does this leave us? In faith we seek to take our bearings in the light of our relationship to this Other. By the creative will of God we live "before" a God from whom every other being receives its being and to whom every action goes. God is indeed Alpha and Omega, in the beginning and at the end of all that is (Rev. 21:6; 22:13). All things do live, move, and have their being in this God (Acts 17:28). Yet because it is the will and work of God to create freedom, this circle of divine causality is very much open. God is closer to us than any other; perhaps this is what Paul Tillich was getting at in speaking of God "theonomously," as an "inner other."[96] The categorically supreme God is to *that* extent first in our action. Strangely, though, to act "within" or preveniently may seem a lesser thing in comparison to the objectifiable and sense-perceptible action on us of other others. One can understand that someone might conclude that God does not "act" at all, or indeed that there is no God to act. And one can understand a temptation to "trump" such conclusions by claiming that all actions are simply the actions of a God who does not compete with nondivine agency.[97]

Such temptations are to be resisted. In this effort to sketch human life in relation to the action of God the freedom essential to genuine relationship must not be lost. This commitment will make a difference as theologians sort through schemas designed to relate divine and human action. Peter Hodgson has helpfully gathered theories of God's action ("personal action," "primary cause," "two perspectives and languages," "uniform action," "process") and added his own notion of "God in history as Gestalt," a structure of praxis, a pattern . . . that guides, lures, and shapes historical process.[98] Religious experience of relationship to God (as, for example, in prayer and worship) will be best served by recognizing a God who wills, feels, knows—and acts, without having to claim that this God can simply be located and limited alongside other agents, as we can. Once again, it is the first order testimony of experience which drives the attempt to formulate a notion of "transcendence in relationship."

If Christian faith is rooted in the stubborn sense that we are in relationship with God, theology must not be permitted to jettison this enlivening vision. Thus I have stressed that we do have the freedom to reject the will of God—a point whose absolute denial would certainly imperil the moral unity of any God ruling the universe we occupy. In this I am disagreeing with those theologians who argue that if God is granted inner access to an emerging moment, that moment is denied freedom.[99] Such an argument seems to give insufficient attention to the reality of genuine otherness in relationship. In every relationship and so in this inner relationship there is no monopoly of power. Moreover, to speak of God as uniquely creator is to be reminded that it is the will of this God to create and know the other. "Before" such a God the Philippian exhortation makes sense: "Work out your own salvation with fear and trembling; for it is God who is at work in you, enabling you both to will and to work for his good pleasure" (Phil. 2:12b-13).

If that is the will of God, then the fact of our freedom counts in principle for the fulfillment rather than the frustration of God's freedom. Of course if freedom is only a necessary and not a sufficient condition for that which God seeks in creation, place is made for the frustration represented by divine suffering. But even this suffering need not be seen as simply diminishing the role of God. There may be debate about what Dietrich Bonhoeffer meant in writing from prison that "only a suffering God can help," but Christians who gather around crosses ought to be at work on the proposition that a suffering God *does* help.[100] As we respond to our Creator's will, God does "suffer" the world in joy and in sorrow. But just so does God know the world with an unrivaled completeness and intimacy. So even the act of sinful rebellion is not complete in itself. An event is real as it eventuates in real effects in its future. But as my rebellion reaches its future it meets a God acting there "first" in the light of a full knowledge of all the events coming together to constitute that emerging moment. Joseph's word may ring down through the centuries: "Even though you intended to do harm to me, God intended it for good, in order to preserve a numerous people, as he is doing today" (Gen. 50:20).

This does not remove the sense of risk, and it certainly should not be used to justify human evil. Even apart from evil, to say that God wills to act universally does not make everything just the same. God's will is to act in relationship, and God, one may presume, is wise enough to know that some times are fuller than others. Thus Keith Ward, noting that we have come to understand the universe as an "integral" but nonmechanistic web, speculates:

> God can determine just so many outcomes as leave the general probability laws of nature intact; and he is likely to determine those which have a focal structuring position within an integral system—a key position in an unstable dynamical system far from equilibrium—which will maximize novel patterns or consequences for good within the system as a whole.[101]

"Determine" is not a particularly relational word, but perhaps One who has the security of self-determined will is the more able to act in relationship with the patient wisdom of tactical judgment.

GOD'S KNOWLEDGE OF THE OPEN FUTURE

It seems to be the nature of *homo religiosus* to reach for that which lies beyond human grasp. To say that God acts with complete knowledge of past and present, for example, is not to say that God knows the future as present. Such "comfort" is bought at far too dear a price.[102] Such an understanding would rob our relationship with God of the living character needed to sustain a significant life of prayer and devotion. In reaching avariciously to lay claim to the future, the believer may be blind to the ways in which God uses effectively full knowledge of the past. Thus Rowan Williams writes of the "memory" of God:

> Because the life of God is not a life with worldly limits, worldly constraints on its possibilities, the memory of suffering here is—we might say—embedded in an inexhaustible life. So when he returns to us the memory of

what has been done, it is a memory inseparably bound to a reality which guarantees the hope of healing because its resources and possibilities cannot be exhausted or extinguished by the world's destructiveness.[103]

We need to struggle here to hold together words like "guarantee" and "hope." Once again: to celebrate the truth that God is first is not to forbid God from creating and loving that which is truly other. And so, to cling to the truth that God determines the will of God is not to lose access to the way in which that will becomes effective by working with infinite sensitivity with the plenum of particularities characterizing the spatiotemporal process we have already described as open.[104] This God is not a capricious God, but God's constancy is that of living will in relation to which I will know surprise—the more so, if I expect the monotonous security of a machine. Again we do well to reject the disjunctive logic of "all or nothing at all." Since we do live in relationship—within the space-time continuum, with other creatures, and before the One who is first, we have something to do. If I had no freedom, my challenge would be at best to understand that fact in the face of the persistent illusion of responsibility. Were I alone free, I would lack the genuine challenge of newness to be known in relation to the freedom that is other than my own. But it is not so, for we do live "on the boundary," in relationship with otherness. For good or ill, our faith is not exempted from this circumstance. Thus we ask: "Given this account of life on the boundary, what may we say of faith on the boundary?"

5

TO BECOME
OTHER IN FAITH

For Christians, faith is not exempted from the experience of otherness. Their faith is engaged in meeting those differences which characterize human life generally (chap. 2–4) and the differences which the other faiths and unfaith represent (chap. 6). Faith is caught up in such differences; it does not by itself create or control them. This follows from the nature of faith. Faith may indeed be an active thing, a living power (for good *or ill*) for the believer. But the believer will agree with the student of religion that faith happens on earth, to historically situated beings. Moreover, faith itself acknowledges a derivative status, for it claims to act in relation to reality that does not depend on faith for being—God, others, even oneself. Faith may make an idol, but not a God. Faith may feel called to save the world, but to do so requires attending to the world in which faith finds itself. Thus to be true to itself—and to be true—faith in various ways faces toward realities that are not itself.

FAITH'S DIRECTION

I argued in chapter 1 that the ground on which faith finds itself is increasingly characterized by the experience of otherness. Such seemingly unsteady ground may be perceived by Christians as a veritable shaking of the foundations. The tendency to regard the other as threat does not go on holiday at the door of the church. On the other hand, in that first chapter, I proposed that the life of faith cannot be oriented, cannot get its bearings, without recognizing precisely such disorientation. To know well this ground that "the others" represent is a necessary step if the believer is to live faithfully and fruitfully. But it is insufficient. Accordingly, I have attempted some excavation beneath the surface on the site where faith seems "situated." Such digging as Part One represents suggests that human life cannot be understood apart from a deep structure of otherness, for it is—respectively—life *within*, *with*, and *before* the other. Thus to meet the other is not a contingent matter, though of course the particular meetings of particular others are that. Human life is inextricably life with otherness. If in happening upon a boundary we dig beneath the surface, we come to find that boundaries run through the very center of our being, for they mark the relationships that come together to constitute that being. The dramatic increase in the quantity and intensity of our specific experience of otherness stands out unmistakably for us, but it can be adequately understood only if it is related to the deep dialectic of difference and connection or root rhythm of relationship which is constitutive of who we are.

Very well, let us suppose that is so. But the very excavation of the ground has made clear that central to the challenge of human freedom are the choices to be made with regard to the other. There are deep differences outside us that are not to be dissolved in a sentimental abstracting from the concrete choices we face. Those choices involve deciding among very distinct ways in which we can respond to the very various others that we meet. More specifically, to be a Christian is also to be faced, objectively and subjectively, with such choices. Thus in these last two chapters we begin to explore how Christian faith may live well with the challenge of the other, both in its own life (chap. 5) and in relation to those who are other with respect to faith (chap. 6). We can claim to do here nothing more complete than to "explore," for the call of otherness, while always the Christian's mark, seems harder to hear with discrimination in this turbulent time. This much is clear: Christian faith will *mis*understand itself if it regards the reality of otherness as wholly external to itself. To do so would be to *dis*regard that to which it is called; indeed, that which is at work in it. This chapter's title may introduce our theme pointedly enough; the Christian is to become other in faith.

BEING AND BECOMING AS CHRISTIAN

That we will become other in some sense is evident simply from an analysis of our human being, as surely as Christian faith fits and forms that humanity. Our analysis in Part One clearly stressed that the self is not a substance, so that with Jürgen Moltmann one will need to say that "*being* human means *becoming* human."[1] Surely one would expect some change or development—some becoming other—over the years in a Christian life span and over the centuries of the church's existence. Why should we expect the formation of Christian faith to contract itself into a drama of a single act of fleeing the pulse of change enlivening the human coil? But the call to become other is not merely a matter of adopting some currently available human casing for an essentially unchanging spiritual core. That would still be an external relationship to change. The Christian faith in itself calls the believer ahead to a life that is new. Moltmann is also right in this:

> Between the experienced justification of the sinner and the hoped-for glorification of the person justified lies the path of sanctification, which has to do with "putting on the new human being, created after the likeness of God" (Eph. 4:24; cf. also Col. 2:10). So likeness to God is both gift and charge, indicative and imperative. It is charge and hope, imperative and promise. Sanctification has justification as its presupposition, and glorification as its hope and its future. In the messianic light of the gospel, the human being's likeness to God appears as a historical process with an eschatological termination; it is not a static condition.[2]

Moltmann's way of putting this may seem strained or stilted. There are many ways in which Christian faith speaks of this becoming other. Yet a number of current studies suggest that somehow we seem to have failed effectively to speak of and otherwise work for human maturity in faith.[3] Why might this be so?

Perhaps Christians have heard in such speaking and working the specter of human arrogance. It might seem wiser (safer?) to say things like "sanctification is (simply) getting used to justification." Such caution is understandable, not the least in Reformation circles. There it is stressed that sinful pride can corrupt the Christian's response to the call to become other in faith. We could, for example, act as if such becoming were our own fine achievement. That would be an offense against God. But the understanding of the relationship with God presented in chapter 4 suggests that one may sin as surely by withholding from God the praise, the response, which is due in view of what God has done and is doing for and in and

through us. If "the One who is first is for us," if (because of the will and
work of God) divine transcendence is to be found in relationship so that
we do live "before" God—if these claims be granted, then it does not
honor God to act as if growth in Christian faith and life were somehow
an assault on God's glory. Martin Luther can hardly be said to have been
blind to the dangers of human hubris which usurps the role of God. But
he knew as well that God's action *for* us comes to have actual effects *in*
us. In a sermon he speaks of "two kinds of Christian righteousness." The
first is that alien righteousness of Christ "by which he justifies through
faith." But he goes on to say this:

> Therefore this alien righteousness, instilled in us without our works by grace
> alone—while the Father, to be sure, inwardly draws us to Christ—is set
> opposite original sin, likewise alien, which we acquire without our works
> by birth alone. Christ daily drives out the old Adam more and more in
> accordance with the extent to which faith and knowledge of Christ grow.
> For alien righteousness is not instilled all at once, but it begins, makes
> progress, and is finally perfected at death.[4]

Luther understands that "the second kind of righteousness is our proper
righteousness, not because we alone work it, but because we work with
that first and alien righteousness."[5] Luther was not the only Christian to
hear a call to new life in faith. There will be different ways to put this.
The differences are not trivial. There are important issues involved in
whether one speaks with a Luther of a second righteousness or with, say,
contemporary Roman Catholic theologian Anne Carr of "transforming
grace within" or with Methodist John Cobb of how "his righteousness is
formed in us."[6] I will address some of those issues in formulation in this
section. But the central logic of Christian faith is such that the World
Council of Churches could prepare for its Seventh Assembly in Canberra,
Australia, in 1991 with these words: "In the Spirit the community of
believers experience the nearness of God and participate in the saving grace
and the liberating presence of the living Christ, thus becoming the instrument and sign of God's transforming action."[7]

DIRECTION FOR PILGRIMS

Thus the Christian life is not without direction. To be in the spacetime
continuum is not a merely external placement. The Christian is "on the
move," going somewhere. The map for Christian existence covers the
whole span of life and indeed—as we shall discover—reaches beyond this
life. Perhaps map is the wrong metaphor, for it might suggest excessive

clarity about both destination and itinerary—directions, not just direction. The Christian does not purchase conviction by squandering the capacity to recognize complexity and own up to ambiguity. There will be situations where the Christian will simply be uncertain as to what Christian discipleship requires. But a sense of direction has the tensile strength necessary to survive in situations where the brittle firmness of "positions" cannot. The Christian faith does bestow the living strength of a sense of direction. I will argue that this is not merely a formal focus of learning to live toward a future for which one works and waits in the present, though that itself does worthy service in freeing the Christian from knee-jerk resistance to change. But this direction can be given sufficient material formulation, so that it will permit the Christian discriminately, though tentatively, to connect with and critique the myriad of voices and movements that claim to announce the new and salvific world.

DIRECTION AND THE DECISIVE GOSPEL
I said that faith's sense of direction spans the whole of life. Just so, it is rooted in the reality of God the creator's will and work for life and as such bears sufficient material embodiment for the criteriological task just mentioned. Before we unpack that direction, it seems wise to identify within the work of God that for which gospel language is to be used. Failure clearly to make clear distinctions—and connections—at this point can be the source of all manner of difficulty. And fear of falling into one extreme or the other (loss of distinction, loss of connection) can be the all-too-earthly ghost that spooks the Christian into passivity or fanaticism. One may be confident—and glad—that diversity will continue to exist within the Christian family with respect to how this relationship is to be formulated. But those differences do not keep a family resemblance from showing through. I do not propose here to announce that resemblance, for I realize that my phrasing is particular and no doubt affected by the context of my effort in this book. But I write as one who hopes that when one professed Christian meets another and observes the gait, the pattern of articulation, the shape of the nose—the physiognomy of faith, the former can say of the latter, "That's who he is" *and* "That's who *we* are."

Faith's sense of direction is derived from the will and work of God. I have already written of how the superiority of categorical difference is to be found in a will that is independent in origin, determinative of the action of the one who wills, and unchallenged by inner instability.[8] The will and work of God are one in purpose, and they extend to all that God has made. Whatever distinctions are to be made must not be permitted to threaten this fundamental unity. Lutheran talk of "two kingdoms" is often interpreted in ways that would threaten the unity. But Walter Altmann refuses to trace such interpretation back to Luther himself:

> Luther never meant to make the church and the state autonomous entities. It was the responsibility of the political authorities to achieve economic, political, and social reforms which would also affect the church, and it was the task of the church to confront the political authorities with God's will. Thus the so-called "two kingdoms" can be distinguished regarding their duties and means, but they overlap each other in terms of space. Besides, they are together based on one foundation—God is the Lord of both—and they have a common goal—the good of all humanity.[9]

God wills and works for "the good of all humanity." Some such inclusive formulation is essential in speaking of faith's direction, though we may have more reason today to warn against an anthropocentric bias in even this broad phrasing. Dorothee Soelle speaks of "the indivisible salvation of the whole world."[10] "World" has the right range to it. But how is the specific reality of Jesus of Nazareth to be understood within such cosmic claims? In chapter 4, I aligned myself with the view that roots the work of God in Jesus in the Creator's will for relationship, so that one might say in a dramatic speculation: the God we confess in Mary's baby would have come even had there been no sin.[11] But the world is not without sin. So it is that Christians speak most surely of the forgiveness of sin when they speak of Jesus. In such speaking, the specific treasure of the gospel is heard, for the gospel speaks of a good that depends on God alone. That is why the apostle Paul can write: "Who will bring any charge against God's elect? It is God who justifies. Who is to condemn? Is it Christ Jesus, who died, yes, who was raised, who is at the right hand of God, who indeed intercedes for us? Who will separate us from the love of Christ?" (Rom. 8:33-35a, alternate reading of v. 34).

Such sentences are surely existentially paradoxical—"against the opinion" (*doxa*) in any culture that agrees with George Bernard Shaw that "forgiveness is a beggar's refuge; we must pay our debts!" But I have suggested that this challenging Christian claim really refers to no metaphysical miracle.[12] In every relationship there is independence as well as interdependence. In Jesus, Christians find the decisive independence of the other, raised to a unique power. Here there is witness to a God who, as Kierkegaard put it, "with the omnipotent resolve of his omnipotent love" can lay claim to all humankind—indeed, to the whole creation which "has been groaning in labor pains until now" (Rom. 8:22). This gospel is, indeed, the true treasure of the church, and Christians do well to safeguard it so that the singularity of God's decisive action is not obscured.[13]

But if this singular word of the gospel is spoken well and often, it will lead us to see that God's decisive and independent action in the Christ is to the end of fulfilling the Creator's will. Paul links creation and re-creation in testifying to the otherness of that will: "It is the God who said, 'Let light shine out of darkness,' who has shone in our hearts to give the light of the knowledge of the glory of God in the face of Jesus Christ" (2 Cor. 4:6).

Our being and our new being are given by God alone, but in love God does not will to be alone. And so, I have said, we come to exist in actual relationship "before" God such that we bear the gift and task of responsibility.[14] Thus in celebrating the decisive work of God for us in Jesus, Christians speak of the gift of faith, but they should not deny that the work of God is great enough to create a genuine other with freedom and responsibility.[15] Our worship of God does not collapse into the circle of God adoring God. The God of whom Christian faith speaks is a creator God who wills to be in relationship. And so we can speak in this chapter of the specific sense of direction given to the Christian.

TO SERVE THE CREATOR'S WILL

This re-creative God who acts for the redemption of all is none other than the God who is creator in the most primordial and comprehensive sense. This God is one God with fundamentally one will. The Creator's categorical superiority bears on the content of the creature's task and on the discharge of that task. As to content, the logic of the new creation reflects originating creation both in *that* the creature is given a task and in *what* that task entails. So it is that Christians will be freshly motivated in their redemption to "return to creation" and to the work of *co*-creation. I have stressed that such human work as created and re-created does not steal from God; rather, it is precisely the Creator's will which such effort serves.[16] Moreover, it seems a particularly fitting testimony to the unity of the Creator's will and work that persons who do not acknowledge God as their creator still can know and do what God intends in the world. God's will to create and empower the other (for *each* other, we shall want soon to add) is that potent. There will be more to say of this in speaking in the next section of resources.

So: in sharing the treasure of the gospel, the Christian bears testimony to the decisive and independent work of God in Jesus *and* the Christian finds herself or himself returned to work anew in service to the creative will of God. There are misunderstandings to be avoided here. (1) The Christian in zealous passion might be tempted to overstate the difference represented in Christian discipleship. I have already said that the Creator God works within the creature without acknowledgment and even in spite of actual defiance.[17] Christians are not elevated above service of the Creator's will, whatever differences may characterize the clarity and intensity of their motivation. (2) To say that the Christian is "returned" to creation may be misleading in a second way. It is not merely that in a fundamental sense one has not been away. The language of "return" may mislead by implying that the structure and style of the service (whether knowing or unknowing) of creation is essentially static. Over against this, it must be said that while the independent re-creative work of God in Jesus is indeed "once *for all,*" the structures and strategies that well discharge our co-creative responsibilities are highly mutable.[18] The theologians of liberation have helped us understand that all social structures are made *through* human beings and many seem sadly to be made simply *by* human beings in defiance of the Creator's will. Yet the reality of change, the throb of temporality we have charted in Part One,—such matters do not in principle derive from sin or from the need to correct oppressive human structures but rather may be supposed to characterize the very work of God in this world. The call of the new sounds *for* creation and *against* sin.

This mutability bears on Christian participation in the work of co-creation. If God is not done with the world, but works freshly in the flow of history, it should not surprise the Christian that we both know and do "in part." Yet this seems hard to realize. Sharon Welch has written insightfully in criticism of the "Euro-American middle class" understanding of "responsible action":

> To act means to determine what will happen through that single action, to ensure that a given course of events comes to pass. This understanding of

responsible action leads to a striking paralysis of will when faced with large, complex problems. It seems natural to many people, when faced with a problem too big to be solved alone or within the foreseeable future, simply to do nothing. If one cannot do everything to solve the problem of world hunger, for example, one does nothing. One can even argue against partial remedies, actions that address only part of the problem, as foolish.[19]

THE ROLE OF THE OTHER

Very well, mutability entails incompleteness in vision and execution. But even a partial response calls for some material specification of God's creative will. The perspective I am commending is to focus on the role of the other. We are to become other—which can be understood *formally* as hearing and heeding God's call to maturity—in *material* relation to the one who or that which is other. The two uses of the word "other" are indeed two here, but I aim to show an essential connection. The difference and connection can be seen in that in the first or formal usage, the change is within the continuity of personal identity. So, materially, the invocation of the other is certainly not a magic wand to collapse all difference. The transformation that takes place within the person opens *that person* to the other. The Christian prays for a "closer walk" but does not seek to dissolve into the maker of heaven and earth. The Christian seeks the intimacy of "communion, not union," as I have said.[20] And in responding to God, the Christian is newly drawn into a relationship with another "other," with all the others. It is customary for Christians to recognize this other—a common phrasing is "the neighbor"—as the object of our action, as the one *to whom* we are sent in "faith's direction." But I am speaking about the reality of the other in the very content of the call itself. The theme can be announced prepositionally: in this chapter, I am trying to make clear that the call is to become other *for*, *with*, and *through* the other.

The prepositions stand apart in dramatic difference. They can best be understood in an explication of how Christian faith identifies the other. Here there are distinctions to be made that could easily be glossed over in a mantra-like repetition of the word "other." The Christian may well ask, "Who is my neighbor?"

1. When Jesus was asked that question, he praised the Samaritan who found his neighbor in the one who fell among thieves (Luke 10:25-37). Accordingly, Christians have emphasized concern for the wounded and

those most vulnerable to wounding.[21] And who are they? The World Council of Churches' Bible studies for the 1991 Canberra assembly spoke for a strong Christian consensus in challenging the churches: "To join the powerless of the earth—the poor, the exploited and the marginalized—and those who try to be with them as they seek truth and freedom."[22]

2. Parker Palmer notes that in the description in Matthew 25 of the last judgment, special emphasis is placed on feeding the hungry, giving drink to the thirsty, clothing the naked, visiting the sick and imprisoned, and— seemingly, a categorical shift—*welcoming the stranger*. He wisely remarks:

> What the stranger has in common with the criminal, the sick, the hungry and ill-clothed people of our land is that all of these are outcasts, ignored by the comfortable and well-to-do. All of these are objects of fear, a fear which runs so deep we have invented entire institutions to keep such folk "out of sight, out of mind." In fact, all of these people are strangers. It is their strangeness which puts us off; we are estranged from all of them.[23]

Who is "the other"? It is this one who is different, who is hard to understand, who perhaps is perceived as threatening "our way" of being in the world. Such an other is apt to be feared, to be fought, to be subdued and controlled. It is this other one who seems to face us increasingly in the current setting I described in chapter 1 as "the critical massing of the many." In that chapter, I indicated that turning the Christian generally to the "neighbor," the biblical direction gives special emphasis to "the stranger":[24] "You shall not oppress a stranger; you know the heart of a stranger, for you were strangers in the land of Egypt" (Exod. 23:9, RSV).[25]

THE OTHER AS STRANGER

3. A narrow reading of this theme is to be resisted. Our discussion in chapter 2 of nature as other certainly should prepare us to recognize this neighbor as exceedingly vulnerable today.[26] Moreover, beyond and beneath all such dramatic expressions of visible otherness and vulnerability, one may well be directed to the stranger in every "other." Every person with whom we share the planet is a unique center of freedom and feeling. There is some strangeness there to be cherished and protected. In the generalizing and homogenizing maneuvers of an efficient (and fearful?) modern consciousness, we may neglect or oppose this element. We may, in the language of chapter 3, stress that the "ordinary one" whom we meet is indeed given

to us but ignore the otherness of the given. In the witness to God's re-demptive action the biblical writings target specific oppression ("the land of Egypt"). But the imperative is rooted in the reality of the Creator's indicative will for diversity. The Christian is directed particularly to (*a*) the vulnerable and (*b*) the stranger and (*c*) to that which is such in all persons. The connections invite reflection. Michel Foucault has shown how certain ideas—of madness, of illness, of crime and delinquency, and of sexuality—serve the purposes of dominant social systems. But his work leaves the reader with the question of whether the truly fundamental pa-thology is not the denial of the difference which the Christian would recognize as given in creation.[27]

4. Similarly, without taking up the next section's subject of resources, one may simply note that such a broader reading will need to include strategies and structures that do not reduce compassion ("feeling with") to what would always have to be a frustratingly finite—and yet dizzingly infinite—number of I-Thou relationships.[28] Such relationships will continue to have a place in the Christian sense of direction, as the circumstances and choices of life connect particular individuals, but even there Christian responsibility calls for something more. Robert Hoeferkamp puts the point directly: "If in the past it was possible to limit love for the neighbor to individual works of charity, our present consciousness of the social nature and conditioning of life no longer permits such a limitation. Today love must be directed to the collective neighbor."[29]

Faith, thus, resists the reducing of the short word other to a single meaning. But in each case the emphasis has been on service *for* others. Caught up in that challenging and complex call, one might trivialize the sense in which *the Christian* is indeed called to *become* other. Thus I speak here of becoming other *with* the other.

"PUTTING ON" THE OTHER

The point is that the Christian's own self does not remain the same in this process. That might seem self-evident in any serious talk of becoming other. But strangely we seem to have stopped short of such seriousness, as if the "becoming" were the external exertion of an essentially self-identical self destined to return to itself after these heroic exploits out beyond the safe boundary of selfhood. There would be neither change nor vulnerability in such an arrangement. To the contrary: in the Christian faith's sense of direction there is a responsibility that drives to the very core of the Christian's own selfhood. No less than that may be involved in what Luther spoke of as "putting on one's neighbor."[30] How is this to be understood?

In chapter 3, I wrote of "the claim of self and other" and noted that it seems mistaken and dangerous to formulate the direction as self-sacrifice.[31] That we are to love our neighbors as ourselves does not amount to offsetting an indicative evil with an imperative good. Here I mean to advance that earlier discussion by way of indicating that the direction that faith receives looks also beyond the clumsy or crafty effort to calculate a balancing of interests. How does this work? "Is" and "ought" keep company in the dialectic of relationships constituting self and other. According to chapter 3, it *is* the case that our relationships are mutually constitutive—though not exhaustive—of our selfhood. Clearly, if the ethical imperative drives those selves apart, it sets up what the therapists call a "lose/lose" situation. The person who gains his or her life in that sense does indeed lose it. Rather, the self's being is—and the self's becoming is to be—*with* the other.

In a similar analysis Michael Sandel has critiqued liberal political theory, as represented by such a figure as John Rawls, for a view of the moral agent as "a pure, unadulterated, 'essentially unencumbered' subject of possession."[32] Such a self, Elizabeth Bettenhausen points out, is "given prior to community and related to it only by the feelings and sentiments of co-operation."[33] Sandel argues that such a self cannot be held to be subject to a good that is not grounded in itself—that is, to a truly social good:

> The good of the community cannot reach *that* far, for to do so would be to violate the priority of the self over its ends, to deny its antecedent individuation, to reverse the priority of plurality over unity, and to allow the good a hand in the constitution of the self, which on Rawls' view is reserved to the concept of the right.[34]

Bettenhausen locates a similar dynamic in faith talk that isolates a justified self, setting up the destructive disjunction between self-interest and self-sacrifice:

> This self, however, is simultaneously bound to be the "servant" of the neighbor but, as subject, without any means of relationship with the neighbor. Only by denying the common natural humanity which the justified self shares

with others, ie., only by "self-sacrifice," is the justified self able to "be a little Christ" to the neighbor.[35]

The direction evident in the descriptive account of Part One cannot support such disjunction. It connects far more readily with feminist writers who have put the matter in this way:

> Our bodies are formed from the bodies of two other people; our personalities are created by the regard given us by others. If we begin with a social anthropology and imagine a self constituted by our connection with the earth and with other people, . . . (ethical action) does not require self-sacrifice but is, rather, a movement in which the self is enlarged.[36]

UNIVERSAL NEGATION, UNIVERSAL QUESTIONING

This may be starting to sound rather sweet. If that is so, I have failed to state adequately the challenge involved in faith's direction. The clearest obstacle is the dark reality of human sin. Clearly, the rhetoric of the other has no safe passage through the enemy's lines. The socially constituted self is certainly capable of corrupting the called-for movement of faith in a decision to "enlarge" what is precisely a false self (though with its own social conditioning, of course). Indeed, the twentieth century's sad history suggests that to say we are "capable" of such sin understates the matter. Hence theologians argue that "if justification proceeds by way of negation, then the judgment is indeed universal and all causes are relativized."[37] God is God, after all, and so we need to be saved from our virtues run wild in idolatry. Such universal negation is indeed needed to protect the singularly justifying work of God. But such negation is misapplied if it prevents the Christian from seeking direction to serve the creative work of God.

Perhaps the clarity of the universal negation is best reflected with respect to the creative work of God by a universal questioning of any claim to capture or freeze the Creator's will. Such questioning does not derive simply from the stark recognition of sin, for it fits the finite and temporal fabric of our creatureliness and finds natural expression precisely in the dialogical character of our life together, as we have been describing it.

In that questioning dialogue we do become other *with* the other. The preposition (*with*) does not dissolve in some monistic soup. Self and other serve each other in coming together, but they do not cease to be other than each other. Such a cessation of otherness would also signify loss of selfhood, if Peter Hodgson is right in arguing that "freedom is precisely presence-to-self in, through, and with otherness; it is intrinsically communal, social, synthetic."[38]

One is drawn to this other. I will speak shortly of how one finds essential resource there. Yet that which draws one is indeed other and calls the self to something that is truly new. This is how one comes to speak as Eberhard Jüngel does of love "as the event of a still greater selflessness within a great, and justifiably very great self-relatedness" so that "the loving ego experiences both an extreme distancing of himself from himself and an entirely new kind of nearness to himself."[39] This is how it is that—facing the "benign alienation" (Edward Farley) of finitude and the willful violation of sin—one struggles to "make the world safe for diversity."[40] It is not at all sweet, for freedom must be protected and enhanced against the twin demons of domination and capitulation. This is, to say it one more time, how it is that the specific neighbors—the hungry, the imprisoned, the ill-clothed, the stranger—rise up to claim our attention. Those specific vulnerable ones require special attention—a need suggesting what social philosophers have called "the difference principle": "the principle that permits only those inequities that work to the benefit of the least advantaged members of society."[41]

One is thus seeking an intensification of the creational diversity in unity, unity in diversity, through recognition and appreciation of the other.[42] A study of the twentieth century does not suggest that it is easy to know and follow such direction. Christians have had to resist in the name of their faith, when human diversity has been subjected to authoritarian violence.[43] As the century closes, it is clear to us that "the bid is raised" as the scale of irreversible consequences tips heavily in what Jonathan Schell has called "the agriculture of time."[44]

The transformation by which the Christian is called to become other for and with the other is, it seems, not a sweet and easy, "natural," development. Business as usual will not suffice. Resources are needed in the face of the complexity of creation and the opposition of evil. Faith is not without such resources.

FAITH'S RESOURCES

The other is resource: Christian faith struggles to claim this promise. Faith's true direction is followed not merely *for* the other (lest compassion become self-violation) and/or merely *with* the other (lest mutuality amounts to "you scratch my back and I'll scratch yours"). As the Christian responds to the circumstance and call of "life together," genuine transformation takes place *through* the other.[45] In lifting up the other as resource in this section, I do not intend to relinquish the understanding gained in the first section. Indeed, one can only speak of the Christian's development *through* the other, if it is remembered that life is (to be) *for* and *with* the other. Otherwise, claiming the other as resource could easily be twisted into manipulation. That is clear. It may be less clear that in such an offense of commission a sin of omission would be found as well, for the other as mere means proves no true power for faith's response to God's directing call. In such manipulation the perpetrator does not receive what deep and serious difference can contribute.

THROUGH THE OTHER

Perhaps one can keep the "through" linked with the "for" and the "with" by emphasizing the role of "admiration" toward that which is truly different. Luce Irigaray employs this notion in speaking of sexual difference and provides this description: "keeping the two sexes unsubstitutable in the fact of their difference. Maintaining a free and engaging space between them, a possibility of separation and alliance."[46] Winnicott wrote of the "potential space" that a "good enough" mother seeks to create for the developing child. Now a "space between" emerges to challenge one who is no longer a child.

Without such knowing, indeed honoring, of difference the notion of responsibility collapses. This truly other one makes a claim on me, from outside myself, to affirm what I can never be. But in admiration there comes into view the possibility of the self becoming other in a way that transcends the existing identities of self and other. Mark Kline Taylor has linked Irigaray's notion of admiration with anthropologist Paul Rabinow's understanding of the dynamics of "the liminal," "the kind of life known 'betwixt and between' differentiated persons, groups or worlds" in which a "realm of tenuous common sense" is mutually constructed through dialectical questioning. In the space between I can see the other as other and I can be surprised by what comes about in my own being. Taylor points out that admiration and liminality need each other:

> Without an identification and affirmation of concrete differences through admiration, liminality becomes a free-floating and disengaged mode of living and thinking. . . . Conversely, without the sense of suspension, shock, and disorientation that characterizes liminality, admiration would be little more than a compilation of differences, of incommensurable worlds.[47]

This is wisely said. I particularly want to emphasize the sense that in this relationship the other does actually become resource in the "becoming other" of the Christian.

GIFT, RISK, AND TASK

Perhaps "resource" has connotations that suggest an external, even an optional, relationship. In that case, the word would fail me, for I mean to speak of the internal relationship of self and other. Recalling our discussion in chapter 3, we could speak here once again of "gift and task." The internal relationship of self and other is first of all life "within, with, and before the other." Thus a theologian (Rita Nakashima Brock) can write evocatively of "the original grace" of "heart" in which we find "incarnate in ourselves the divine reality of connection, of love."[48] Or, less flamboyantly but still very evocatively, a psychologist (Heinz Kohut) can conclude from his studies that the capacity to empathize is part of "the innate equipment of the human psyche."[49] Theologically, one might be moved to hear here an echo of the fact that on faith's confession there is only one creator and that in some deep sense evil is parasitic on the good.

We are created as resource for each other. We are to become other through each other. This is gift. But it is a precarious gift. Thus Alfie Kohn in writing of "the brighter side of human nature" can speak of empathy as "heritable," but he must soberly add that "hurting is also natural."[50] A theologian might rather say: hurting is so widely present that we must indeed grant that such evil has become second nature for us. And so gift becomes task and in that volatility lies the possibility of turning away from and/or against the actual other and in turn trivializing and externalizing the resource to be experienced there. Against such dark possibility become reality again and again the Christian is called to the strategies of liminal admiration, which are already the task side of the gift of creation.[51] Thus Taylor speaks powerfully of affirming in theory and practice unsubstitutable differences *and* of being "given toward the others one affirms" so that one undergoes "the disorientation, sense of homelessness, play and suspension" to be known in discharging the task.[52]

THE GOD RELATIONSHIP AS RESOURCE

Who is the other in whom such resource resides? Most fundamentally, of course the Other of whom the Christian must speak is God. In chapter 4, I have written of how all persons, indeed all creatures, exist "before" God.[53] Christian faith gladly confesses that the gift of existence does not depend on faith. But God does will that faith exist on earth. And so the

Christian turns consciously to God, crying out, "I believe; help Thou my unbelief!" We should not need to be reminded that the Christian faith does have to do with an actual relationship, the relationship with God. In relation to God the Christian hears a call to faithfulness in life and thought. But Christian faith trusts that the call of God is not without the gift of God. Surely with regard to this most fundamental other it ought to be clear that we are not speaking of a merely external relationship of an essentially abiding self-contained human self.

What difference, then, does this relationship to God make to the believer? How is there here "resource"? Three aspects may be distinguished:

1. At one level, Christians have rather readily understood their identity in terms of their relationship to God in the sense that their status, who they are, depends on the will and work of God. Who am I? In faith the Christian clearly says: "I am one loved by God, (and so one) forgiven by God." And that does make a difference, as Jüngel makes clear in commenting on Luther's understanding of the freedom of a Christian: "According to Luther, the Christian as free lord is master of all. Not even death, that instance of temporal life in dispute, is exempt. The Christian is master of all, thus also and precisely of bodily life, in the sense that nothing can harm *eternally*."[54]

2. To trust in this relationship to God is to be directed outward in service. Thus Luther will not speak of the Christian as "master of all" without the parallel claim, "a perfectly dutiful servant of all, subject to all."[55] James Gustafson has helpfully analyzed how one gets from the first to the second in his reflection on the bearing for life in the world of the Christian sense of "dependence, gratitude, obligation, and direction."[56] Clearly here is resource.

3. There may, however, be a sense in which Christians have failed to recognize the transformative power of the relationship to God internally. Ann Belford Ulanov writes as an analyst interested in how the person who prays is set free:

> In prayer, we re-collect ourselves and feel touched by what or who we know ourselves to be. We recover a sense of ourselves, now disidentified somewhat from the different roles we take on during each day. For finally in prayer, I am I, for better or worse, before God, and not mother or teacher or wife or lover or some identity I share with my depressed or anxious or dulled feelings.[57]

The contemporary chorus of voices singing the praises of "spirituality" is cacophonous enough to tempt the Christian to the purity of abstinence. That temptation should be resisted. There is resource for Christian becoming in prayer, meditation, and worship, precisely because in the God relationship self-transformation does not amount to self-preoccupation. The God of this God relationship cannot be well contained within the circle of self-interest. Thus the crucial centrality of the biblical witness for Christian piety roots in the fact that, as David Tracy has put it, the text remains stubbornly other than the believer.[58]

Rebecca Chopp amplifies the point in a testimony to the living character of the text. She writes of how "the passage produces a space between our meaning and proclaiming, it comes in the midst of reading and passes, slips, and breaks away from the reader's own controlling intent." What I would call the "gift and task" of reading the Scriptures becomes clear:

> The Scriptures, precisely as received in a feminist hermeneutics of marginality, can no longer be domesticated as good morals, existential comforts, sweet little narratives. There is now, not only in those who read the Bible but in the reading of the Bible itself, a restlessness of Word and words that moves from emancipatory transformation but that can vanish in the midst of us as proclaimers and as hearers.[59]

This other is uniquely empowering, and as continuing creator, God works within to "direct." The Christian believes this is true in a measure of all creatures, as I have said. But the apostle Paul bears witness to an internal relationship of a different intensity which Christian faith entails: "Work out your own salvation with fear and trembling; for it is God who is at work in you, enabling you both to will and to work for his good pleasure" (Phil. 2:12b-13).

THE "PROSPECTIVE" WORK OF CHRIST

The work of God in Jesus is not only a work for us but a veritable work *in* us. Recent Christian reflection offers promising directions for the development of this theme. Thus, for example, F. W. Dillistone understands God's forgiveness to emphasize the "prospective" dimension under the theme of intercession so that "the way will be open . . . to receive the light and walk in the light as reconciled."[60] Or George Rupp has argued that the options for Christian reflection are not to be limited to the "Realist Transactional" view (which "in effect precludes any genuine significance

to historical development under the guise of 'taking history seriously' "),
on the one hand, and to a "Nominalist-Processive" view (where "the effect
of the work of Christ . . . is simply the cumulative change which particular
individuals and their communities experience"), on the other hand. Rupp
argues generally for the processive approach but recognizes the claim of
realism in that "the Christian doctrines of creation and providence affirm
. . . that this process of Atonement is in some sense ontologically grounded
in the very structure and development of the cosmos itself: the kingdom
of God is the goal or telos of creation."[61] In chapter 4, I have already
argued that God's decisive ("transactional," in that sense) act is grounded
in God's creative resolve. It should not surprise, accordingly, that this act
for us becomes creative *in* us.[62]

The relationship to God in faith, thus, is not an external matter, something that conceivably could be removed without altering the Christian's
fundamental identity. In stressing the internal character of the relationship
with God, one might seem to be suggesting that this is a private matter,
hidden away from all others. Our recognition of the otherness of God and,
notably, of "the text" should already serve to indicate that this would be
a misreading of the relationship. The Christian is linked in an essential
way with other Christians. This too is resource for Christian becoming.
The point is not merely that the church is needed to get the individual
Christian, all these individual Christians, established on the way of Christian
becoming. The story of the Christian church is not a vast collection of
isolated "dear Diary" entries, which come together only in their beginnings
and endings. The Christian does not "run the race" as a relay team member,
whose actual connectedness with the team is to be found only in the passing
of the authorizing baton. Rather, the Christian finds essential present resource in life with other sisters and brothers in faith.

CHRISTIAN COMMUNION, HUMAN COMMUNITY
This truth about the importance of a Christian community is prefigured in
the creation of the self in and for human community, as described in chapter
3.[63] In both cases there is no genuine community without actual difference.
Sadly, Christians seem resistant to difference and excessively troubled by
disagreement within the flock. To expect sameness in the life and thought
of the faith is, generously interpreted, to forget that Christian existence
does not cease always to be a particular human identity. Tragically, it may

be to suggest that the mind the church has in it is not that of a servant
God seeking the good of all humankind (cf. Philippians 2) but that of a
tyrant whose image may somehow well be represented by the singularity
of domination, human or divine.[64] As surely as that is not the God of the
Christian faith and as surely as the Christian struggles to live and think
faithfully, there is need for the witness of Christians who are undeniably
"other."

Thus Shirley Guthrie adds a third evaluative criterion to those of Scripture and Christian community:

> We must listen with respect to other Christians who are sexually, racially,
> economically, politically, and culturally different from us. . . . We all read
> into scripture and bring into the church the biases, prejudices, and self-
> interest of our particular sex, race, class, region, political affiliation, and
> cultural environment.[65]

The point here is not to satisfy some external standard of "political
correctness." It is to claim the empowering reality of human diversity for
the Christian's becoming other. Larry Rasmussen put the matter succinctly
in claiming that "the simplest, most important axiom for thinking about
church and society today (is) . . . whom we learn with determines what
we learn."[66] As the Christian is opened up in such dramatic ways, there
may be a readiness to hear the quieter revolutionary and resourceful voices
of otherness. The other is not needed, then, merely as a critical corrective
on human partiality. The point is to claim the good of the diversity of
God's creation more positively for the church, recognizing that in the church
the many members form a whole that is more—and better—than the sum
of its parts. Hence the church will be well advised to stay close to this
creational ground minimizing the proliferation of structure which so easily
serves for the protection of privilege and so for the diminishment of genuine
diversity.[67]

Christians need each other, precisely in their respective otherness I have
been saying, in order to be Christian. The Christian will wisely cast the
net of Christian identity widely, recognizing the great and subtle temptations
to confuse divine oneness with particular human singularity. But the Christian of course recognizes that not all the others are Christians. In this
recognition another call is rooted. To distinguish the church is not to isolate
it. It is for the sake of the world that the church needs to be the *one* church.
But beyond this, one must say that in the call the Christian hears to become

other these others—the non-Christians—are also resource in their own way. In chapter 6, I will speak of how a connection with unbelief needs to be claimed by faith for the sake of faith. Here I am concerned with the Christian's effort to serve the creator's more comprehensive will for life.

In this effort the Christian is called to work *through* the other in that the Christian's vision of the ultimate meaning and ground of human good is not shared by all contributing to that good. Does such difference divide? The Christian is driven by the passion of faith in God. "Because [God] first loved us" (1 John 4:19) the Christian is impelled to the hungry, the imprisoned, the naked—all these "least," in whose suffering Christians face their brother Jesus (Matthew 25). The beginning and the end of the act of love for the Christian are in God. Does not this beginning lay claim to the act? How can the act have actuality if it is not given to God? But the Christian makes common cause with many who do not see matters so. This does not trivialize the Christian's vision. But perhaps the Christian has reason here to consider how the specific clarity that the gospel conveys is related to the broad sweep of what is going on for creaturely well-being without the motivation of Christian faith. It is related, for on the Christian reading it is the Lord Jesus before whom will be gathered all the nations. But matters are less clear in this broader vision. How many are they who may have reason to say in whatever language fits their creaturely condition: "When did we see thee?"

CREATIVE SERVICE IN "THE MIDDLE"

Warned as they are about stunning surprises at the story's end, Christians will not marvel that the means of their creaturely and creative service in the middle of things are not their private possession. Indeed, they will particularly prize the public character of reason: that through discourse and reflection persons of different persuasions can further their fruitful service of humankind. That public character needs to be prized; it needs to be protected. Faith prizes this other instrument, not the least because it can expose the excesses to which the bold enthusiasm of faith's singular passion may lead. Faith, I say, recognizes that the public character of reason needs to be nurtured and protected. If faith has understood that fully and truly human life is "within" the body (chap. 2, above), it will understand that one does not protect the publicity of reason by attempting to isolate it from the particularity of such embodiment.[68] Reason is not a rocket headed for heaven that has jettisoned the humble first stage of its situated launching. It is only as the particular physical and emotional realities of our givenness are shared in the conversation that we have a chance to move together toward a fuller vision of human wholeness. Faith has a special sense for and stake in this. Faith knows that it is called to work through what is "other," reason. Reason is indeed other, and faith does not well claim to do what reason can do. But faith knows the feel of faith and thus can recognize when divine claims are being made in the name of human reason. Sometimes such claims are made directly, extending a human project beyond its range, as when one crosses the border between science and scientism. Sometimes such claims are made indirectly, in narrowing speech to exclude or demean other equally human voices. In both cases the Christian is called to resistance.[69]

The Christian is thus dialectically related to the role of reason in the wider human community. On the one hand, the Christian needs to claim and exercise this common gift with non-Christians for the common good, as I have said, and indeed in the service of the Christian's own venture of faith seeking understanding. On the other hand, as surely as faith reflects on its own treasure, it finds itself prowling on the boundaries and at the foundations of human self-understanding. Perhaps some currently regnant reason wants to let what is partial be regarded as universal and what is temporary be eternally frozen as embodiments of human meaning and well-being. Something that humans well crafted in one situation may not serve fruitfully in another. In any case, human beings do not make good gods. So perhaps Charles Winquist is right in suggesting that theology "can become a mode of public liminality if theologians can learn to live with the tension of being in the margins of the dominant secular culture."[70]

TRANSFORMING SOLIDARITY

I have been trying to develop the theme that there are resources available for faith *through* the other. Clearly, there are such resources in the enabling presence of God, Christian communion, and human community. Such resource must not be blandly portrayed as something simply conveniently available, so that the other would be within reach but still kept at arm's length, as it were. Dorothee Soelle counters such a view in writing of how suffering is transformed through communication and solidarity:

> The way leads out of isolated suffering through communication (by lament) to the solidarity in which change occurs. . . . By giving voice to lament one

> can intercept and work on his suffering within the framework of commu-
> nication. . . . That sort of thing is conceivable only in the context of a group
> of people who share their life—including their suffering—with one another.
> One of them can then become the mouth for others, he can open his mouth
> "for the mute" (Prov. 31:8).[71]

Such dramatic experience of solidarity in suffering can underscore for us the deeper dimension of resource. The resources of which we have spoken are not available "through" the other, in the sense that the other can be used and then dispensed with. Faith should be able to see this. The Christian would not seek the gifts of God without God. And these other others are given to us as resource in like manner. There is power available for transformation, to be sure, but it is a different power from what we normally recognize. One can speak of it as "power with" rather than "power over."[72] One can speak of power as both producing and *undergoing* effects.[73] Through the other there is power to change and to be changed. David Tracy has drawn once again on the more dramatic voice of difference to make this point:

> The voices of the others multiply: the hysterics and mystics speaking through
> Lacan; the mad and the criminals allowed to speak by Foucault; the primal
> peoples, once misnamed the primitives, defended and interpreted by Eliade;
> the dead, whose story the victors still presume to tell; the repressed suffering
> of peoples cheated of their own experience by modern mass media; the poor,
> the oppressed, and the marginalized—all those considered "nonpersons" by
> the powerful but declared by the great prophets to be God's own privileged
> ones. All the victims of our discourses and our history have begun to discover
> their own discourses in ways that our discourse finds difficult to hear, much
> less listen to. Their voices can seem strident and uncivil—in a word, . . .
> other. And they are. We have all just begun to sense the terror of that
> otherness. But only by beginning to listen to those other voices may we also
> begin to hear the otherness within our own discourse and within ourselves.
> What we might then begin to hear, above our own chatter, are possibilities
> we have never dared to dream.[74]

I have cited this long passage not merely because of Tracy's eloquence but because one can hear here a testimony to the gift and task of a truly new power in relationship.

Christian faith should be able to see this, I say again. Douglas John Hall writes of how "in the theology of Bethlehem and Golgotha" our suffering, "though abysmally real, is given both a new perspective and a new meaning—and the prospect of transformation": "God meets, takes on, takes into God's *own* being, the burden of our suffering, not by a show of force which could only destroy the sinner with the sin, but by assuming a solidary responsibility for the contradictory and confused admixture that is our life."[75]

Somehow, then, faith needs to speak of power in relationship. This fits the fabric of our human condition: that we are made in and for relationship. Perhaps that is why the drive for invulnerability seems precisely that which makes one vulnerable.[76] This vulnerability is not the opening to the other in which the self is challenged by truly new possibility "in the space between." It is the weakness found in isolation, not the least in domination. But what of a godly vulnerability? Michael Sandel has written of how our connectedness bears on our knowing and doing the good. If we are not "wholly unencumbered subjects of possession, individuated in advance and given prior to our ends," what then? He writes: "We . . . must be subjects constituted in part by our central aspirations and attachments, always open, indeed vulnerable, to growth and transformation in the light of our revised self-understandings."[77]

Sandel sketches a vision of a "wider subject than the individual alone, . . . a community in the constitutive sense":

> And what marks such a community is not merely a spirit of benevolence, or the prevalence of communitarian values, or even certain "shared final ends" alone, but a common vocabulary of discourse and a background of implicit practices and understandings within which the opacity of the participants is reduced if never finally dissolved.[78]

Sandel does not claim to speak on behalf of faith; faith does not require him to do so. In precisely such a reasonable account, open to public scrutiny, faith finds a resource that reminds it of its own store. "Shared final ends" together with abiding "opacity"—that statement of human solidarity is a fair and hopeful description of Christian communion as well. The prepositions "for," "with," and "through" come to converge. And so prompted from outside, faith will want to add to the list that Sandel makes of what is at work that is "more than the individual." Faith trusts that God is at work. As Christians seek to serve the Creator's call in this time, they hope for the kind of change that speaks of another time. Faith looks beyond the muddled middle we share to speak of a telos.

FAITH'S TELOS

In speaking of this, we surely are exploring unknown territory. We speak of that which we do not possess, for the telos of which Christian faith speaks is indeed other than what we now know. Why, then, does faith so speak—rather than settling for staying modestly within the boundaries of what we now know? If the answer is, "Because faith believes the promise!" we must ask, "Why?" It seems important at the outset to be clear about what is claimed. Or, to put it differently, "Why is this talk of telos not threat rather than promise?"

THE MORAL CALL FOR METAPHYSICAL CHANGE

Christians are not satisfied with the ways things are. "The way things are" does include the kind and degree of "becoming other" which the Christian now experiences. But in faith the Christian looks to a future that is qualitatively "other" than the gaining—and losing—ground which is now experienced. There is a moral dimension to this hope. The Christian can claim the language of the tormented American poet John Berryman: "The only really comforting reflection is not 'we will all rest in Abraham's bosom' and rot of that purport but: after my death there will be *no more sin*."[79]

Berryman's suicide hardly stands as a vote of confidence, but he knew what was needed—and what he could not find in life as he knew it. The battle against sin must come to an end, if life is to reach its true goal. Moreover, even if one could somehow manage to stand with those who speak of reaching Christian perfection in this-worldly sanctification, the moral challenge is not silenced. At the end of chapter 3 we sounded the cry, the claim, of the innocent victims of sin. Helmut Peukert spoke for them: "This generation has inherited everything from the past generations and lives on what they have paid for. . . . Is amnesia, the utter loss of historical memory, the presupposition of happy consciousness?"[80]

Thus the moral outcry for a truly other future seems itself to require a metaphysical change. Stated in terms of the individual, perfection seems to require that we *cannot* sin, for the constant threat of backsliding cannot be accepted as the fitting accompaniment for the beatific state. Stated in communal terms, without a telos we have no practical moral access to countless (relatively) innocent victims in the past. Any life that reaches its goal without responding to these claims is surely *im*perfect.

NATURAL AND METAPHYSICAL EVIL

This moral call for metaphysical change is joined by other voices. The vast suffering which depends on and indeed derives from our natural connectedness must somehow be addressed. The child dying of inoperable cancer of the throat may have a moral claim against other human beings in view of what they have done to nature and so, perhaps indirectly, to the child. But such harm comes about *through* nature, and not all of it seems to flow from human choices. It is perhaps possible to build a case that "understands" the causes of such suffering in relation to the Creator's will for a genuine relationship with humankind. Keith Ward provides such a statement:

> The universe exists in order to bring into being a creative, contingent, free realization of purpose in a communal and evolving personal form of being, related to God as its source, ideal and guiding power. The sub-personal basis of contingent creativity is the factor of randomness, which eliminates determinism but at the same time eliminates absolute control. Where changes are partly random, there must be failures and imbalances as well as fortuitous and productive interactions. The sub-personal basis of rational purpose is the predictable law-likeness of being, which eliminates anarchy but also eliminates continuous providential adjustment of the laws. Where changes are law-governed, there must be particular cases in which general laws are disadvantageous or destructive as well as cases where they provide the basis for constructive planning. The sub-personal basis for a developing community of beings is a plurality of emergent forces, which eliminates monotony but also eliminates complete harmony. Where many individual substances each develop by interaction with each other, conflict and domination are as inevitable as co-operation.[81]

Such a statement, while probably beyond belief in an individualistic culture, does make sense. The "natural" suffering that human beings and other animals undergo is, we are told, to be understood as coming about through God's will for relationship with an "other," with "others," characterized by genuine freedom. But then the lives of all these suffering ones surely do place a great additional weight on any measurement claiming to outline the future perfection of freedom. I have been arguing that the creation of freedom itself cannot be justified unless freedom is a necessary means to an end in which freedom passes into something that is not less personal but that is yet not subjected to the uncertainties of contingency.[82] More than that, one must say: unless that end is reached, all the instances of "natural" suffering, which have come out about in turn through nature-as-means enabling freedom-as-means, cry out that life has not reached its perfect telos.

Finally, this metaphysical thirst for something truly other arises in facing the ultimate enemy, death. In chapter 2, I suggested that in the understanding of Christian faith death as a biological reality does not derive fundamentally from sin.[83] Claus Westermann states the matter very directly: "Man, just because he has been created, carries within him limitation by death as an essential element of the human state."[84]

So it seems. But to accept death in evolutionary wisdom and even to welcome it as the cessation of suffering is to assume the reality of life (and death) as we know it. Such acceptance does not deny loss, and it is not strange that Christians join others in hoping for some victory over this final enemy.[85] Moreover, we sense that "victory" could not mean merely adding an (even indefinite) quantity of years to our threescore and ten. At some point we sense that "more of the same" would amount to a passable hell rather than a pure heaven.

So we look to something we do not now possess. We hope. But of course it does occur to us, even if not prompted by the questions of others, to wonder whether this hope is not in vain. Two questions occur in that wondering: (1) What would do, if it were true? (2) Can this be true? We have begun a response to the first question. At least we have indicated that if this life is to be truly said to have a telos, it must be something other than what we now have. There must be newness, discontinuity. We must actually "become *other*" in a qualitative sense. Sin, suffering, and death stand between us and any such telos.[86] A metaphysical change is needed, by which contingency gives way to certainty and ambiguity to clarity. There is biblical speech of this sort. "Then" death will be swallowed up in victory (1 Cor. 15:54; Isaiah 28), every tear will be wiped away (Rev. 7:17), we will see "face to face" (1 Cor. 13:12), as we "enter into the joy" of the Master (Matt. 25:21).

CONTINUITY, METAPHYSICAL AND MORAL

But this newness would not do unless it could be shown that in such change it is truly *we* who become other. That is, somehow there must be sufficient continuity so that this glorious future can be said to be truly ours. What is entailed by this requirement?

What would suffice to constitute significant continuity with our present identity and being? There are metaphysical requirements. No doubt we hope for greater unity than we now experience, but the oneness of simplicity would not seem to constitute a fulfillment of the diversity we now experience. If God is to be "all in all" (1 Cor. 15:28), the "in" must remain to mark some difference. So, too, on the account in Part One "becoming" seems to be written so deeply into our very being that there must be movement of some sort within the telos. This seems a fair inference from the structure of Christian hope, as Peter Hodgson sees the matter: "For me it seems intuitively right to say that, just as God does not cease to be God in virtue of God's immanence in the world, so also the world does not cease to be the world in virtue of the world's immanence in God."[87]

In this exploration I am asking how the logic of Christian hope for a telos might meet what Paul Ricoeur has called "the need to consent in some global sense to the goodness of the necessity in being." Ricoeur distinguishes biblical "eschatological" consent from Stoic consent, which in rational detachment denies the self's feelings and passions, and from Orphic consent, which "loses the self completely in an ecstatic and exhilarating admiration of being which dissolves all particularity."[88] If we are seeking metaphysical continuity, that is, if we are speaking of that which seems necessary in our very being, it would seem that the telos would somehow have to include the range of being within which we have our life. A God who brought into being a telos for such as we are would have to be one who could "create new heavens *and a new earth*" (Isa. 65:17a).

In his vision Isaiah says that "the former things shall not be remembered or come to mind" (Isa. 65:17b). In chapter 4, I appropriated Kierkegaard's language of "God forgetting" to convey the decisiveness of divine forgiveness.[89] There is evident appeal in this. Yet surely our sense of human responsibility is such that some kind of moral continuity would also need to be included in any telos meeting the needs of faith in its becoming. Christians will not speak of God being bound in a karma-like necessity, but the biblical speech of a law of the harvest ("you reap whatever you sow," Gal. 6:7) cannot simply be disregarded. The rich man and Lazarus both find their places in God's future, but it is precisely *their* places that they find (Luke 16). At the very least the moral integrity, which matters to us despite and even within our moral failings, must be discernible in the fact that the hoped-for future does not double back to anesthetize the Christian facing the moral claim to be heard in the call of the God of present and future.[90]

Could a telos characterized by this dizzying combination of continuity and discontinuity be true? Could faith appropriately look to such a future? Or is the faith that hopes in such a way to be dismissed as one or another form of wish fulfillment?[91] Clearly, nothing requires that we produce evidence of the existence of that which by hypothesis is future. But the continuity claimed for this telos requires that the notion can be coherently developed and, more than that, invites consideration of the question of how the hope seems reasonably to "fit" as telos for aspects of our present experience of self, world, and God. In what remains of this chapter, I can only offer some exploratory comments.

THE FIT: NONCONTINGENT TIME

It is important that the question about the "fit" of the telos not be phrased in ways that ask how there could be movement to the telos from a present reality that is understood in essentially static terms. Any true telos to which we could look would require continuity with our present experience. But what is that experience? The burden of Part One was to make the point that what we now know as life is *within, with, and before* the other. In this life there is change, some of it quiet and some spectacular. To begin with chapter 2's theme of the broad sweep of the spatiotemporal process, there are considerations here that may connect with faith's hope for a telos. We have already noted the point celebrated in Gödel's theorem: that, as Thomas Torrance puts it, scientific concepts and propositions "cannot be completely formalized within closed systems, for their contingent intelligibility by its very nature requires to be completed beyond itself, that is by meta-theoretical relation to ever higher and wider systems of understanding."[92] In this finding concerning *how* we study reality, what is suggested about *that which* is being studied?

In a remarkable speculation entitled *God Within Process*, Eulalio Baltazar has tried to fill out the vision of the Roman Catholic paleontologist and "amateur" theologian Pierre Teilhard de Chardin.[93] Of particular interest is Baltazar's suggestion of a movement within what we loosely call

"time" which in fulfillment could yield "activity without contingency"—
that is, the kind of metaphysical discontinuity-and-continuity which seems
formally required by faith's telos. The "no more sin" of which Berryman
spoke would seem to require a life that would be without the possibility
of sin (the tradition's *non posse peccare*) and yet truly alive—"active."
Baltazar prepares the way in three steps:

> At the lowest level of the evolutionary process, time is contingent in the
> sense that electronic and atomic radiations are short-lived, measured in
> millionths of a second; the movement is chaotic, diffused, haphazard, in-
> determinate as shown in the cloud chamber or the Brownian movement of
> molecules; the time is transient because entropy takes over; the movements
> are lost instead of being collected in the thing and perfective of the thing.
>
> As we go higher up, however, the entropy is counteracted by a higher
> form of movement—life. Compared to the physical, transient random and
> fragile motions of the atoms and molecules, life is directed, better organized,
> longer-lived, more stable and immanent. . . . There is an advance in inte-
> riority, and with this advance time comes to a greater possession of itself. . . .
>
> In man, time has become human temporality, human history. Compared
> to the infrahuman level's spacetime dimension, human time is able to gather
> the past, the present and to a degree the future. . . . Through human con-
> sciousness, then, time for the first time becomes consciously purposive, and
> hence non-contingent; time becomes transparent to itself, interior to itself,
> and hence immanent. Human temporality represents the fullness of time of
> the infrahuman spacetime dimensions; toward it they tended as to their
> eschatological future or "eternity" in order to be.[94]

And what is the telos for human temporality, and so for all of evolutionary
time gathering itself in humankind? Time gathered into "activity without
contingency" would seem to address the agenda that moral evil posed for
the individual. What of finitude, clearest in the stark reality of death? Some
contemporary cosmologists stand on tiptoe to speak with Teilhard of an
Omega Point. Thus Frank Tipler in conversation with Wolfhart Pannenberg
can draw on information theory to suggest that in a closed universe (ex-
panding to a maximum before collapsing) "the resurrection of the dead in
the sense of Pannenberg would seem inevitable in the eschaton."[95]

Obviously there are all sorts of questions to be put to the likes of Baltazar
and Tipler. To take Tipler's dizzying proposal: What if the universe is not
closed? Would the possession of complete information, yielding full sim-
ulation of the past, amount to the presence of a person? But it surely is a
matter of no little interest to faith that reflection by some scientists on what

we now seem to know elicits such a process of proposing and then questioning. Perhaps the qualitative change entailed in faith's telos can be anticipated in reality as we now experience it. Indeed, perhaps something of such a telos is now experienced. If that were the case, we would be well advised to listen to Native American and feminist writers who commend a softening of strict linear thinking in a conception that seems more like a spiral than a line or a circle.[96] In listening to such contemporary voices, the Christian may come to reflect again on John's dialectical talk of the timing of telos: "But the hour is coming, and is now here" (John 4:23).

THE FIT: SELF TRANSCENDED AND FULFILLED

There are comparable suggestions to be found in our present life *with* the other, in our understanding of the human person. In chapter 3 we spoke of how human identity is coming to be understood to be constituted (though not exhausted) by internal relationships with other realities. One framework employed in such understanding is the process philosophy of Alfred North Whitehead. Whitehead found "the complete problem of metaphysics" formulated in the first two lines of a well-known hymn: "Abide with me; Fast falls the eventide."[97] In the last part of his magnum opus, *Process and Reality*, Whitehead turned to "the question whether the process of the temporal world passes into the formation of other actualities, bound together in an order in which novelty does not mean loss." Among his reflections is this attempt to build on the experience of relationship in a temporal sense:

> An enduring personality in the temporal world is a route of occasions in which the successors with some peculiar completeness sum up their predecessors. The correlate fact in God's nature is an even more complete unity of life in a chain of elements for which succession does not mean loss of immediate unison.[98]

Whitehead did not convince all his readers, not even all his followers.[99] But there are interesting possibilities available in the "softening" of the self represented by the internal relationships of the "peculiarly complete summing up." Baltazar has built on Teilhard de Chardin's vision; Marjorie Hewitt Suchocki has done so with Whitehead's. Her work in "process eschatology," *The End of Evil*, addresses both the questions of intelligibility and credibility with which we are concerned in this section. Her discussion of the second question is particularly complex and has not escaped criticism from within the process community.[100] But I find particularly interesting Suchocki's appropriation of a soft relational self to speak intelligibly of the qualitative change present in faith's telos:

> One could say that occasions are resurrected directly, and persons indirectly insofar as the particular togetherness of occasions created just this person. This would mean, then, that in God *all* events or times of a person are present, and not simply the final event in the total series of the soul. In God, finite personal identity is "thick," much deeper than the "thinness" of seriality. The wholeness of a person's life is present, and not simply the concluding moment. One could envisage then a multiple transcendence of personality in God: first transcendence of seriality into the fullness of the self; second, a transcendence of selfhood through the mutuality of feeling with all other selves and occasions, and third and most deeply, a transcendence of selves into the Selfhood of God.[101]

Baltazar's speculations accept formally the structure that linearity provides, while making much of the material maturation of "time." Suchocki's proposals, dissolving many boundaries, seem to disengage hope for "everlasting" life from such linearity individually and cosmically.[102] Classical Christian thought walks a fine line here, as Keith Ward's statement indicates:

> The Eternal is not far off in time; but breaks in now. . . . We must look for an eternal fulfillment of every present, by its relation to the Being which Christ brings near. . . . If we ask about the ultimate end of the universe, we are not thinking of many billions of years in the future. . . . We are, in the theistic context, thinking of the endless flourishing of finite persons, made one in the infinite ocean of Divine love. Clearly, this will not be in the present physical structure of the universe, which, by the presently known laws of physics, is bound to decay and die. Human fulfillment, then, is to be found beyond the boundaries of our presently known physical cosmos.[103]

Perhaps Suchocki's speculations could also provide a way of approaching the claim for some moral continuity, for some moral accountability, in any telos. As the Christian ponders such questions once again, some biblical passages may not seem quite so strange. What did Paul mean when he wrote: "The fire will test what sort of work each has done. . . . If the work is burned up, the builder will suffer loss; the builder will be saved, but only as through fire" (1 Corinthians 3:13-15).[104]

In such passages there is much that is not clear. Arland Hultgren provides a biblical framework for reflection in his discussion of "justification and eschatological peril" (including the 1 Corinthians 3 text). He is hopeful about the "abundance of grace":

> One cannot charge Paul with a mechanistic or mechanical view of the redemption of humankind. Salvation cannot be thought of apart from a living faith, in which God is truly God for the believer, and the possibility of perishing (nonsalvation) is real. The saved are those who believe the gospel, and there is a distinction between them and those who are perishing (1 Cor. 1:18). Yet the direction and thrust of Paul's thinking is that ultimately that distinction will pass away through the divine "negation of the negation," which is always unsettling to a piety that seeks to maintain the negation against those who are perishing.[105]

It is clear that Paul meant to say to the Corinthians that "no other foundation can any one lay than that which is laid, which is Jesus Christ" (1 Cor. 3:11, RSV). Before one addresses issues of "universal salvation," much fresh theological work is needed on what it might mean that we are called to "build on" that foundation, and indeed on who "we" are both "now" and "then." Without such work the churches will increasingly confuse honest folk who greet unreflective telos talk with the question: "What can this mean?" I have been saying that Christian reflection is encouraged to do that work and perhaps even assisted in the doing by attending to our present experience of life within the spacetime continuum and with the human other. But surely it is our experience of God, our life before this Other, that most significantly drives and informs this effort. The anticipatory openings toward a telos are taken seriously by faith, for faith lives in relationship to God. I have claimed that, in this relationship, direction and resource are given for faith to become other. And it is here that faith learns to live in hope toward a telos. Jürgen Moltmann recognizes this in distinguishing relationship to God from pantheism: "Whereas simple pantheism [all is God] sees merely eternal, divine presence, panentheism [all is *in* God] is able to discern future transcendence, evolution and intentionality."[106]

Moltmann is concerned to make the point that we must link God's immanence in the world with God's transcendence. He chooses to do that through the theme of Spirit:

> The Spirit preserves and leads living things and their communities beyond themselves. . . . It is not the elementary particles that are basic, . . . but the overriding harmony of the relations and of the self-transcending movements, in which the longing of the Spirit for a still unattained consummation

finds expression. If the cosmic Spirit is the Spirit of God, the universe cannot be viewed as a closed system. It has to be understood as a system that is open—open for God and for his future.[107]

The God in whom faith trusts for a true telos is a God who has willed and worked that which is qualitatively new. This is a God who wills to be in relationship, who seeks the other. This is a God who in creation says, in Kierkegaard's language, "Be even over against me." And when humankind uses that freedom to be not merely "*over* against," but against God? Looking to Jesus, the Christian declares with Paul that "nothing can separate" her or him from this God's love.

THE MORAL FIT

A telos of the type we have described has the right rhythm—freedom finding its fruit in a noncontingent relationship—to fit such a God who makes creatures out of nothing and loves sinners unconditionally. Christian appeal to the resurrection of Jesus relates to this context. This appeal does not ask us to leap to an assertion with no connection to anything else in the faith or life we know as human beings. That death does not triumph over God's deed in Jesus fulfills the life of the Nazarene and bids to make our lives truly whole.[108] In this resurrection witness, it is God who is to be believed. The claim is that *God* raised Jesus from the dead. The Christian trusts "the One who is first." The saying "I, when I am lifted up from the earth, will draw all people to myself" (John 12:32) bears witness to none other than the God known in present personal experience. Thus the Christian finds Paul's response appropriate: "And all of us, with unveiled faces, seeing the glory of the Lord . . . , *are being transformed* into *the same image*" (2 Cor. 3:18, emphasis mine). I say the rhythm is right; the telos connects with what we now experience in relationship with God. This is not to deny that there is much theological work to be done in the filling out of the fit. Paul precedes his claim that all of us are being transformed with the assertion, "Where the Spirit of the Lord is, there is freedom." Again the issue of in what way and measure our choices contribute to that telos must be faced. Paul Fiddes, for example, makes this offering:

> Decisions and experiences in this life matter: they are building what we are. Since God's aim is the making of persons, he has the certain hope that we will be "glorified," but the *content* of that end depends upon human responses, for the content of the end is persons. . . . There is room then for tragedy as well as triumph in God's victory over suffering.[109]

Even if Christian telos talk can be intelligibly filled out, it remains a matter of hope. It could be merely a coherent delusion. But our consideration of the second question, "Can this telos be true?" has led us remorselessly back to the first question, "What would do?" No telos will do that denies our responsibility and with that our reality. "Where the Spirit of the Lord is, there is freedom." Now we may put the question, "If freedom is fundamental in our humanity and in our Christianity, what would do as grounds for faith in such a telos as described?" The fact of our freedom bears on both the objective content of the claim and on the subjective process of claiming. Some ambiguity in answering both the questions of intelligibility and credibility fits rather than frustrates freedom. Freedom and responsibility could be frustrated (1) by the content of the claim or (2) by the making of the claim in a way that denied the finitude and fallibility of our human knowing. And (3) it would also be frustrated if the function of such telos talk consistently proved to be to anesthetize the Christian. Such an outcome would turn against faith itself, for that matter.

In Christian faith we are called to become other. In faith we trust a God who can bring about real change, a God who has done so in creation and re-creation. In all of its speaking, faith seeks to worship one God, a God who is one. And so faith's vision of the future does not trump what is being played out from the hand(s) dealt in creation and re-creation. When the tormented rich man asked that he might return to earth to warn his five brothers, he was told: "If they do not listen to Moses and the prophets, neither will they be convinced even if someone rises from the dead" (Luke 16:31). The gift and call of God reaches humankind in present experience. To claim that such experience itself must be validated by a privileged knowledge of the future is indeed to trivialize the present relationship to God. Perhaps the moral paralysis linked with some Christian recourse to the future is simply a more dramatic and developed form of such trivialization. "What" we claim and "how" we claim it do keep company.

So faith hopes for this telos but joins those who protest when talk of the future contributes to moral paralysis in the present. Faith trusts that somehow Christian hope connects the Christian in opportunity and responsibility with the "becoming" to which truly human life beckons. In that connecting, Christians in faith find themselves meeting many who do not seem to share their faith. At such boundaries of Christian faith a further call is to be heard.

6

TO BE WITH THE OTHERS IN FAITH

We began in chapter 1 with the nearly undeniable fact of our human experience of otherness. I argued (1) that people in the West are undergoing this experience with an increasing frequency, approaching a critical mass and (2) that they are doing so at a time when our Enlightenment sense of reality is under attack, if not in a state of collapse. It may not be necessary or possible to puzzle out just how the intensification in meeting human others and their worlds, on the one hand, and the erosion of a sense of orientation in "our" world, on the other, are causally interrelated. They come together to draw the self outside itself: I lose the "world" surrounding and sustaining my self's identity as its center and I meet someone "alongside" me (not in *my* world, to whatever degree that world still exists for me).[1] I meet many such others. We sense that these meetings matter. There may be peril and/or promise in them, but we sense in any case that things— that *we*—will not be the same. We are talking about the very stuff of our living. The first part of our task, thus, was to orient by owning up to the growing sense that in these confusing days something is dying and something is being born. I did not make clear what rising sun(s) one might see who is so oriented, but I did suggest that the compass of Christian faith seems well suited for travel across boundaries.

In Part One we paused to study the terrain. As one digs around in the experience of living, one finds that boundaries mark relationships characterized by distinction and connection. We are perhaps most commonly aware of our relationships *with* other human beings—the occasioning theme of the first chapter's disorienting orientation. But in digging beneath the surface of that relationship we encountered the boundaries marking our lives as life within and "before" otherness as well. Such an understanding can inform one's reflection as one moves ahead to explore life on the boundary. In chapter 5 we explored the claim of Christian faith concerning otherness: that we are to become other for, with, and through the others. The emphasis was on the word the believer hears, directing her or him in faith outward into some world, ahead into some future—into God's world and God's future.

DISCERNING THE DIFFERENCE OF OTHER FAITHS

But the believer who seeks so to live in faith quickly meets those who are other *in faith*. To live faithfully and fruitfully on the boundaries one surely must somehow deal with the reality of this otherness in faith. If Christian faith directs the Christian to the other (chap. 5), that direction cannot be effectively followed without reflection on the faith or unfaith that characterizes the lives of the others. We will, of course, "be with" those others for good or ill. But how well we are with them—to what effect—clearly depends on to what degree we relate to them as they define themselves with respect to faith. Who are the others, whom Christians meet with respect to faith? People of other faiths are such, as are persons who profess no faith. As we make our claims in faith we come up against both. In 1990 delegates at the Eighth Assembly of the Lutheran World Federation appropriately spoke of "the witnessing vocation of the church among people of *other faiths or no faith*."[2] I will emphasize that Christians also have much to learn from listening to each of these groups. Accordingly, I hold them together in this chapter.

Connection and difference will characterize the Christian's relationship both to people who profess no faith and to persons of other faiths. An error easily made would be to proclaim one's linkage with those who are believers (how ever so "other") and to deny any connection with the unbelievers. Each of these moves might tend to reinforce the other. Recognizing these temptations, I choose to emphasize difference in speaking in this section of the other faiths and connection in speaking of unfaith in the next section. In the closing section of the chapter, I will draw the two together again in asking how the Christian may live faithfully and fruitfully in faith on the boundary.

SIGNIFICANT DIFFERENCE

This section is titled "Discerning the Difference of Other Faiths." What is it to be discerning when faced with the other faiths? How is the Christian to regard the differences among the faiths? Paul Martinson has suggested that these differences are hardly a trivial matter:

> We must always be alert to difference. The common makes relationship possible; difference makes it significant. Generally people do not give their lives for that upon which we all agree or find we have in common. People give their lives because of that which is different. Difference is fraught with significance.[3]

One needs to be prepared to face genuine differences in the faiths. Empirical study does not lead one naturally to the view that the faiths are somehow all expressions of one fundamental reality we might call "religion." Consider, for example, the differences in belief systems. Such differences cannot be dismissed as, say, decorative propositional variety for some supposedly more primordial singular essence. For the Christian, faith is understood to entail a relationship between the believer and God such that the Christian may speak of the revelation of God. In this there is a knowing *of* God and a knowing *about* God. Accordingly, it will not do to collapse Christian faith into a subjective passion that, it is suggested, cannot be distinguished from the passion characterizing adherents of the other faiths.[4] (One notes the assumption that the faiths apparently could/would not differ in their passions.) It is not helpful for the believer—or, I might add, for the unbeliever—simply to lump all the faiths together, disregarding difference in belief—not to mention conflict and contradiction. John Cobb, who has worked steadfastly to call Christians into and even "beyond" dialogue, has seen that we do not make progress in these matters by denying difference. Thus he has written: "What is supremely important to the Buddhist is not what appears supremely important to the Christian. 'Christ' and 'Buddha' do not name the same reality."[5]

The Christian in faith does make claims purporting to be true. Christians, for example, find ways of saying "the One who is first is for us" and in doing so speak of Jesus of Nazareth. Such speaking cannot be both true and false. It may be part of the privatizing of faith to act as if such claims are neither importantly true nor importantly false so that it matters not whether such claims are accepted or rejected in other faith orientations. Against such trivializing distortions one must say that if we do not "discern the differences," we surely do not know who the others really are, and—given the inevitability of our life with them—we very probably do not know who we are.

In facing the differences, we must sort out the significances. "True" and "false" may state the options rather too flatly. Throughout this book I have in effect argued that to be automatically repelled by difference is to resist the rhythm of reality which pulses with otherness. But I have just argued that the difference in content that contradiction represents cannot be accepted without trivializing the faiths. So: which differences truly enrich, and how do they do so? Is contradiction the only criterion limiting inclusion? Is it always a criterion? How is one to judge materially with regard to faith and the faiths? These are the questions caught up in the matter of discernment.

What help can I hope to give for meeting this challenge to sort out the significances? It should not surprise when I say that the very best I can do is to provide some guidance as each reader takes up this challenge personally. It is not merely that in faith each individual bears some irreplaceable personal responsibility for judgment. Surely faith communities do not simply dissolve into their millions of members when the issue of judgment arises. But the ruler for the measuring to be done as individuals and communities cannot be made available within the paragraphs that I can write in this final chapter. This is not simply a comment on my own limitations in knowledge of the other faiths. The unavailability of a ruler for judgment measurements follows from what has been said in Part One in excavating life in relationship. The sorting out of the *different* differences takes time. To offer a chart firmly fixing the relative truth and error of the faiths is to be "done early" with a task that Christian thinkers have at best only well begun. Moreover the measuring needed eludes us not only in length but in breadth or depth. The cognitive claims of faith are not trivial, precisely because they are grounded in the many-textured complexity of faith's life in relationship, involving prayer, worship, disciplines of obedience, and the like. In quest of orderly typologies one must not safely abstract from the living stuff of the reality of the relationship.[6]

What life and faith call us to, then, is precisely the sorting out of the different differences in dialogue. I have critiqued two positions that would divert from such dialogue: (1) what is sometimes called a pluralist position in which differences, no matter how dramatic, pale before an alleged, but cognitively inaccessible, unity, and (2) what would most likely be an exclusivist position in which one has at hand a standard such that what remains to be done is nothing other than simply to "measure" the other faith(s). Similarly, in sorting out the differences, one must not seek to ascend to some position beyond positions, forsaking the ladder of one's own particularity in order to put every (other) faith in its place. I do not seek to do that. Thus I write as a Christian, but at a time when Christians and persons of the other faiths are increasingly coming into actual relationship with each other. What one can do is to consider what the claims of Christian faith suggest by way of orientation, as one seeks to discern the differences. In what ways might the Christian understand these differences?

THE REACH OF GOD'S REVELATORY LOVE

The Christian *cannot* faithfully understand these differences to exclude the *people* of the other faiths from the reach of God's love. The Christian Scriptures as a whole say what the first letter of Paul to Timothy does in particular: it is indeed *all* whom God desires "to be saved and to come to the knowledge of the truth" (1 Tim. 2:4). Our human moral sense agrees: a God who would not desire all is not *good enough* to be God. Moreover, if what was said in chapter 4 about God's "categorical superiority" is true, we cannot regard God's will to save all as some benevolent inner disposition yielding no active effect.[7] A God who desires all but is capable of reaching only some is not *great enough* to be God. Thus it is that when Christians respond to the logic of their faith they speak as did the members of an ecumenical consultation of Protestant, Roman Catholic, and Orthodox theologians at Baar, Switzerland, in 1990:

> The Bible testifies to God as God of all nations and peoples, whose love and compassion includes all humankind. We see in the Covenant with Noah a covenant with all creation. We see His wisdom and justice extending to the ends of the earth as he guides the nations through their traditions of wisdom and understanding. God's glory penetrates the whole of creation.[8]

Or more succinctly at the Seventh Assembly of the World Council of Churches in Canberra in 1991: "The Bible testifies to God as sovereign of all nations and peoples, *whose love and compassion include all humankind*."[9]

To say that the Creator God in love wills to be at work to bless all persons is, of course, not necessarily to bestow a blessing upon all human faith. But it lays the foundations for recognizing that God does will to be known. We have sounded the Christian conviction that God's transcendence is a transcendence *in relationship*, so that the categorical difference between God and us is expressed precisely in the radical character of God's commitment to humankind. In a relationship, knowing has a natural place. In knowing the other, I am affected by the other; I take something of the other into myself and I can give something of myself to the other pertinently. Moreover, if it is God's intention to bring the human to maturation in relationship, that will not occur without some kind of knowing. Knowing seems to be too basic an aspect of human being to be left behind in any state of fulfillment. It makes more sense to say that whereas we know only in part in the present, then—in completion—we will "know as we are known," then we will know "face to face" (1 Corinthians 13). A God who seeks a saving relationship with all will seek to be known by all. Accordingly, Christians will find some way to speak of a revelation by God that is indeed "general."[10]

PAUSING BEFORE THE HUMAN POLE

With this we may seem well on our way to baptizing the dizzying diversity of the religions of humankind. That would seem an odd way to go about "discerning the differences." But we need to pause to ponder the other, the human, pole of the relationship in terms of which we are seeking to understand God's universal will to reveal and to save. What follows from faith's recognition that our knowing of and about God is a human knowing? At the very least one must say with the apostle Paul: "But we have this treasure in earthen vessels, to show that the transcendent power belongs to God and not to us" (2 Cor. 4:7, RSV). This cuts more than one way. On the one hand, the affirmative movement toward the people of other faiths may be seconded if Paul's point serves to reduce our condescending arrogance. Thus no less committed an advocate of missions than Lesslie Newbigin can remind us that the "Christian story" serves as "lenses" we are to "look through, not at."[11] Would it not be strange if North European humanity were to turn out to be the perfect vessel for Africans and Asians—

or even Americans? In recognizing revelation in relationship, we refuse to collapse the relationship: God may be one, but clearly we human beings in true faith will be many. How many? Do not Christians need to distinguish between internal and external pluralism? Is the Christian able to sweep in not only African Christian hymn rhythms and Asian procedures for Christian polity[12] but also Islamic rejection of trinitarianism as tritheism and Buddhist suspicion concerning the personalizing of the ultimate? Diversity is to be expected, clearly; but in what sense could one speak of *one* treasure in the face of conflict and contradiction? For faith to recall the human element in the relationship is to be reminded of several considerations.

1. We are finite. In chapter 4 we said that to live "before" God, in God's unfailing presence, is not to "possess God as an item of knowledge to be classified and filed away."[13] If it is God's treasure we seek to cherish and share, we will not want to proceed in such a way as to deny the otherness of the treasure.[14] Yet a faith claiming that God's transcendence is "in relationship" will work for relatively more adequate formulation of the revelation.[15]

2. If even the high priests of science have come to speak of "fallibilism," we will not want to claim exemption for our theological vessels.[16]

3. Moreover, to remember that we know "in part" only (1 Corinthians 13) is to be open to the possibility that (quite apart from error) apparent contradictions may not be actual ones, if the assertions are to be understood as addressing different aspects of one reality. They *may* not be, or they may be. A closer look at the whole configuration of religious meaning in question is needed.

4. In our finitude we possess the freedom we experience in contingency. We can not only happen to go wrong, we can also *will* to do so. Surely the twentieth century has taught us that this is not merely a theoretical possibility. In freedom human beings can and do reject even the revelation of God. There is no reason to exempt human religious capacity from the possibility and the reality of sin. Here is where the distinction between God's treasure and human vessels cuts the other way, warning us against unlimited openness.[17] We need to ask how human sin may show itself in particular religious practices and teachings—indeed, in

principle even in particular religions as such. Thus the "Baar document" wisely urges us to:

> speak with honesty and with sadness of the human wickedness and folly that is also present in all religious communities. . . . Any adequate theology of religions must deal with human wickedness and sin.[18]

CONSTITUTIVE CONVERSATION

Clearly, the Christian is thus driven into actual conversation with the person of another faith. Only in such conversation, in such actual contact, can one "discern the differences," distinguishing enriching differences from the mistaken or malevolent elements in any religion. Does the call for such conversation claim a position of privilege exempt from critique? In the final section of this chapter, I will respond to this question in discussing the nature of a faithful and fruitful dialogue. But as one prepares to enter this conversation, two other things are needed in faith's orientation: a sense for criteria and an element of expectation.

To enter the conversation with criteria is not to trivialize the conversation. Quite the contrary. Conversation between, say, a Buddhist and a Christian is not apt to be either honest or productive, if they come together saying, "I don't believe anything, you don't believe anything—let's talk!" The dialogue to be sought requires listening *and* speaking. Thus at Curitiba in 1990 the Lutheran World Federation expressed a commitment to "hold . . . the interrelationship of witness and dialogue as integral to Christian mission and self-understanding."[19] In witness, criteria are given. But they are not given in a wooden way and cannot be applied mechanically. They are given precisely *for* the conversation in its actual course, as Carl Braaten has recognized: "The Christian claim is not a proposition that can be proved true or false by arguments taken from Scripture or tradition; it is proving itself rather in the concrete historical process, under the conditions of world-historical encounters with other religions and worldviews."[20]

In such an understanding, of course, the criteria cannot themselves ᵊmain safely outside the conversation. They enter the conversation with ᵗher in order to be effective. But it is clear that they will also be tested ᵌs and can be transformed in the process. Thus the Christians at ᵊlose their statement with this: "We feel called to allow the ᵊligious dialogue to transform the way in which we do ᵊove toward a dialogical theology in which the praxis of dialogue together with that of human liberation, will constitute a true *locus theologicus*, i.e. both source and basis for theological work."[21] To recognize in this way the constitutive character of interreligious dialogue is not to abandon the faith that brought one to this dance.[22] The Christian participates as a Christian. But Christian faith is a living thing and will not be unaffected by the dialogue.

CREATION AS COMPREHENSIVE CONTEXT
Our theologies will not emerge from the dialogue unchanged, but with what criteria do we begin? The criteria for the dialogue process should reflect our differences and our connection. The participants in the conversation are called to represent accurately their particular faiths. But they speak together not only as Buddhists or Hindus or Christians (where difference may be the more obvious) but as human beings (for whom some kind of connection is to be affirmed). While we have learned to mistrust the ministrations of universal reason, human beings do seek meaning, do strive to make sense of things. Minimally, therefore, certain formal criteria suggest themselves. The participants in the conversation will seek clarity, consistency, coherence—without neglecting the richness of their experience.

What of material criteria? For the Christian the fact that the conversation is between actual human beings suggests a soteriological standard. Christians who debate among themselves about theocentric and christocentric approaches may be drawn in dialogue "back/ahead" to a genuinely gospel emphasis: a "soteriocentric" approach. Here I find Paul Knitter's approach attractive and am intrigued by his claim that such an approach "seems more faithful to the data of comparative religions."[23] So the Christian will ask: "Does what I meet in the other seem to work there for genuine salvation"?

Our earlier discussion provides a way to approach this question. Given the discussion of the relationship between creation and redemption, we will seek not to define salvation narrowly. The Christian will ask: "Is there here evidence of growth toward the fulfillment of God's creative intent, is there the kind of transformation that the Christian seeks in love?" I take it this is the kind of question World Council of Churches delegates were thinking of at Canberra when they said this:

> The Holy Spirit is at work in ways that pass human understanding; the freedom of the Spirit may challenge and surprise us as we enter into dialogue

> with people of other faiths. The gospel of Jesus Christ has taught us the
> signs and fruit of the Holy Spirit—joy, peace, patience and faithfulness (Gal.
> 5). Dialogue challenges us to discern the fruits of the Spirit in the way God
> deals with all humanity.[24]

Christians claim that the Holy Spirit is not another spirit than the one
that brooded over the waters (Gen. 1:2) as otherness was given being.
Human connection and Christian specificity come together in this emphasis
on creation, so that one employing such a criterion can avoid beginning
with the presumption of criteriological privilege.[25] Christians of diverse
stripes come together to trust that it is the Creator God who saves. Hence
the Christian will expose any claimed state of "salvation" (including the
Christian) to scrutiny in terms of its fit with the experience of being human—
an experience for which the Christian does not claim a patented understanding.[26] Even within the Christian community there is significant variety
in understanding, as for example when Christian voices from south of the
equator caution northerners from understanding justification without reference to vindication. One should not expect salvation to mean simply one
thing for a world characterized by otherness in *that* and in *what* God creates.
The question is, "Does what I meet in the other seem to work *there* for
genuine salvation?"

Yet this breadth does not anesthetize Christian judgment. One will work
for distinctions such as the one Paul Tillich proposed between divine and
demonic "ecstasy," with the status of the human functioning as a crucial
variant in such distinctions.[27] Moreover, claims to salvation can be critiqued
where it becomes evident that the role of the Other has been usurped. Thus
Darrell Jodock ponders "the absence of a lively enough and profound
enough sense of transcendence" in the Peoples' Temple of Jim Jones:

> Once this particular leader came to be regarded as divine rather than as one
> witness to the active presence of a transcendent God, and once this particular
> movement became itself the hope of the world rather than an embodiment
> of something much larger than itself, perspective was lost.[28]

If the Christian does not confuse the vessels and the treasure, there will
be less temptation to limit the work of God to the work of Christians.[29]
What, then, may the Christian *expect* in the conversation? To expect something in the conversation is, of course, not to prejudge the conversation.
But even as the Christian comes with criteria, the Christian may well hope
that the other's faith will not be silent when the question of salvation is

asked. Perhaps that is why Protestants, Catholics, and Orthodox Christians could together go so far as to say of "peoples and nations" (once again, at Baar in 1990):

> We affirm that God has been present in their seeking and *finding*, that where there is truth and wisdom in their teachings, and love and holiness in their living, this like any wisdom, insight, knowledge, understanding, love and holiness that is found among us is the gift of the Holy Spirit. We also affirm that God is with them as they struggle, along with us, for justice and liberation.[30]

At Canberra in 1991 the World Council used some of the Baar language (the covenant with Noah as a covenant with all creation) but seemed more cautious: "We witness to the truth that salvation is in Christ and we also *remain open* to other people's witness to truth as they have experienced it."[31]

The Baar language, bold as it is, is conditional: "*where* there is." Conceivably, it seems, there might be no truth and wisdom or love and holiness to be found. But there needs to be something unconditional in the Christian expectation at this point, as I understand it: *that all persons must somehow have effective access to the saving grace of God.* We have not always expected that. We may have spoken of "general revelation," following Paul in Romans 1 and 2, but have been very clear that such revelation cannot save.[32] Our Christian revelation then becomes "special" indeed. If this emphasis escalates into holding that those who die without receiving that revelation are lost, our own God becomes a demon and our own election a principle piercing the one heart of humankind.

Christians will struggle to know how to think about this expectation. At least three options appear as matters of emphasis. (1) I am particularly drawn toward the foundation given in the doctrine of creation, as that is thought together with the conviction that in Jesus of Nazareth God acted decisively for all the creation. God's commitment to work to claim all is sealed in the flesh of Jesus, and now (in Kierkegaard's words, "to speak foolishly") God "must go on" in the service of that will. Henceforth anyone who stands in relationship with the God of creation stands in relationship with that God, the one who acted in Jesus, the only God there is. The point here is precisely to recognize the unconditional element in the relationship God has with the other. "Revelation" is not such an unconditional element; it calls for reception. In chapters 4 and 5, I have written of how the element of independence or difference in relationship is raised to a higher power when we speak of a God whose superiority is categorical. Given that the transcendence of God is (by the will of God) in relationship, we are drawn to ponder what the "for God" significance of the event of Jesus means for us.[33] We will seek to understand that what is decided by God's work in Jesus will not be undone.

Somehow, I say, our formulations must meet the challenge that the persons of other faiths are understood to be granted access to the saving work of God. (2) One may move from the beginning (creation) and middle (the work of Christ) to the end of history to speak of God as the power of the future fulfilling all religions.[34] Does this move represent confidence or desperation? Does it entail granting "ontological priority" to the future? (3) Or, one may claim as a third option the existential choice of actualizing this expectation through the missionary witness itself. In any case, the expectation serves the logic of that witness, even as it opens the missionary to hear what God may be saying through the other.

There may be other ways of formulating this expectation, and some combination of formulations may serve us well. But we must question any reading of the Christian faith that does not permit us this expectation. We do not need to expect more than this. What has or will come of such gracious opportunity cannot be settled apart from the actual course of human freedom and surely cannot be known apart from the actual course of the conversation. Wolfhart Pannenberg, who can see farther than most of us, wisely writes:

> Human experiences of salvation are as ambiguous as other human experiences. It all depends on whether there is communion with God, the God of Israel and of Jesus. Such communion is promised to Christians, provided they do not desert their faith. . . . When it comes to the basis of our Christian confidence in our future salvation, if the spiritual life that Christians experience among themselves remains ambiguous, how could it be less ambiguous in the case of the non-Christian? We may hope that God will look graciously upon them as we hope for ourselves.[35]

Pannenberg helpfully reminds us that in any talk of ultimate salvation, the Christian's position is that of one being judged, not doing the judging. Indeed, if one holds with Pannenberg that there is a difference in that "the Christian has the promise of God in Christ," one will underscore the note of responsibility, recalling that "from everyone to whom much has been given, much will be required" (Luke 12:48). By the will of God, human beings are truly other than God, and I argued in chapter 5 that the issue of human responsibility-in-freedom cannot simply be disregarded in any talk of the telos for faith. While one may be drawn to speculate about that ultimate future (with Suchocki and Baltazar), we do not know how that ultimate future comes together. Indeed, we do not know about the *present* history of freedom. Or do we?

We may be in doubt about what to say regarding the other faiths. We may seek discernment in the face of these differences. But what of those who offer no candidate faith for inspection? What of unbelief?

CLAIMING THE CONNECTION OF UNFAITH

There may indeed be important differences—and *different* differences, as I have said—among the faiths winning human assent. But something different from all of these meets us in the figure of the unbeliever. Later I will emphasize that unbelief itself is not a monolithic reality. The Christian will do well to recognize that. There are differences to be discerned *within* unbelief. But first one needs to face the fact that unbelief—unfaith—is different *from* faith.

Perhaps no single definition of faith will serve to encompass human religious diversity. But it is possible for believers to recognize unbelief when they meet it. And this does happen. Indeed, increasingly all the faiths—different though they be—seem to sense the need to resist the inroads of unbelief (though, of course, this does not eradicate the differences among the faiths). Unbelief does exist. There are those who will not speak of anything superior to human being, who will acknowledge nothing worthy of worship. Search as one will in the lives of such persons, one finds no religious ritual or cult, no spiritual practice of meditation or communion to contradict their profession of unfaith.

Somehow Christians have been slow to acknowledge such difference. Perhaps the sin of which Christians often speak— pride—is to be seen in this. It is surely arrogant to classify persons of other faiths as "anonymously" Christian. It may be similarly self-serving to refuse to take the unbeliever at her or his word.[36] In facing unbelief, the Christian can drive into more than one ditch. To fail to recognize the reality of unbelief is to seek to inhabit some world other than this one. Yet once the reality of difference which unbelief entails sinks in, the Christian may be tempted to deny any sense of connection.

Perhaps it is the strength of faith that becomes its weakness in both responses. (1) Faith has an all-consuming character; it does not easily recognize that the actual difference of unbelief exists. Given the preciousness of faith and given its apparent "givenness," how can it be that someone simply disbelieves? May it be that faith senses a threat in this? (2) But if I cannot credibly deny that the unbeliever exists, at least I do not need to accept the risk of being linked significantly with this other. It is understandable that such a risk is hard to accept. Faith is held dear by the believer and faith and unfaith are not the same thing. Nonetheless, the call to the Christian to be "with the others" entails claiming the connection with unfaith.

CREATURELY CONNECTION

What connection? The Christian is linked with the unbeliever in more than one way, even on the Christian faith's own self-understanding.

1. Clearly, the Christian means to worship the God in whom all things live, move, and have their being (Acts 17:28). It is no attack on the goal of faith in Christ to recognize that the "ought" of the goal is grounded in the "is" of a God, who is "first" and can be "for us" apart from human knowledge. What would be an attack on the logic of Christian faith is precisely that disjunctive thinking which issues a declaration of independence for human existence as such, so that all connection with God comes to depend on conscious knowing and believing.[37] To the contrary, understanding how the relationship to God is not limited to faith, the Christian can faithfully speak of forms of connection with unbelief that do not deny the real difference between faith and unfaith. I will mention three.

a. There is the connection represented by faith's claim *that* unbelievers and believers equally have their existence from God the creator.

b. There is the connection represented by *what* we find we have in common in life. Max Stackhouse has tried to say something of this in quite concrete terms:

> Study or travel in other cultures immediately reveals a simple but profound fact: whether German or Indian, whether Marxist or Hindu, people are human. Everywhere they fall in love, suffer, rear children, work, eat, try

to stay out of trouble, worry about their health, seek some control over their environment, sing, play, weep, organize social systems, participate in various rites and festivals and face death. . . . The word "humanity" conveys something real.[38]

Thus David Augsburger, surveying such ethnographic data as those gathered in Yale University's Human Relations Area Files, comments: "Similarities are most pronounced on the biological level, increased variation appears in the psychological, greater variety exists in the interpersonal and social, with the greatest contrasts occurring in the institutional and the broader worldview levels."[39] The Christian who lives with unbelievers in a family or community knows such human connection quite concretely. My unbelieving sister or brother and I are together in our life and we do not need the permission of our faith or unfaith to be so. The Christian experiences her or his humanity as the vehicle and perhaps even in some sense the telos of her or his transforming Christianity, but the reality of the person's humanity is thereby confirmed, not denied. Perhaps the Christian is to "do everything in the name of the Lord Jesus," but the doing does not stop being human for that reason. My sisters and brothers and I are together as we come into this life and walk through it in diverse perils and pleasures toward an end that awaits us all.

c. Moreover, do we not stand alongside each other, yes even together, in a still more primary sense? As a Christian, the believer holds that this is so—in faith the Christian regards what I have spoken of in chapter 3 as the "givenness of the other" as the very work of God. The Christian's faith and the unbeliever's unfaith do not erase the truth that they are both created through and with the other(s), including *each* other as circumstances (increasingly) indicate. Thus to speak of our creatureliness is not simply to claim connection by identifying common (formal and material) but wholly independent relationships with the one Creator; it is to speak of actual linkages among us in sharing human life.

THE CRITICAL CONTRIBUTION

2. Are we connected also in our *believing*, in our *disbelieving*? Without denying the difference, without disregarding the unbeliever's own word of denial, and without trivializing the precious gift of faith, can one claim a connection? The short answer, I believe, is yes. Distinctions and qualifications clamor to be made, of course—but they will serve to solidify the yes by clarifying and specifying it.

a. Faith is not possession but pilgrimage. Therefore it is not strange that the word of confession is "I believe; help my unbelief!" (Mark 9:24). Is this a confession of faith, of sin? Yes and yes. And perhaps the two are not so far apart in the human person before God. The believer needs the unbeliever's reminder that one's faith is always, as Kierkegaard would put it, "over 10,000 fathoms of water."

b. It seems clear, then, that human faith in God may be a gift, but it is surely not the self-contained circle of God believing in God. Hence, "we walk in danger all the way" not only because we can disbelieve but because we can believe. The psalmist was right: zeal for God's house— or for what one wrongly claims to be that—does tend to be all-consuming (Ps. 69:9). Is Morris Cohen's language really too strong?

> Religion *has* made a *duty* of hatred. It preached crusades against Moham-
> medans and forgave atrocious sins to encourage indiscriminate slaughter of
> Greek Orthodox as well of Mohammedan populations. It also preached
> crusades against Albigenses, Waldenses, and Hussite Bohemians. . . . Cruel
> persecution and intolerance are not accidents, but grow out of the very essence
> of religion, namely its absolute claims.[40]

There is perhaps no need here for a detailed account of the sins of commission and omission characterizing Christian history.[41] But there does need to be an active recognition of the way in which the believer needs to claim the connection with the principled unbeliever, who will not let service to some God who dwells in light inaccessible work against the brother or sister who is seen. Dorothee Soelle finds such a protest in Job: "Why does the Almighty allow evil? . . . Once the question is radically raised, no answer can be given within the context of an understanding of God that combines justice and omnipotence. Job is stronger than God. Job's thinking has led to atheism for moral reasons."[42] For how many people have the crimes against humanity committed in the name of Christianity counted against the God who came as the suffering servant in Jesus?

c. Furthermore, the believer needs to consider a similar salutary connection even with those unbelievers whose protest may not be anchored in those human values the Christian's own faith would mean to serve. Herbert Richardson has written of how atheism may flourish in transitional periods between dominant matrices of meaning. Or it may take the form of boredom, when a traditional "intellectus" is dying from within.[43] At such times the Christian's connection with unbelief is well claimed by the

Christians to yield a burden of proof to be borne by the formulation of faith presently (previously?) presiding over Christian piety. The account in chapter 1 suggests that our time may be such a time.[44]

3. Thus far I have stressed how much the Christian believer has to gain from claiming the connection with unbelief. But the connection is also to be claimed in order that the Christian may give something of value in this relationship. The admonition of 1 Peter is not halfhearted: "Always be ready to make your defense to anyone who demands from you an accounting for the hope that is in you" (1 Pet. 3:15).

THE NEED FOR NEW WINESKINS
In various ways unbelief is demanding such an accounting, inviting the Christian to speak clearly and directly. Some of this speaking will continue to be in the cadences of direct evangelical address. The Christian does not understand the gospel to be good news for Christians alone. If there is One who is truly "first" and if that One is "for us," there is a message to be shared. The Christian's own store stocks provisions for this task, though sensitive selection will be needed if the effort is to be genuinely effective. The news of the gospel is good enough to fit each human situation in its particularity. If "the good seed" falls into "burned over" ground, particular care in cultivation will be needed. And the field will represent other specific forms of human difference. It is tempting for the Christian spokesperson to regard as good fruit a comfortably familiar replication of (what at least once represented) a particular grasp of Christian existence. In a setting that calls for a truly fresh hearing, that replication may represent the dependency and incipient artificiality of a hothouse culture.

Moreover, given the recognition of temporality discussed in chapter 2, it is clear that the Christian has no abiding city in any particular formulation of the Christian story. Themes and motifs that were once understood as support can shift to become problems and challenges, as a study of the church's affair with a notion of verbal inspiration suggests. As the believer continues on his or her pilgrimage the questions of the unbeliever will often point the way for what is—or is becoming—the believer's own quest. Question and quest, preaching and teaching, dogmatics and apologetics may not be so far apart in this journey. Thus, often what will serve the Christian church best will be the structure of conversation in which both parties have active roles in the flow of question and response.

DOES THE UNBELIEVER KNOW GOD?

In the final section, I will speak of the method(s) suitable for this conversation, of the approach and style that can serve faith on the boundary. But here one needs to ask: What should the Christian assume about the unbeliever in this conversation?

A partial answer has already been given in this section: the Christian's own faith makes clear that every human being stands in relationship with God. More than that, I have stressed that the logic of Christian faith suggests that in being for us God wills to be known by us—though the "for us" cannot be collapsed into the "by us." So, are we to say that the unbeliever does know God? Are we about to obliterate any distinction between faith and unfaith? In responding, I can build on what was said in chapter 4 regarding life "before" God: that all persons have experienced the activity of God (cf. Amos 9:7, e.g.) and "can know—indeed in some sense do know God."[45] In *what* sense?

There are biblical passages indicating that one may choose to undertake actions which serve the will of God without knowing that the actions bear that significance: "He judged the cause of the poor and needy; then it was well. Is not this to know me?" (Jer. 22:16). Indeed, such deeds are said to serve no less than the one called the Son of Man himself (Matt. 25:31ff.) Many Christians would bear testimony that they know professed unbelievers who seem concretely to incarnate this possibility by acts of compassion and courage. May there not be an enabling knowing of God of a sort in this then? This moral witness may be the most focused and forceful incognito in which the knowing of God clothes itself, but one wonders as well about the grounding sought in metaphysical inquiry into the real or the purity of form sought by the artist.[46] May there be other "rumors of angels" in such signals of transcendence as a sense of humor or a sense of safety?[47]

The psalmist spoke of a deer panting after the water brook (Ps. 42:1), and Augustine wrote: "Thou hast made us for Thyself and our heart is restless, until it repose in Thee."[48] There does seem to be a human quest for the qualities of transcendence which the Christian claims in speaking of God. May Pascal have been right in phrasing this divine word to the human quester: "Thou wouldst not seek Me, if thou didst not possess Me"?[49] Perhaps the Christian in self-examination will conclude that it is precisely religion's offenses against humanity which keep the unbeliever from acknowledging that which or the one whom he seems to know.

Perhaps. But other possibilities exist as well. One such possibility is considerably darker. We have come increasingly to see that in at least some knowing and not-knowing the will is powerfully at work. Certainly it may be that in some unfaith the Christian faces a human will that wills sinfully not to know. The danger with this view is that one might find this interpretation all too convenient as a way of dismissing the challenge in what is a valid difference in the knowing of God. Surely this option will not be quickly chosen by any Christian who has sat with an earnest person who cries out, "I want to believe, but I simply can't: I don't believe there is a God." One will rather choose to think with that person about what counts as evidence, about how much "evidence" is sufficient within a framework of freedom.[50] Nonetheless, the Christian will recognize that culpable ignorance is possible.

Once again, we are driven toward the actual conversation, toward the question, "How may one live faithfully and fruitfully on the boundary?" But in turning to that question, one needs to carry another question along. How do we avoid the trap of looking for in the other—or making the other into—simply what we ourselves already are? We easily get into the business of doing all sorts of conceptual acrobatics to show that the atheist or agnostic is (or can be made into something) somewhat like us or might have what always ends up being a pale copy of what we so clearly possess. If our sketch of the realities "within, with, and before" which/whom we live suggests the truly fundamental character of relationship, what shall we make of that as we face the reality of honest and thoughtful unbelief? To employ the language of Christian particularity, may God love with a radicality that can somehow reach out to encompass even the difference between belief and unbelief? Instead of focusing on judging the other, would it not be wise to ask, "What, in any case, may God intend for me through this one who as a professed unbeliever seems truly other?" Only as that radical question is kept before us can we undertake the task of considering how we can be *well* with these others in faith. Asking that question will mean that we meet more nearly on level ground. That will make a difference as we begin talking.

LIVING FAITHFULLY AND FRUITFULLY

It is this to which we are called. In the light of the constitutive presence of the other in life (indicated in Part One) and in the face of faith's intensifying relationship to otherness (as sketched in this and the preceding chapter), some concluding remarks are necessary.

CONVERSION AND CHANGE

"To be with the others in faith" is in a sense not an optional matter. The time when a Christian could live as if there were no others in faith has passed and does not seem likely to come again soon. The adverbs "faithfully" and "fruitfully," on the other hand, point to a life that is not at all inevitable. The adverbs may not seem to be equally in need of defense, for does not the first simply repeat the point of the subject? Yet to speak of faith living faithfully is to be reminded of the possibility of apostasy. Sadly, meeting the other can be an occasion for the soft or quiet infidelity in which one does not claim one's identity as a Christian as one enters into the conversation. To seek shared ground with the person of another faith— or, better, to celebrate the discovery of such ground—is not to aspire to the unoccupied territory of faithless neutral ground. Similarly, the Christian may be called to "claim the connection" with unbelief, but none of the ways in which we have just spoken of that entail abandoning the faith.[51]

It may not seem as clear that the Christian is called to live "fruitfully." Indeed, one form of piety seems to make a point of juxtaposing faithfulness to "success" or "effectiveness." Such piety, perhaps in understandably robust resistance to particular cultural definitions of "success," gives away the faith's own call to "fruit bearing." What, then, is involved in living fruitfully on faith's boundary? This vivid language depicts a development characterized by some combination of continuity and discontinuity. So the Christian enters the conversation faithfully seeking ways the gospel can be good news for the other. The Christian expects the word of truth to work powerfully in the witness given in dialogue. It is important that the change anticipated is not understood to abolish difference. For example, the other who is converted to Christianity in the conversation will not cease to be other. All the human dynamics of difference that provide the "vessels" for the other's other faith or unfaith surely should not be expected to disappear when the universal good news of the gospel is heard and believed.

The challenge is so to live on this boundary that one's faithful witness is fruitful *for the other*.

Similarly, the Christian finds the question of fruitfulness turning back on herself or himself. The Christian will thus ask: "How have I been— am I being—changed through this conversation?" After all, the description in Part One of life's dynamic of difference cannot suddenly be so bracketed that this meeting yields no effect at all. And would not the discussion in chapter 5 of the Christian becoming other for, with, and through the other imply that one is called to live fruitfully also when one meets the faith of the other? If the conversation has been fully fruitful, both parties will be changed somehow for the better. The Christian cannot appropriately enjoy the success of welcoming the newly converted, without asking and an- swering the question of what fruitful difference the conversation has made within him or her. Has the understanding of the Christian claim been enriched in hearing the other's living witness regarding the ultimate? Has the defense of the history of Christendom been softened, been qualified, by hearing the earnest protest of the unbeliever? Even without assuming a positive response on the part of the other, one asks after the fruit of the meeting: have, for example, new possibilities for thinking and living the faith been evoked in the conversation with the other?

To live faithfully and fruitfully—the adverbs belong together.[52] The conversation will not be fruitful if the participants do not honestly represent their stance vis-à-vis faith. And if no fruit is borne in the conversation— for and within the other, for and within the Christian—one must ask whether the conversation has been faithful. This is not a triumphalistic declaration. Once again, to accept the criterion of fruit bearing is not to assume that the other will be converted. If through the conversation the Christian finds the other the more strongly confirmed in a course of life with respect to faith which the Christian cannot—on pain of contradiction—endorse, the Christian still may fruitfully ask, "What may I learn about what it means that God creates and seeks to save those who are truly other than God— including me?" There is something for the believer to learn in the con- versation, apart from the conversion of the other, even precisely in the reality of nonconversion. Such recognition of the internal implications of fruit bearing is not the private property of Christian faith. Indeed, John Cobb has argued: "That one norm that can be applied with relative ob- jectivity to the great religious traditions has to do with their ability, in faithfulness to their heritage, to expand their understanding of reality and its normative implications."[53]

The adverbs belong together. We are called to live faithfully and fruitfully on the boundary. And the two "categories," the other faiths and unfaith, are well held together here too. If I have been able to "claim the connection" with unbelief, I will not, in "discerning the differences" with respect to the other faiths, fail to ask what genuine connection faith itself may represent. But in discerning significant differences among the faiths, I will not approach the unbeliever with a plea to connect with me by believing just anything at all.

THE ENEMIES OF THE CONVERSATION

If the adverbs do belong together, who are the real enemies of faith on the boundary? This may not be so easily known. The person who questions some specific belief or indeed Christian faith as a whole may be inviting the Christian in conversation to give an accounting for the hope that is in him or her (1 Pet. 3:15). This person is no enemy if the question is earnest enough to carry with it an actual willingness to listen to the response. The enemies would be those who work against any real conversation. One can do that by denying the participants their identities with respect to faith— at least for the conversation. Or one can do that by defining those identities in such a way that the conversation could not be mutually fruitful, so that some combination of continuity and discontinuity could not characterize the change known by both members of the conversation.

Thus the identity of the other can be compromised. I have already written of the need to "discern difference" and to "claim connection." But one's own faith identity can also be so defined as to oppose fruitful conversation. Thus for the Christian a "Christian enemy" would be a person who would define Christian identity in such firm and fixed terms that the African would have to become middle American, or the "man [or woman!] 'come of age'" would have to hit skid row in order then to acquire Christian identity. Or, less obviously perhaps, that firm and fixed "enemy" conception of Christian identity would prevent any significant development in the "victorious" Christian's own Christian existence. The danger of a wooden definition of Christian identity looms not only for the individual Christian but also theologically in the dialectical task of claiming the "faith once delivered to the saints." Francis Schüssler Fiorenza argues that "foundational theology" must take as its starting point "the givenness of the religious dimension of human life," but he wisely adds that "the originating interpretations have a reception-history, produce consequences and effects, lead to modifications, reinterpretations, shifts in argumentation, and new paradigms."[54]

Rebecca Chopp has written insightfully of how women as other can be marginalized in a number of ways: by systemic devaluing, by their effacing, by their being cast as on the border of order-threatening chaos.[55] More broadly, the Christian who attends to the reality of the other can by extension be similarly devalued, effaced, and cast. The third move is particularly interesting. Chopp employs Toril Moi's portrayal of what I recognize as an "enemy" maneuver:

> Women seen as the limit of the symbolic order will in other words share in the disconcerting properties of *all* frontiers: they will be neither inside nor outside, neither known or unknown. It is this position that has enabled male culture sometimes to vilify women as representing darkness and chaos, to view them as Lilith or the Whore of Babylon, and sometimes to elevate them as the representatives of a higher and purer nature, to venerate them as Virgins and Mothers of God. In this first instance the border line is seen as part of the chaotic wilderness outside, and in the second it is seen as an inherent part of the inside: the part that protects and shields the symbolic order from the imaginary chaos.[56]

There is imaginary chaos, and there is chaos that is real and fruitful. In any case, it is clear that to identify the "enemy" we need to consider not merely *what* is held but also *how* that stance is taken.[57]

A LIVING CONVERSATION

We can best speak of "how" this stance is taken by claiming the context given in the verb in our subtitling phrase: to *live* faithfully and fruitfully on the boundary. This "life in conversation" may be what the Christians at Canberra in 1991 called for as a "culture of dialogue."[58] That life can be illumined—clarified and defended—by considering two questions.

First, Does this call imply what John Milbank has criticized as "the idea of dialogue as privileged mode of access to the truth"? Milbank asserts that this idea "assumes that many voices are coalescing around a single known object which is independent of our biographical or transbiographical processes of coming-to-know."[59] Is the call really an ethnocentric denial of difference? If one recognizes the particularity and incommensurability of perspectives, what then? Does not dialogue ask for or assume too much? Or, second, Does it not ask for too little? Is not the air that dialogue breathes that of the cozy seminar room, where everyone quietly understands that all the verbal jousting is really much ado about not very much at all?

I will respond to these questions together by appropriating the dictionary definition of "conversation" as "intimate association or intercourse." This is the language of life. What follows from that? A coming together in life, a having-to-do-with-each-other in living conversation, will be fully *actual*. In a sense, both questions attack dialogue as abstraction from actuality. That actuality can be spelled out in the terms of the participants and their eventful meeting.

1. That I meet the actual other will mean that I meet a particular person in her or his uniqueness. Of course the fact that this person is, say, a Buddhist (and I a Christian) will mean that the conversation will engage our participation in the complex wholes of feeling, thought, and action that the religions represent.[60] Even in this, however, it seems wise to avoid the kind of essentialism represented by the grand typologies that survey courses sometimes sponsor.[61] But, granting that there is a shared communal reality in religion, in a truly actual encounter my concern is to meet the other in the terms not of some textbook outline but of where he or she individually lives and breathes with respect to faith. What ultimately drives this one's daily deeds? What calms this one's middle-of-the-night distress? To what does this other bow the knee? Why? What would this one give up last? If she or he could speak only one sentence to a child, what would it be? As one works thus with the actual empirical content of faith, one may be surprised by what one meets. For example, the membership in the categories conveniently classified as other faiths and unfaith may turn out to be not as clear as supposed at the outset.

2. If the conversation is to occur for me actually I must be truly there— fully involved. Once again, from my side it is not Christianity that speaks but this particular Christian. The questions just posed to draw out the actual other with respect to faith need to be put to me as well. That what the liberation theologians speak of as the "social location" of faith's speech is fully pertinent to the conversation will be evident as we respond to such questions.[62] What must be avoided is the tendency to suppose that I have

a self and an identity fully secured somewhere else, held back—not giving itself and not at risk in the conversation.[63]

3. And of course in this conversation this actual Christian and this actual other must actually meet with respect to the reality of faith. In a genuine meeting of true others much must not be settled in advance. Something new occurs, I have said, in a truly "fruitful" meeting. Perhaps one might say that something (materially) unexpected is to be (formally) expected. This requirement for genuine conversation can be understood to follow from the logic of the gospel itself. In the first section of this chapter, I argued that the Christian is called to the unconditional expectation that "all persons must somehow have effective access to the saving grace of God." But that "somehow" does not itself render a judgment about particular traditions with respect to faith, and surely not about the actual individual person who stands in some relation of adherence to such a given tradition. The complex freedom of the individual and the genuine contingency in the meeting rise to block such judgments. We are open to the conversation; we *need* the conversation. Thus David Lochhead appropriately writes:

> The Gospel, except in the case of Judaism (where it must be said "If Judaism is not of God, then neither is Christianity") provides no warrant for an *a priori* valuation of other traditions. . . . Openness to the world, which we understand as the arena of God's activity and as the object of God's love requires of us that we listen.[64]

If Lochhead is right, the Christian faith seems to invite a moment of self-transcendence. Because I am a Christian I am called truly to listen to the other—though, of course, also to speak. But in truly listening I am opened to something that is actually other.[65] This is where talk of "passing over and coming back" or of acquiring a "second first language" belongs.[66]

We cannot claim to know in advance what will transpire, as we both listen in this actual meeting of others. Of course each participant brings criteria and convictions to the meeting; this conversation is, after all, actually to involve them and must do so in their givenness. But in the meeting one does face the new possibilities that the genuinely other introduces. My Christian estimate of Buddhism, of this Buddhist person most directly but also indirectly of Buddhism, may be radically transformed. My estimate of Christianity may itself be transformed. Paul Martinson catches nicely the unpredictability:

> All kinds of change are possible. Maybe a false idea about the other, a careless cliché, will be blown away. Perhaps we will discover a new attitude,

a new pattern of relating to others. Maybe new insights never before considered will come. We will learn. To learn is to change. Change may even mean conversion. Whether mutual witness brings about many "small" conversions (one remains in one's faith but holds it in a new or changed way) or a single "big" conversion (one ceases to be Christian and becomes Buddhist, or vice versa), change is sure to come.[67]

INCOMMENSURABILITY: OBSTACLE AND INCENTIVE

It does seem that such an understanding of living actual dialogue does not ask too little. But how is this meeting possible? In asking this question, we might be stunned into silence by the talk of "incommensurability" between our paradigms to which we made reference in chapter 1.[68] Did not Thomas Kuhn, who thrust this theme into the center of the Anglo-American discussion, argue that "the proponents of competing paradigms must fail to make complete contact with each other's viewpoints" because (in addition to other reasons) they "practice their trades in different worlds"?[69] That we see and know through paradigms surely must be acknowledged. But this does not need to yield the pessimistic solipsism often associated with this theme. True, there is no neutral, universal, ahistorical framework for understanding and evaluation. If that is what the Enlightenment was about, we are clearly post-Enlightenment people. There is no such universal order to keep order: because/*therefore* we are given to each other in our particularities *as other*. Kuhn's "*complete* contact" is not needed; perhaps it is not even to be desired if the creativity of difference and individuality are to be affirmed. Thus Richard Bernstein has shown how incommensurable languages can be compared and rationally evaluated in multiple ways: there are always points of overlap and crisscrossing.[70]

To broaden a theme from chapter 3, we are speaking of how "the other is given." The other, the actual other—nature, our bodies, the other human person, God—is given to us in our living, in the experience that makes up the stuff of our existence. Thus we are not locked in our linguistic prisons, because language does depend on something other than itself: the actual experience of life together with the other. I cannot offer here a detailed prescription for the recovery of a modified or critical realism. There is much work to be done in this regard. But John B. Cobb seems to me to point in the right direction:

> In short, language does create our worlds. But it does so by highlighting features of a common world that, in its totality, is so rich and complex that

no language will ever encompass it all. Different languages highlight different features. Communities order themselves to the features highlighted in their language, neglecting others. But the neglected features are still there, and they still function even when they are not thematized. When communities that have developed quite differently interact, each may learn about features of its own experience that it has neglected and thus expand its own grasp of reality.[71]

"They still function even when they are not thematized"—Cobb's calm sentences are speaking about the dizzying and nurturing fact that, more flamboyantly ciphered, the other is given for us. Experience is given for our linguistic work of selection and ordering. Thus it does indeed make sense to speak of "social location" and to include in cross-cultural analyses not only varieties of intellectual systems and convictions but, as Mark Heim argues, "functional structures for maintaining identity and meaning or legitimating authority [and] yet others [varieties] attending to the economic conditions . . . and those which take up the organization of power."[72] And, second, the other's acts of linguistic ordering, with their consequent distinctive influence on later experience, are themselves given to us in particular meetings through the reality of a world-making process which we do not create with our words. Given this second point, Beverly Harrison well says: " 'Objectivity' here means openness to others' history and to the critical claims that history bears and also the ability to learn from others' historical experience."[73] Thus Alasdair MacIntyre, who cannot be credibly charged with ignoring the historically contingent character of our "tradition-constituted and tradition-constitutive inquiries," has lately been writing of how potentially creative dialogue can take place between incommensurable standpoints.[74]

In this actual meeting of actual others it is clear, then, that no single method holds sway. Such a single method would be another abstraction. We meet to work together at meeting.[75] We come to the conversation with our criteria—with our methods—for this conversation, this "intimate association or intercourse," is a living thing. In this chapter we have been seeking to attend to the testimonies of faith. Perhaps Lochhead is right in understanding the Christian faith as calling to dialogue. Perhaps it is even the case that Cobb is right in supposing that all the great religious traditions seek to "expand their understanding of reality." But it is not first faith in which the call to dialogue is rooted. The analysis of *life* on the boundary presented in Part One of this book surely sounds such a call to any living faith. The conversation with the others in faith is grounded in the rhythm of change, the pulse of the new, which characterizes all life.[76] What follows from that fact?

AN EARTHLY AND TIMELY CONVERSATION

In speaking of life on the boundary, we spoke most comprehensively of the space-time continuum. Just so, this conversation will be "here"—in this particular place with this particular other with the particular given-to-each-other which obtains. And in the meeting we know that to have such a "given" beginning is not to be at the end of the process. The dialogue is "now." Time's arrow reminds us that the present is not the future. We are other than each other here in this place, and in that "spatial" instability or volatility we sense that the next moment will itself be new in relation to this one.

So it is not the case that the end is sure, but we merely cannot yet know the what and the when of that end. The end is not known because the end is not yet. The present process will have its efficacy, good and/or evil, in that future. In the language of chapter 5 we will "become other *through the other*." That is faith talk, but such talk is grounded once again in the reality of life on the boundary. Thus Richard Schweder writes:

> The expression "thinking through cultures" is polysemous; one may "think through" other cultures in each of several senses: by means of the other (by viewing the other as an expert in some realm of human experience), by getting the other straight (rational construction of the beliefs and practices of the other), by deconstructing and going right through and beyond the other (revealing what the other has suppressed and kept out of sight), witnessing in the context of engagement with the other (revealing one's own perspective on things by dint of a self-reflexive turn of mind).[77]

I ask again: What does such living "thinking through" mean for faith on the boundary? It means, among other things, that Christians should not come to the conversation with an eschatological trump card ready to be played if the going gets tough.[78] Statements of hope about the future do not double back to lift the speaker preemptively out of the contingency of dialogue and carry her or him ahead to an end that is certain. Thus the Christian who speaks of the ultimate future can be held accountable in the present for such speaking, can be asked for the *present* reason for the hope that is in him or her (1 Pet. 3:15). Of course, in speaking of the future the Christian is not bound simply to project the droning on of the present, ad infinitum. We were just speaking, after all, of the future as indeed other. But it makes sense that the other of that future will be such that this present will be able to be recognized as "given" for it. In the pertinent section of chapter 5, I have tried to offer such statements, focusing on the material issue of what would count as salvation "then."[79] The same rhythm of continuity and discontinuity may surely be expected by people of faith in their believing up to that "then."

Such an uncertain life on the boundary is difficult. Is it too difficult? Clearly, some find it so. Perhaps this question itself cannot be answered "now" once and for all. Perhaps we have come back to what was suggested in chapter 1: that faith is the right stance for life on the boundary.[80] The Christian bids to believe in God the Creator. Such faith does not cast a holy cloak over the evil we do. But the fundamental reality of otherness—our spatial standing together and our temporal unfolding to some common future—is not something we have worked in our defiance or our diffidence. Indeed, it is rather the denial or exclusion of genuine difference which seems dear to the heart of darkness. Christian faith can, then, welcome this life on the boundary as gift and task. In the gift of life on the boundary, there is resource for the task that faith finds on its boundary. In our living, there is instruction for our believing, as surely as faith proves itself in illuminating and directing that living.[81] This circle is not vicious if it is the open circle of life.

And so the Christian can accept the ambiguity by which our knowing finds its fit with the freedom of our creaturely doing. It is possible to take up this boundary life in faith. To such a Christian to do so seems all right, if not easy. It is all right to remain on earth with earthen vessels, to exist in history where the end is not yet. The "ground" on which this faithful person stands turns out to be a boundary and the boundary a path—a path we do not walk alone, for the other is given.[82]

NOTES

Preface

1. Elizabeth A. Johnson, *She Who Is: The Mystery of God in Feminist Theological Discourse* (New York: Crossroad Publishing Company, 1992), 216.
2. Catherine Mowry LaCugna, *God for Us: The Trinity and Christian Life* (New York: Harper San Francisco, 1991), 304. While I have not emphasized specifically trinitarian speech, there are numerous points where I find LaCugna's work particularly helpful. Two such are her discussion of God's transcendence and immanence (pp. 322ff.) and her anthropological discussion (chapter 8). Her recasting of the distinction between the immanent and economic Trinities certainly challenges much conventional Christian speech about God. LaCugna deals with concerns I have in this connection in her conversation with Piet Schooneberg (cf. p. 219, regarding "the freedom of divine self-expression in salvation history, *and* the freedom of the recipient to accept the divine self-communication") connection and Walter Kasper (cf. p. 220, regarding the need to convey "that there is something *new* about God because of God's entry into history"). Even more fundamentally, the challenge is to unpack LaCugna's summary formulation: "While the world is the gracious result of divine freedom, God's freedom means *necessarily* being who and what God is. From this standpoint the world is not created *ex nihilo* but *ex amore, ex condilectio,* that is, out of divine love" (p. 355.)
3. Ted Peters, *God—The World's Future: Systematic Theology for a Postmodern Era* (Minneapolis: Fortress Press, 1992), ix.
4. Patrick R. Keifert, *Welcoming the Stranger: A Public Theology of Worship and Evangelism* (Minneapolis: Fortress Press, 1992).

Chapter 1. The Critical Massing of the Many

1. Salman Rushdie, "A Pen Against the Sword: In Good Faith," *Newsweek*, 12 February 1990, 53. Emphasis his. Rushdie's subsequent apology to the Muslim community is, I take it, only another entry in his chapter in this history.
2. The point is that the dominant group uses itself as the standard by which others are judged. *Perhaps* one can speak of plants and fish as exotic, but it at least verges on ethnocentrism to speak in this way of another human being. Tony Hillerman, novelist of the Navajo people, makes the point well in *Talking God* (New York: Harper Paperback, 1991), 290, in the challenge put regarding the selectivity and message evident in museum collections: "I, being Talking God, ask you who have come to look at this display of masks to look around

you in this exhibition, and throughout this museum. Do you see a display of the masks of the gods of the Christian, or of the Jew, or of Islam, or of any other culture strong enough to defend its faith and to punish such a desecration? Where is the representation of the Great Jehovah who led the Jews out of their bondage in Egypt, or the Mask of Michael the Archangel, or the Mother of the Christian God we call Jesus Christ, or a personification of Jesus himself? You do not see them here. . . . Here you see the gods of conquered people displayed like exotic animals in the public zoo. Only the overthrown and captured gods are here. Here you see the sacred things torn from the temples of Inca worshippers, stolen from the holy kivas of the Pueblo people, sacred icons looted from burned tepee villages on the buffalo plains."

3. Ben Wattenberg, *Minneapolis Star Tribune*, 11 March 1991.

4. The most striking expression of this debate may have been the skirmishing between the arts community and governmental concern expressed to and through the National Endowment for the Arts—most dramatically with regard to the photographs by Robert Mapplethorpe.

5. "Counsel for Lutherans with Respect to Interfaith Worship," Division of Theological Studies, Lutheran Council in the U.S.A. (1986). Earlier (1984), the Council had issued "Counsel for Lutheran-Jewish Celebration." Similarly, the World Council of Churches has issued many such statements. See, e.g., "Guidelines on Dialogue" (1979, 1982, 1984) and "My Neighbor's Faith—and Mine" (1986). In "Dialogue with People of Other Faiths" (1986), the National Council of the Churches of Christ in the U.S.A. particularly addressed relationships among Christian, Jewish, and Muslim communities. These are only a small sample of this literature.

6. Among the many commentators, Ted Peters characteristically offers a balanced view. See Peter's column, "Theology Update," in *dialog* 25, no. 3 (1986): 226–31; and idem, "Discerning the Spirits of the New Age," *Christian Century* 105, no. 25 (31 August 1988): 763–66, for a fuller bibliography. It is interesting that this is the matter at issue in the warning issued in December 1989 by the Vatican's Congregation for the Doctrine of the Faith against fusing Eastern and Catholic meditation: "Christian meditation is not submersion in an impersonal divine atmosphere, in an abyss without face or form."

7. Joseph Campbell with Bill Moyers, *The Power of Myth* (Garden City, N.Y.: Doubleday & Co., 1988).

8. Starhawk, *The Spiral Dance: Rebirth of the Ancient Religion of the Goddess* (San Francisco: HarperCollins Publishers, 1989), 24.

9. I. I. Rabi, quoted in Jeremy Bernstein, *Experiencing Science* (New York: Basic Books, 1979), 45–46.

10. Margaret R. Miles, "Hermeneutics of Generosity and Suspicion: Pluralism and Theological Education," *Theological Education*, Supplement (1987), 36.

11. Gayraud S. Wilmore, "Theological Education in a World of Religious and Other Diversities," *Theological Education*, Supplement (1987), 162. The forms of diversity that Wilmore discusses are non-Christian faith communities, denominationalism, ecclesial, theological, liturgical, ethical, and spiritual.

12. Stephen Toulmin, *Cosmopolis: The Hidden Agenda of Modernity* (New York: Free Press, 1990), 108. Toulmin offers this summary: "Human actions and experiences were *mental* or spontaneous outcomes of reasoning; they were performed willingly and creatively; and they were active and productive. Physical phenomena and natural processes, by contrast, involved brute matter and were *material*: they were mechanical, repetitive, predictable effects of causes; they merely happened; and matter in itself was passive and inert." Emphasis his. See also Toulmin's discussion (pp. 109–17) of the "timbers" on the "Nature Side" and the "Humanity Side" of the Modern Framework. Toulmin's study is notable for arguing that the modern world had two distinct origins: "If we follow this suggestion, and carry the origins of Modernity back to the late Renaissance authors of Northern Europe in the 16th century, we shall find the *second*, scientific and philosophical phase, from 1630 on, leading many Europeans to turn their backs on the most powerful themes of the *first*, the literary or humanistic phase" (p. 23, emphasis his). He also emphasizes historical reasons for these developments (see, e.g., p. 36). Studies that have influenced my interpretation of the Enlightenmnent but that are not otherwise noted here, are Peter Gay, *The Enlightenment: An Interpretation*, 2 vols. (New York: Alfred A. Knopf, 1966–69); Ernst Cassirer, *The Philosophy of the Enlightenment* (Princeton: Princeton University Press, 1951); and Basil Willey.

13. See particularly the second and sixth of the Meditations on First Philosophy, René Descartes, *The Philosophical Writings*, trans. John Cottingham, Robert Stoothff, and Dugald Murdoch, 2 vols. (Cambridge: Cambridge University Press, 1984).

14. Toulmin, *Cosmopolis*, 72–74. Toulmin takes his title from the Stoic theme that "social and natural regularities alike are aspects of the same overall *cosmos + polis = cosmopolis*" and he adds: "The practical idea that human affairs are influenced by, and proceed in step with heavenly affairs, changes into the philosophical idea, that the structure of nature reinforces a rational Social Order (p. 68). See also Toulmin's discussion (pp. 127–28) of the form of the family burial ground as illustrating the social power of the traditional image of the planetary system. Descartes's famous "piece of wax" passage put it this way: "The perception I have of it is a case not of vision or touch or imagination—nor has it ever been, despite previous appearances—but of purely mental scrutiny; and this can be imperfect and confused, as it was before, or clear and distinct as it is now, depending on how carefully I concentrate on what the wax consists in" (Descartes, *Philosophical Writings*, 2:21).

15. David Hume, *An Enquiry Concerning Human Understanding*; and idem, *Inquiry Concerning the Principles of Morals* (New York: Liberal Arts Press, 1957).

16. The phrase is Arnold Schoenberg's. In the discussion of these postclassical developments in music and art I am much influenced by the work of Wes Aardahl.

17. John Cage is cited in Rob Tannenbaum, "A Meeting of Sound Minds: John Cage and Brian Eno," *Musician*, no. 86 (1985): 70.
18. Toulmin, *Cosmopolis*, 153, discusses such developments under the heading of "Re-renaissance Deferred," arguing that we have here an attempt to "revive the rationalist dream of a clean slate and a return to abstract fundamentals."
19. G. W. F. Hegel, *On Art, Religion, Philosophy*, ed. J. Glenn Gray (New York: Harper & Row, 1970), 112.
20. Michael Murray, quoting Stravinsky's set designer, from the liner notes to *Stravinsky: the Rite of Spring, Lorin Maazel, The Cleveland Orchestra* (Telarc Record, 1980), DG 10054.
21. Compare Toulmin's discussion (*Cosmopolis*, 148) of nineteenth century romanticism as rationalism's mirror image.
22. See Elizabeth Frank, *Jackson Pollock* (New York: Abbeville Press, 1983), 66.
23. Frank, *Jackson Pollock*, 111. Originally quoted in Selden Rodman, *Conversations with Artists* (New York: Devin-Adair, 1957), 82. For Stravinski, see Robert Craft, ed. *Dialogues and a Diary* (Garden City, N.Y.: Doubleday & Co., 1963), where the composer insists that these objective elements "are emotive themselves."
24. Langdon Gilkey, *Society and the Sacred: Toward a Theology of Culture in Decline* (New York: Crossroad, 1981), 6.
25. Jürgen Habermas, *The Theory of Communicative Action*, trans. Thomas McCarthy (Boston: Beacon Press, 1984), 1:342.
26. Richard Faulk, "In Pursuit of the Postmodern" (Paper delivered at Claremont, Calif., conference, Toward a Post-Modern World, 16–20 January 1987), 3.
27. Fritjof Capra, *The Turning Point: Science, Society and the Rising Culture* (New York: Simon & Schuster, 1982), 32–33. Cf. his *The Tao of Physics: An Exploration of the Parallels between Modern Physics and Eastern Mysticism* (New York: Random House, 1975). The scope of Capra's claim was anticipated already in 1978 by Nicholas Yonker, who wrote of an emerging "Planetary Age," which was to join four earlier periods: the Primitive, Early Civilization, the Axial Age, and Modernity. See Nicholas Yonker, *God, Man and the Planetary Age: Preface for a Theistic Humanism* (Corvallis, Ore.: Oregon State University Press, 1978).
28. Perhaps most attention has been given to Bill McKibben's dramatic lament, *The End of Nature* (New York: Random House, 1989), in which the otherness of nature is at issue. A different and yet fundamentally related theme was posed in a question at the Twenty-fifth Nobel Conference, Gustavus Adolphus College, in October 1989. If "we have begun to think of science as a more subjective and relativistic project, operating out of and under the influence of social ideologies and attitudes" (conference program), is not science "as a unified, universal objective endeavor" over? I will discuss this question in chap. 2. A greater consensus seems to exist among theologians that theology must face the challenge of *"the transition from the Eurocentric age to the*

age of humanity as a whole" (Jürgen Moltmann, *Paradigm Change in Theology: A Symposium for the Future*, ed. Hans Küng and David Tracy, trans. Margaret Kohl [New York: Crossroad, 1989], 221). Emphasis his. Certainly the most sweeping apocalyptic is heard in the deconstructionist voices. Mark C. Taylor, e.g., states: "God, self, history, and book are, thus, bound in an intricate relationship in which each mirrors the other. No single concept can be changed without altering all of the others. As a result of this thorough interdependence, the news of the death of God cannot really reach our ears until its reverberations are traced in the notions of self, history, and book. The echoes of the death of God can be heard in the disappearance of the self, the end of history, and the closure of the book" (Mark C. Taylor, *Erring: A Postmodern A/theology* [Chicago: University of Chicago Press, 1984], 7–8). Each of Taylor's categories will be considered in Part One.

29. Toulmin, *Cosmopolis*, 84.

30. Mary Hesse, *In Defense of Objectivity* (London: British Academy, 1973), 280. One may contrast Hesse's outline with Richard Bernstein's portrayal of the elements of modernity: "The idea of a basic dichotomy between the subjective and the objective; the conviction that human reason can completely free itself of bias, prejudice and tradition; the ideal of a universal method by which we can first secure firm foundations of knowledge and then build the edifice of a universal science; the belief that by the power of self-reflection we can transcend our historical context and horizon and know things as they really are" (Richard Bernstein, *Beyond Objectivism and Relativism: Science, Hermeneutics, and Praxis* [Philadelphia: University of Pennsylvania Press, 1983], 36). For useful summaries of the trends mentioned in the philosophy of science, compare William C. Placher, *Unapologetic Theology: A Christian Voice in a Pluralistic Conversation* (Louisville, Ky.: Westminster/John Knox Press, 1989), chap. 3; and Wentzel van Huyssteen, *Theology and the Justification of Faith: Constructing Theories in Systematic Theology*, trans. H. F. Snijders (Grand Rapids: Wm. B. Eerdmans Publishing Co., 1989), part 1.

31. Peter C. Hodgson, *Revisioning the Church: Ecclesial Freedom in the New Paradigm* (Minneapolis: Fortress Press, 1988), 11–19. Similar discussions are available in Douglas John Hall, *Thinking the Faith: Christian Theology in a North American Context* (Minneapolis: Augsburg Publishing House, 1989); and Hans Küng, *Theology for the Third Millennium: An Ecumenical View* (New York: Doubleday & Co., 1988).

32. I have been particularly influenced at this point by Curtis L. Thompson's discussion in his forthcoming work, *The Othering of Freedom in Love*. See also Lawrence E. Cahoone, *The Dilemma of Modernity: Philosophy, Culture and Anti-Culture* (Albany: State University of New York Press, 1988).

33. Mark Edmundson, "Prophet of a New Postmodernism," *Harper's Magazine*, December 1989, 63.

34. Toulmin, *Cosmopolis*, 177. Emphasis his.

35. Cahoone, *Dilemma of Modernity*, 193. Emphasis his. If one argues that the modern view itself represented a truncation of reason and reality, one could

argue that the changes dramatized in deconstruction actually represent more fully the self-destructive tendencies of the modern world. John B. Cobb, Jr. has made this point ("Theology in the U.S.A.: Whence and Whither," Center for Process Studies, Claremont, Calif.). Cobb also remarks that "the dominant community of physicists has moved parallel to the deconstructionist post-modernism. . . . It has taken a mathematical turn analagous to the linguistic one, and it has rejected concern for how mathematics relates to a non-mathematical reality" (p. 15). See also the distinctions ("deconstructive," "liberationist," "conservative") suggested in David Ray Griffin, William A. Beardslee, and Joe Holland, *Varieties of Postmodern Theology* (Albany: State University of New York Press, 1989).

36. Cahoone, *Dilemma of Modernity*, 71–72. Emphasis his. See, e.g., his discussion in chap. 5, "Subjectivism Without the Object: Husserl," and in chap. 6, "Subjectivism Without the Subject: Heidegger."

37. Taylor, M. C., *Erring*, 157–58. Cf. Simone de Beauvoir, *The Ethics of Ambiguity*, trans. Bernard Frechtman (New York: Philosophical Library, 1948), 14–16; and Kai Nielsen, *Ethics Without God* (London: Pemberton, 1973).

38. William Dean, *History Making History: The New Historicism in American Religious Thought* (Albany: State University of New York Press, 1988). Dean makes the point of the impossibility of any primordial escape and does so instructively in the context of American religious thought.

39. Michel Foucault, *The Order of Things: An Archaeology of the Human Sciences* (New York: Random House, 1970), 375. Emphasis his. For Jacques Derrida, see *Of Grammatology*, trans. Gayatri Charravaorty Spivak (Baltimore: Johns Hopkins University Press, 1976). I certainly do not want to suggest that there are not significant differences among the deconstructionists, but here I am simply making the point that they come together in blocking off any escape from history.

40. Richard Rorty, *Philosophy and the Mirror of Nature* (Princeton: Princeton University Press, 1979). It does not follow, I realize, that the edification must be solipsistic. See Bernstein R., *Beyond Objectivism and Relativism*, 204–5, 91, for a reading of the "incommensurability thesis" as openness rather than closure. Cf. Rorty's later book, *Contingency, Irony, and Solidarity* (Cambridge: Cambridge University Press, 1989).

41. Jay Efram and Michael D. Lukens, "The World According to Humberto Maturana," *Family Therapy Networker* 9, no. 3 (May–June 1985), 25. Chilean biologist Maturana seems to have powerful influence in some family therapy circles. Cf. Lynn Hoffman, *The Foundations of Family Therapy* (New York: Basic Books, 1981); and Paul Watzlawick, ed., *The Invented Reality: How Do We Know What We Believe We Know?* (New York: W. W. Norton & Co., 1984), for the formulation of the "constructivist" view. In "A Frog's Eye View of the World," *Networker*, May–June 1985, 32–43, Richard Simon succinctly states Maturana's theme: "Scientific observation is bound to the

biology of the observer. . . . Science is not a way of knowing a world that exists apart from us, but a particular way of living together."

42. Milan Kundera, *The Art of the Novel*, trans. Linda Asher and David Bellos (New York: Grove Press, 1988, 1986), 41.

43. Toulmin, *Cosmopolis*, 186–88.

44. Hall, *Thinking the Faith*, 198: "Our kairotic moment is nothing less than the bankruptcy of the worldview which brought us into being and sustained us for some centuries. This conception of humanity and the world has proved incapable of absorbing the negating factors which it itself helped to produce. Until we are prepared to examine critically and openly this *fundamental* failure, our concentration upon less ultimate problems will only confuse the issue and deepen the real problem." Emphasis his.

45. Cf. Cahoone, *Dilemma of Modernity*, xv.

46. See Russell Jacoby, *The Last Intellectuals: American Culture in the Age of Academe* (New York: Basic Books, 1987), for a development of this point.

47. Alasdair MacIntyre, *After Virtue: A Study in Moral Theory* (Notre Dame, Ind.: University of Notre Dame Press, 1981), 8. Cf. idem, *Whose Justice? Which Rationality?* (Notre Dame, Ind.: University of Notre Dame Press, 1988).

48. Robert Bellah, *Habits of the Heart: Individualism and Commitment in American Life* (Berkeley and Los Angeles: University of California Press, 1985), 75–76. Bellah makes clear that expressive individualism and utilitarian individualism agree in this fundamental point.

49. Karl-Otto Appel addresses this concern in "The Need for, the Apparent Difficulty, and the Eventual Possibility of a Planetary Macroethics of (for) Humankind" (Paper delivered at the Sixth East-West Philosophers' Conference, University of Hawaii, 1989): "That type of human interaction that is mediated by the world-market is steered, so to speak, by signals like prices and carried through by the communication-medium of money; hence it is an interaction at far distance by anonymous relations that leave almost no chance for a face to face meeting of human beings with moral feelings" (p. 5). Appel points out that the contemporary challenges will not be met by stressing specific role or function responsibility within a social system (as in Arnold Gehlen's philosophy of institutions) or by appeal to "quasi-instinctive dispositions of humankind" (Konrad Lorenz). See also Hans Jonas, *The Imperative of Responsibility: In Search of an Ethics for the Technological Age* (Chicago: University of Chicago Press, 1984). Richard Falk writes: "The modern circumstance is groundless in the fundamental, ultimate sense of endowing our existence with a meaning beyond our mortality. When my death means everything, the death of others means nothing. The ethos of the terrorist becomes as natural as it is detestable in such a world. And this pertains whether those relying upon terror do so with kidnappings and hijackings or with covert operations and high techology attacks on civilian targets. The revolutionary and the functionary have become mirror images in this age of terror" (Falk, "In Pursuit of the Postmodern," 4).

50. Carl E. Braaten and Robert W. Jenson, eds., *Christian Dogmatics*, 2 vols. (Philadelphia: Fortress Press, 1984), 1:xvii. Braaten and Jenson both served as editors of *dialog*. I realize that in the important matters of gender, race, class, and the like one can find very little diversity in this group. Yet the difficulty of holding together the kind of voices represented in the *Dogmatics* can be witnessed in the pages of the journal, perhaps particularly in the years following 1984. See, e.g., the papers of the Call to Faithfulness Conference at St. Olaf College, June 1990, as published in *dialog* 30 (Spring 1991).

51. Dietrich Bonhoeffer, *Ethics*, ed. Eberhard Bethge, trans. N. H. Smith from the sixth German ed. (New York: Macmillan Co., 1955; paperback ed., 1965), 195.

52. Harvey Cox might appeal to such material in making his proposal that the resources for theological renewal "will come not from the center but from the bottom and from the edge," though additional argument will be needed to link his candidates: fundamentalism and liberation theology (*Religion in the Secular City: Toward a Postmodern Theology* [New York: Simon & Schuster, 1984], 21–25, passim. See also Rebecca S. Chopp, *The Power to Speak: Feminism, Language and God* (New York: Crossroad, 1989). Chopp argues that "despite the pluralism within modern Christianity, there is, nonetheless, a fundamental accommodation of modern Christianity, as seen from the marginality of feministic discourse, to the social symbolic order."

53. See Thomas Ogletree, *Hospitality to the Stranger: Dimensions of Moral Understanding* (Philadelphia: Fortress Press, 1985). See also Keifert, *Welcoming the Stranger.*

54. This theme of unity is not unchallenged. An obvious challenge is to be found in the notion of double divine predestination. Yet even Calvin can place that affirmation in the context of divine justice. See John Calvin, *Institutes of the Christian Religion*, trans. Henry Beveridge, 2 vols. (Grand Rapids: Wm. B. Eerdmans Publishing Co., 1964) where everything is disposed and directed "to its proper end by incomprehensible wisdom" (1:176). We are not to blame God for our crimes (1:186), "for he who has fixed the boundaries of our life, has at the same time intrusted us with the care of it, provided us with the means of preserving it, forewarned us of the dangers to which we are exposed and supplied cautions and remedies, that we may not be overwhelmed unawares" (1:187). Similarly, we are to "confess that the reprobate suffer nothing which is not accordant with the most perfect justice" (2:254). Martin Luther certainly makes distinctions between God hidden and God revealed. See Brian Gerrish, "To the Unknown God: Luther and Calvin on the Hiddenness of God," *Journal of Religion* 53 (July 1973): 263–93. Yet Gerrish cites Luther as follows: "Begin from below, from the Incarnate Son. . . . Christ will bring you to the Hidden God. . . . If you take the Revealed God, he will bring you the Hidden God at the same time" (pp. 278–79). It is clear that at least the *knowledge* of the unity of God lies beyond us (see the "three lights—nature, grace, glory"—in *The Bondage of the Will*), but the believer is called to trust in this. I will discuss this issue more fully in chap. 4.

55. Steven G. Smith, *The Argument to the Other: Reason Beyond Reason in the Thought of Karl Barth and Emmanuel Levinas* (Chico, Calif.: Scholars Press, 1983), 103. Smith is discussing Levinas's *Totality and Infinity: An Essay on Exteriority*, trans. Alphonso Linguis (Pittsburgh: Duquesne University Press, 1969).

56. See the discussion of this point in Vico, Herder, Collingwood, Gadamer, and Hans Robert Jauss in Giles Gunn, *The Interpretation of Otherness: Literature, Religion and the American Imagination* (New York: Oxford University Press, 1979), chap. 4.

57. Loren Eiseley, *The Night Country* (New York: Charles Scribner's Sons, 1971), 148.

58. Wallace Stevens, *Opus Posthumous* (London: Faber & Faber, 1957), 237.

59. Victor Turner, *The Ritual Process: Structure and Anti-Structure* (Ithaca, N.Y.: Cornell University Press, 1969), 110.

60. Ogletree, *Hospitality to the Stranger*, 3.

61. Lutherans, e.g., find a number of ways to express this point. On the one hand, there is the theme that creation is "purer" than humankind, as expressed by Gustaf Wingren, *Creation and Law*, trans. Ross Mackenzie (Philadelphia: Muhlenberg Press, 1961), 101–2. In his *Credo: The Christian View of Faith and Life* (Minneapolis: Augsburg Publishing House, 1981), Wingren puts it nicely: "One could describe the whole of the Christian faith as faith in the Creator. Nothing would fall outside of that. The cross of Christ, baptism, the resurrection of the dead, would all find a place within that whole." This is Wingren's particular emphasis, though he acknowledges that the whole of Christian faith could also be understood through the second or third article (pp. 18–19). On the other hand, even of the human it is insisted by Lutherans (using Aristotelian categories), against the position of Flacius, that sin has not become human substance. See the Formula of Concord, Art. 1.

62. Bonhoeffer, *Ethics*, 201.

63. I am thinking of the motif that Mircea Eliade emphasized in his study of the religions. See Mircea Eliade, *Myths, Dreams, and Mysteries: The Encounter Between Contemporary Faiths and Archaic Realities*, trans. Philip Mairet (London: Harvill Press, 1960), 34–38, on the "escape from historical time."

64. David Ignatow, *Rescue the Dead: Poems* (Middletown, Conn.: Wesleyan University Press, 1968), epigraph.

65. I find helpful Mark Kline Taylor, *Remembering Esperanza: A Cultural-Political Theology for North American Praxis* (Maryknoll, N.Y.: Orbis Books, 1990), 68–69, for the distinction between "Christian discourse" and "extradiscursive affairs," which "pertain to the larger contexts within which Christian discourse is maintained and within which it labors."

66. See M. K. Taylor, *Remembering Esperanza*, 24ff., for a critique of "method of correlation" theologies. Edward Farley, in *Good and Evil: Interpreting a Human Condition* (Minneapolis: Fortress Press, 1990), draws richly on non-theological and theological materials. But I find it confusing that Farley tries

to reserve the theological discussion to a Part 2, following consideration in Part 1 of the nontheological.

67. David Tracy, in Moltmann, *Paradigm Change in Theology*, 462. I hope to make clear that I am not wanting to say with Tracy that "all is interpretation" (p. 463). Farley, *Good and Evil*, 1–26, does a marvelous job of arguing that our experience of the world is "to some degree sharable and communicable," so that "language cannot be reduced to the voicing of differences."

68. Placher, *Unapologetic Theology*, 12. Emphasis his. Cf. note 30 above.

69. Mark Kline Taylor has described well "the postmodern trilemma": "To acknowledge tradition, to celebrate plurality, and to resist domination—all taken together. The problem is that in attending to and developing any one of the three traits, postmodernists often find themselves unable to attend to and develop the others" (*Remembering Esperanza*, 40). I hope that the "extradiscursive" effort at excavation in Part One will set the stage for an attempt to address the dilemma in Part Two. In any case, I do not understand the voicing of particular Christian testimony in the conversation to entail what Paul Lakeland well criticizes as "premature or even preemptive recourse to scriptural evidence" (Paul Lakeland, *Theology and Critical Theory: The Discourse of the Church* [Nashville: Abingdon Press, 1990], 82).

70. Rushdie, "A Pen Against the Sword," 53.

Chapter 2. Life Within the Other

1. Loren Eiseley, *The Star Thrower* (New York: Harcourt Brace Jovanovich, 1978), 216–17. Perhaps awareness of the part/whole relationship is conveyed by the diversity of our experience of the whole. In this connection Jonathan P. Strandjord considers the "Varieties of Temporal Experience" in *Process Studies* 17, no. 1 (Spring 1988), 19–25, noting particularly the variable rate of "lived time."

2. Stephen Toulmin, *The Return to Cosmology: Postmodern Science and the Theology of Nature* (Berkeley and Los Angeles: University of California Press, 1982), 260. Emphasis his. It does not seem contradictory to speak of the modern identity crisis that develops when each individual must create her or his own symbolic home. See Peter Berger, Brigette Berger, and Hansfried Kellner, *The Homeless Mind: Modernization and Consciousness* (New York: Vintage Books, 1973).

3. Robert John Russell, "A Response to David Bohm's 'Time, the Implicate Order and Pre-Space,' " 209–18, in *Physics and the Ultimate Significance of Time*, ed. David Ray Griffin (Albany: State University of New York Press, 1986), 211. For a much-cited discussion of the three arrows of time (thermodynamic, psychological, and cosmological), see Stephen W. Hawking, *A Brief History of Time: From the Big Bang to Black Holes* (New York: Bantam Books, 1988), 145–53. Peter Coveney and Roger Highfield offer a very accessible discussion and defense of irreversibility in *The Arrow of Time* (New York: Fawcett Columbine, 1990).

4. Ilya Prigogine and I. Stengers, *Order out of Chaos* (London: William Heinemann, 1984), 285. On the quest, see Coveney and Highfield, *Arrow of Time*, chap. 8, "A Unified Vision of Time," esp. 288ff.

5. Ian G. Barbour, "Bohm and Process Philosophy: A Response to Griffin and Cobb," 167–71, in Griffin, *Physics and the Ultimate Significance of Time*, 168. Earlier in the volume Griffin cites Einstein as follows: "The non-divisibility of the four-dimensional continuum of events does not at all, however, involve the equivalence of the space co-ordinates with the time co-ordinate. On the contrary, we must remember that the time co-ordinate is defined physically wholly differently from the space co-ordinates" (p. 24), citing Albert Einstein, *The Meaning of Relativity* (Princeton: Princeton University Press, 1950). See also Barbour's first volume of Gifford Lectures, *Religion in an Age of Science* (San Francisco: Harper & Row, 1990), 108ff. Insisting (p. 110) that temporal change *does* occur in every frame of reference, Barbour speaks of "the temporalization of space" rather than "the spatialization of time." Emphasis his.

6. Cf. Smith, *Argument to the Other*, 71: "The absence of the Other is the ground of time itself, i.e. of truly new and different instants." Turning the matter the other way, through time, we reach the other.

7. Søren Kierkegaard, *Philosophical Fragments*, ed. Howard V. Hong, trans. David Swenson (Princeton: Princeton University Press, 1962), title page.

8. Odil Hannes Steck, *World and Environment* (Nashville: Abingdon Press, 1980), 94.

9. Claus Westermann, *Blessing in the Bible and the Life of the Church*, trans. Keith Crim (Philadelphia: Fortress Press, 1978).

10. Wingren, *Creation and Law*, 30: "The '*opus proprium*' of God, which is to give and which is seen most clearly in the Gospel, is already operative in Creation and is expressed in the primary fact of life."

11. Toulmin, *The Return to Cosmology*, 262–63.

12. See the warning in Coveney and Highfield, *Arrow of Time*, 207.

13. James Gleick, *Chaos: Making a New Science* (New York: Penguin Books, 1987), 5, 8, 117, 152. Compare Dr. Ary Goldberger's heart studies at Harvard of how "healthy is chaotic" in that there is need for the heart to change rhythms in response to other changes in the body, or Walter Freeman's work at Berkeley on chaos or "noise" in brain activity (*Minneapolis Star Tribune*, 16 January 1989).

14. Jeffrey S. Wicken, "Theology and Science in the Evolving Cosmos: A Need for Dialogue," 45–55, *Zygon* 23, no. 1 (March 1988): 52. Emphasis his. He adds: "Nucleic acids and proteins, for example, are relationally constituted by their functional roles in organisms, and their behaviors are regulated by those wholes. At a higher level of the organic hierarchy, the identities of organisms are relationally constituted by their ecosystemic roles." See also Jeffrey S. Wicken, *Evolution, Thermodynamics and Information: Extending the Darwinian Program* (New York: Oxford University Press, 1987).

15. Barbour, *Religion in an Age of Science*, 111–12.
16. Ted Peters, ed., *Cosmos as Creation: Theology and Science in Consonance* (Nashville: Abingdon Press, 1989), 13–14. Cf. John Polkinghorne, *One World: The Interaction of Science and Theology* (Princeton: Princeton University Press, 1986).
17. See chap. 1, note 63, above. While I greatly appreciate Matthew Fox's emphasis on creation, I sometimes hear such an Edenic motif in his writings. See Matthew Fox, *Original Blessing: A Primer in Creation Spirituality* (Santa Fe, N.M.: Bear & Co., 1983).
18. For a helpful distinction between the authoritative and the authoritarian, see Donald Evans, *The Logic of Self-Involvement* (London: SCM Press, 1963), 170–73.
19. One thinks of strong tendencies in various forms of Eastern religious thought (though assorted Western pietisms might serve as subtler illustrations). Paul Varo Martinson offers this summary statement: "In Confucian and Taoist concepts of time we seem to have something akin to an endless series of replicating moments; the destiny of actual life is to replicate at this moment in time and space the natural rhythms of primordial reality (Taoism), or the moral rhythms of social reality (Confucianism). Buddhism, in turn, tends to radicalize and absolutize the moment. No longer is there a meaningful past/ present/future movement, for the present absorbs past and future into its own infinity" (Martinson, *A Theology of World Religions: Interpreting God, Self, and World in Semitic, Indian, and Chinese Thought* [Minneapolis: Augsburg Publishing House, 1987], 176–77). Similarly, to speak of the mutual interfusion of past, present, and future seems to yield this result. See Fritjof Capra's much-cited *The Tao of Physics: An Exploration of the Parallels Between Modern Physics and Eastern Mysticism* (Berkeley: Shambhala Publications, 1975). David Griffin, citing the writing of Ryusei Takeda, adds an important qualification: "This idea that the future is as influential upon the present as is the past stands in strong tension with the idea of karma, which pervades all Buddhist thought, according to which the causal influences upon one arise from the past, but that one can so act in the present as to become liberated from bad karmic influences" (Griffin, *Physics and the Ultimate Significance of Time*, 30). Similarly, for an extremely rich illustration of how mythic structures can be employed to dramatize temporal discontinuities, see Lawrence E. Sullivan, *Icanchu's Drum: An Orientation to Meaning in South American Religions* (New York: Macmillan Co., 1988), chaps. 2, 4, 8, and 9.
20. Ian G. Barbour, "Creation and Cosmology," 115–51, in Peters, *Cosmos as Creation*, 131. See also Robert John Russell's intriguing reflection concerning the seven theoretical models permitted by general relativity with respect to the kind of infinities assigned to past, future, and the size of the universe. He comments: "Interestingly, though one can have a homogeneously finite model, no *homogeneously infinite* model, such as Fred Hoyle's steady-state, . . . is possible in standard general relativity!" ("Cosmology, Creation,

and Contingency," 177–209, in Peters, *Cosmos as Creation*, 190–91). Emphasis his.
21. Julian Huxley, *Religion Without Revelation* (New York: Harper Mentor Book, 1957), 189.
22. Richard Eugene Wentz, *The Contemplation of Otherness: The Critical Vision of Religion* (Macon, Ga.: Mercer University Press, 1984), chap. 2.
23. See the discussion of Robert Frost's poem in Gunn, *The Interpretation of Otherness*, 195–98.
24. Philip Hefner, "The Evolution of the Created Co-Creator," 211–34, in Peters, *Cosmos as Creation*, 221. Eiseley's discussion of "the strangeness in the proportion" is in chap. 9 of *The Night Country*, 129.
25. C. F. von Weizsäcker, *The History of Nature*, trans. Fred D. Wieck (Chicago: University of Chicago Press, 1949). It is important as well to recognize the more nuanced distinction that von Weizsäcker introduces: "Nature undergoes history, but she does not experience it. She is history but does not have history, because she does not know that she is history. And why does man alone have a conscious, experienced history? Because he alone has consciousness and experience. And so it does seem to me meaningful after all to see man's distinction not in his historic existence as such, but in his awareness of his historic existence." See Douglas John Hall's discussion of this distinction in *Imaging God: Dominion as Stewardship* (Grand Rapids: Wm B. Eerdmans Publishing Co., 1986), 181–83. See Barbour's illuminating discussion of the differences in the medieval, Newtonian, and twentieth-century worldviews in *Religion in an Age of Science*, 218–21.
26. Arthur Peacocke, *God and the New Biology* (San Francisco: Harper & Row, 1986), 53. He offers this summary: "The continuities of biological evolution extend now to the molecular domain, where increasingly the principles that govern the emergence of self-reproducing macromolecular systems are now well understood both kinetically (Eigen and colleagues at Göttingen) and thermodynamically (Prigogine and colleagues at Brussels)." It would be important to add that continuity does not entail uniformity. "Punctuationist" theorists emphasize that the bursts in species change and the fact that new species form from only a small part of the old species accounts for "gaps" in that it is unlikely that a detailed picture of the changes would be preserved in fossils. Stephen Jay Gould of Harvard has described the life of the earth as "like the life of a soldier . . . long periods of boredom and short periods of terror." On the criticism of the "gradualist" stress on small variation and slow change, see Brian Leith, *The Descent of Darwin* (London: Collins, 1982).
27. Cf. Errol E. Harris, *The Foundations of Metaphysics in Science* (New York: Humanities Press, 1965), 462: "If there is no difference whatever between the parts, they must be indistinguishable; and if altogether indistinguishable, identical, and if identical then not spread out and continuous. There can be no continuum without extension of some sort, and there can be no extension without distinction of parts."

28. Jürgen Moltmann, *God in Creation: A New Theology of Creation and the Spirit of God*, trans. Margaret Kohl (San Francisco: Harper & Row, 1985), 51. Feminist thinkers have been particularly active in pointing out the subjectivity and social enmeshment hidden behind the "objectivity" of scientific method and ethos. Thus Sandra Harding takes aim at what is touted as the "hardest" of the sciences in "Why Physics Is a Bad Model for Physics" (Paper presented at the 1989 Nobel Conference at Gustavus Adolphus College, St. Peter, Minn. [publication forthcoming]). See also the collection *Sex and Scientific Inquiry*, ed. S. Harding and J. O'Barr (Chicago: University of Chicago Press, 1987).

29. Helmut Peukert, *Science, Action and Fundamental Theology: Toward a Theology of Communicative Action*, trans. James Bohman (Cambridge: MIT Press, 1984), xviii. Peukert traces the same line of development in the social sciences in chap. 5. A more dramatic statement is Douglas R. Hofstadter, *Gödel, Escher, Bach: An Eternal Golden Braid* (New York: Basic Books, 1979). Cf. Polkinghorne, *One World*, 25.

30. Peacocke, *God and the New Biology*, 160. Emphasis his.

31. Jeffrey S. Wicken, "The Evolutionary Ecology of Meaning" (Paper presented at the Pannenberg Conference at the Lutheran School of Theology at Chicago, November 1989 [publication forthcoming]), 58. Cf. p. 60 and the discussion in Peacocke, *God and the New Biology*, 142.

32. Peacocke, *God and the New Biology*, 60. John B. Cobb, Jr., and David Ray Griffin, eds., *Mind in Nature: Essays on the Interface of Science and Philosophy* (Pittsburgh and Washington, D.C.: University Press of America, 1978), offers a valuable discussion of this relationship in the terms of process thought. Cf. Cobb's concluding comment: "Reductionism may be countered either by stressing that complex wholes are more than their parts or by showing that the ultimate parts themselves have characteristics of value and subjectivity that are usually denied them. Whitehead is rightly claimed for both of these strategies" (p. 147). Along the second line of response Griffin writes in *God and Religion in the Postmodern World* (Albany: State University of New York Press, 1989), 88: "Developments in physics have led to a world of energetic events which seem to be self-moving and to behave in unpredictable ways. And recent studies in biology seem to demonstrate that bacteria and macromolecules have elemental forms of perception, memory, choice and self-motion." Process thinkers distinguish between wholes in which a new higher-level entity emerges and those in which this does not occur. See the discussion between David Ray Griffin in *Zygon* 23, no. 1 (March 1988): 57–81, and Ian S. Barbour, "On Two Issues in Science and Religion: A Response to David Griffin" (pp. 83–88).

33. Peacocke, *God and the New Biology*, 53. Bill McKibben, in his dramatic account *The End of Nature* (New York: Random House, 1989), notes that "nature, we believe, takes forever" but that "this idea about time is essentially mistaken" (p. 3), since in a few short decades "irrevocable" damage has

been done (p. 45). This nicely makes the point that nature itself participates in the variability of time and should leave open the possibility that one could decide to work freshly with what nature can now be. See Paul Santmire's distinctions between wild nature, cultivated nature, and fabricated nature in "The Future of the Cosmos and the Renewal of the Church's Life with Nature," in Peters, *Cosmos as Creation*, 265–82.

34. H. Paul Santmire, *The Travail of Nature: The Ambiguous Ecological Promise of Christian Theology* (Philadelphia: Fortress Press, 1985). Emphasis mine.

35. See Bruce C. Birch and Larry L. Rasmussen, *The Predicament of the Prosperous* (Philadelphia: Westminster Press, 1978). Cf. Hall, *Imaging God*, 167–74.

36. See Jürgen Moltmann's discussion in "Reconciliation with Nature," in *Word and World* 11, no. 2 (Spring 1991): 117–23, esp. 121.

37. James Limburg makes this point well in speaking of the account in Genesis 1 in "The Responsibility of Royalty: Genesis 1-11 and the Care of the Earth," *Word and World* 11, no. 2 (Spring 1991): 124–30: "The name given to the human species in this first creation account immediately links that species to the earth. The Hebrew *adam*, translated 'humankind,' is a play on *adamah*, the word for ground (see also 2:7). This linkage could be expressed with Latin derivatives by saying that humans are made from humus. Or, with Anglo-Saxon vocabulary, earthlings are made of earth" (p. 125). This issue on "The Environment" contains several valuable articles.

38. See Lynn White's very influential article, "The Historical Roots of Our Ecologic Crisis," *Science* 155 (1967), 1203–7.

39. Steck, *World and Environment*, 105.

40. Hall, *Imaging God*. See particularly chap. 6, "Being-with-Nature."

41. Santmire, *Travail of Nature*, 16ff.

42. See, e.g., Daniel O'Connor and Francis Oakley, *Creation: The Impact of an Idea* (New York: Charles Scribner's Sons, 1969).

43. Moltmann, "Reconciliation with Nature," 119–20, develops the connection of Christ with the wisdom tradition, citing the *Gospel of Thomas* (Logion 77), where there is this unknown saying of Jesus: "I am the light which is over everything. I am the All: the All came forth from me and the All has reached to me. Split the wood; I am there. Lift up the stone, and you will find me there." In the same issue of *Word and World*, see also Vitor Westhelle's development of the mystical tradition's "comprehension of nature as the expression of divine mystery" in "The Weeping Mask: Ecological Crisis and the View of Nature," 137–46. Westhelle notes here "new possibilities for the representation of God" and appeals to Luther for whom "God is not to be sought as the invisible reality *behind* creation and then defined by the arguments of reason. But God is *in* creation without being creation" (p. 145). Emphasis his.

44. Peri Rasolondraibe, in "Environmental Concern and Economic Justice," *Word and World* 11, no. 2 (Spring 1991): 147–55, extends the image of mutually

"shared otherness" of the economic Trinity to the community of life found in the lichen formed by symbiotic relationship between fungi and algae. Thomas Berry has been among the most forceful in arguing that the emphasis on a transcendent, personal, monotheistic deity has encouraged Christians to reduce nature to an object. He is concerned not merely to stress divine immanence but to regard the world as a subject. Thus the third of his "twelve principles" is: "From its beginning the universe is a psychic as well as a physical reality." See Berry's summation and the critical discussion in Anne Lonergan and Caroline Richards, eds., *Thomas Berry and the New Cosmology* (Mystic, Conn.: Twenty-Third Publications, 1987), 15–18, 107–8. In chap. 4, I will consider this matter of a revised notion of transcendence, as that bears on the other boundaries of human being and becoming.

45. Santmire, *Travail of Nature*, 7–8, discusses the "rising acosmic spirit." "Channeling" and "reincarnation" motifs seem, at least in the Western context, to be highly dramatic expressions of a much wider phenomenon.

46. Drawing on Romans and on 1 Corinthians 15, Santmire, *Travail of Nature*, 202–3, offers an ecological reading of Paul, but is more skeptical about John: "John represents a tradition that was predicated on a vision of Christ and the community of Christ first and foremost and . . . John has very little positive regard for human history in general or for the biophysical world as such" (p. 213).

47. E. O. Wilson, in *On Human Nature* (Cambridge: Harvard University Press, 1978), 195, offers the opinion that, in time, mind will be "explained as an epiphenomenon of the neuronal machinery of the brain." Most of the attention of the animal rights activists seems to have been directed to fur trapping and fur ranching, but the first area selected for questioning in the 1989 survey of the American Society for the Prevention of Cruelty to Animals was lab testing, and the questions were introduced by a paragraph that made mention of "such horrifying practices as experimenting on live puppies, deliberately drowning cats with salt water, and dissecting animals while they were still alive." While the public display of passion in this area can be an important resource, it does not guarantee the presence of the careful reflection essential in thinking through the bearing of the distinction and connection characterizing the relationships between human beings and the (other) animals.

48. I am thinking, of course, of the Gaia hypothesis of James Lovelock. His idea, that the earth is a living organism, received a formal hearing by the scientific establishment as the subject of the Chapman Conference, sponsored by the American Geophysical Union in 1988. Cf. Peter Russell, *The Global Brain: Speculations on the Evolutionary Leap to Planetary Consciousness* (Los Angeles: J. P. Tarcher, 1983). On the effort to preserve distinction, see Rosemary Radford Ruether, *Gaia and God: An Ecofeminist Theology of Earth Healing* (San Francisco: HarperCollins, 1992).

49. Persons working in different disciplines converge at this point. Note, e.g., Jeffrey Wicken's concern for the "*interior* dimension" in "Theology and

Science" (p. 55, emphasis his), and, from the other "direction," the work of the psychologist Mihaly Csikszentmihalyi in "Consciousness for the 21st Century," *Zygon* 26, no. 1 (March 1991): 7–25. Csikszentmihalyi, in *Flow: The Psychology of Optimal Experience* (New York: Harper & Row, 1990), moves beyond focus on chemical ingredients or neural writing to the process of "taking control of the body" so that entropy can yield to harmony in consciousness, "flow."

50. Alfred North Whitehead, *Modes of Thought* (New York: Macmillan Co., 1938, 1966), 114. Cf. his remark in *Process and Reality: An Essay in Cosmology*, ed. David Ray Griffin and Donald W. Sherburne (New York: Free Press, 1929, 1957, 1978), 170: "A traveller, who has lost his way, should not ask, Where am I? What he really wants to know is, Where are the other places? He has got his own body, but he has lost them." Rita Nakashima Brock's *Journeys by Heart: A Christology of Erotic Power* (New York: Crossroad, 1988) is a recent effort, influenced by Whitehead, to reclaim the body.

51. I am thinking, for example, of the controversial work of Dr. David Comings of the City of Hope National Medical Center arguing that a long list of behavioral disorders can be found to occur with unusually high frequency in the relatives of people with Tourette syndrome.

52. Robert Plomin, J. C. DeFries, and G. E. McClearn, *Behavioral Genetics: A Primer* (San Francisco: W. H. Freeman, 1980), 8.

53. See the report "Personality Similarity in Twins Reared Apart and Together" by Auke Tellegen and other members of the Twins Studies at the University of Minnesota in *Journal of Personality and Social Psychology* 54, no. 6 (1988): 1031–39.

54. The researchers conclude that genes permeate all these behavioral domains and that environmental influences account for less than 50 percent of the behavior studied.

55. See the criticism in Alfie Kohn, *The Brighter Side of Human Nature: Altruism and Empathy in Everyday Life* (New York: Basic Books, 1990), 10, 29–32.

56. Plomin, DeFries, and McClearn, *Behavioral Genetics*, 9.

57. See Griffin, *God and Religion in the Postmodern World*, 80. While granting that the evidence is controversial, Griffin cites, among others, E. J. Steele, *Somatic Selection and Adaptive Evolution: On the Inheritance of Acquired Characters* (Chicago: University of Chicago Press, 1981), 95–96. Barbour, in *Religion in an Age of Science*, discusses Stuart Kaufman's work on the ways in which protein affects genes (p. 160). It would be important to point out that such instances of "downward" causation do not represent "backward" causation.

58. Willis W. Harman, "The Post-Modern Heresy: Portents of a Fundamental Shift in Worldview" (Paper prepared for the Conference on a Post-Modern World, Santa Barbara, Calif., January 1986), 12.

59. See Philip Hefner, "Sociobiology, Ethics, and Theology," *Zygon* 19, no. 2 (June 1984): 185–207. Cf. Barbour, *Religion in an Age of Science*, 192–94, for the challenge to Wilson to consider both biological and cultural evolution.

60. Oliver Sacks, *The Man Who Mistook His Wife for a Hat and Other Clinical Tales* (New York: Harper & Row, 1987), 39. Sack's reference to art brings to mind the remark of Claude Monet: "The motif is insignificant for me; what I want to reproduce is what lies *between* the motif and me" (Catalog for the Impressionism exhibition [Toledo Museum of Art, 1989], 8). Emphasis mine.

61. See note 32 above.

62. Peacocke, *God and the New Biology*, 52. Emphasis his.

63. See John B. Cobb, Jr., *The Structure of Christian Existence* (Philadelphia: Westminster Press, 1967), for a discussion of this transition. James M. Gustafson, *Ethics from a Theocentric Perspective*, 2 vols. (Chicago: University of Chicago Press, 1981, 1984), 1:270, suggests a distinction between animal purpose and human intent.

64. Peter Singer, quoted in Jeremy Igger, "Ethical Basis for Eating Meat Elusive," *Minneapolis Star Tribune*, 6 March 1990. Accordingly, Singer bases his critique of eating meat on a different comparison: that it entails "sacrificing the major interests of those animals for what is really a minor interest of our own—the pleasures of our palate."

65. Wicken, "Theology and Science," 49.

66. Csikszentmihalyi, "Consciousness for the 21st Century," 9.

67. Roger Sperry, "Science Values and Survival," *Journal of Humanistic Psychology* 26 (Spring 1986): 21. Cf. Sacks, *The Man Who Mistook His Wife for a Hat*, 20: "Whether in a philosophic sense (Kant's sense), or an empirical and evolutionary sense, judgment is the most important faculty we have."

68. Sacks, *The Man Who Mistook His Wife for a Hat*, 20. Emphasis his. It seems important to connect this point with Sacks's strong emphasis on understanding the world not as concepts but "as concreteness, *as symbols*" (p. 177). Emphasis his.

69. Søren Kierkegaard, *The Sickness Unto Death: A Christian Psychological Exposition for Upbuilding and Awakening*, ed. and trans. Howard V. Hong and Edna H. Hong (Princeton: Princeton University Press, 1980), 13. Compare, from a very different philosophical perspective, Rita Nakashima Brock's use of the term "heart," "the union of the physical, emotional, and spiritual" *(Journeys by Heart*, xiv and passim).

70. Roger Sperry, *Science and Moral Priority: Merging Mind, Brain, and Human Values* (New York: Columbia University Press, 1983), 92, puts the matter in this way: "The mental forces do not violate, disturb, or intervene in neuronal activity but they do supervene. Interaction is mutually reciprocal between the neural and mental levels in the nested brain hierarchies. Multilevel and interlevel causation is emphasized in addition to the one-level sequential causation more traditionally dealt with."

71. N. W. Porteus, "Man, Nature of, in the OT," *The Interpreter's Dictionary of the Bible* (New York: Abingdon Press, 1962), 3:243.

72. Frank Bottomley, *Attitudes to the Body in Western Christendom* (London: Lepus Books, 1979), 159–60. Cf. James B. Nelson, *Embodiment: An Approach to Sexuality and Christian Theology* (Minneapolis: Augsburg Publishing House, 1978), chap. 3 on "the dualistic nemesis."

73. See Derrick Sherwin Bailey, *Sexual Relation in Christian Thought* (New York: Harper & Brothers, 1959); and Peter Brown, *The Body and Society: Men, Women and Sexual Renunciation in Early Christianity* (New York: Columbia University Press, 1990).

74. See Bottomley, *Attitudes to the Body*, chap. 12.

75. But see note 44 above.

76. Moltmann, *God in Creation*, 219–20.

77. Claus Westermann, *Creation*, trans. John J. Scullion (Philadelphia: Fortress Press, 1974), 56.

78. Philip Hefner, in Peters, *Cosmos as Creation*, 228–29.

79. Hall, *Imaging God*, 106–7. Hall nicely makes the point (p. 100) that if a substantialist concept of the image is substituted, the Reformers' talk of the image being "lost" "sounds like an absurdity."

80. Hall, *Imaging God*, 178.

81. For a fuller discussion of this formulation, see my locus on "Sin and Evil" in Braaten and Jenson, *Christian Dogmatics*, 1:391–99.

82. See, e.g., Margaret R. Miles, *Carnal Knowing: Female Nakedness and Religious Meaning in the Christian West* (Boston: Beacon Press, 1987), 167–68; Carolyn Merchant, *The Death of Nature: Women, Ecology, and the Scientific Revolution* (San Francisco: Harper & Row, 1980); and Cornel West, *The American Evasion of Philosophy: A Genealogy of Pragmatism* (Madison: University of Wisconsin Press, 1989), 37. This connection is a theme occupying the attention of the very diverse authors in the "ecofeminist" movement. See Leonie Caldecott and Stephanie Leland, eds., *Reclaim the Earth: Women Speak Out for Life on Earth* (London: Women's Press, 1983); and Ynestra King, *What is Ecofeminism?* (New York: Ecofeminist Resources, 1989). Mark Kline Taylor suggests that a "hetero-realist" alienation from one's own body on the part of a man can be articulated in relation to the matrophobic impulse as "a denial of his own body as good in itself, as good outside of dominative, largely genitalized relationships with women." See M. K. Taylor, *Remembering Experanza*, 120.

83. Csikszentmihalyi, "Consciousness for the 21st Century," 24.

84. Lindon J. Eaves, "Content and Method in Science and Religion: A Geneticist's Perspective," *Zygon* 24, no. 2 (June 1989), 217–53, 246.

Chapter 3. Life with the Other

1. Edward Farley, in his comprehensive study *Good and Evil*, distinguishes three spheres: agency, the interhuman, and the social. Farley argues that "the interhuman is primary to both agents and the social because it is the sphere that engenders the criterion, the face (Emmanuel Levinas), for the workings of the other spheres" (p. 29). Discussion of "the face" follows in the body of this chapter.

2. Farley, *Good and Evil*, 35.

3. Levinas, *Totality and Infinity*, 251. Levinas makes the point of inequality (and therewith, I take it, secures the otherness) one way or the other. Thus he writes: "The Other qua Other is situated in a dimension of height and of abasement—glorious abasement; he has the face of the poor, the stranger, the widow, and the orphan, and, at the same time, of the master called to invest and justify my freedom."

4. See the discussion in Smith, *Argument to the Other*, 169. Smith notes that Levinas uses the analogy of Moses for whom God is revealed as having already "passed by" (Exodus 33).

5. Levinas, *Totality and Infinity*, 39. Emphasis his. Thus thought is not competent to comprehend the other within the totality of a system; proceeding by negation, thought witnesses to the infinity of the other (pp. 93, 108).

6. Levinas finds death and eros both testifying to the plurality of existence in that, through them, otherness enters a person's life. See Smith, *Argument to the Other*, 70–71.

7. As cited in Smith, *Argument to the Other*, 74. Emphasis his.

8. Moltmann, *God in Creation*, 221. Emphasis his. Moltmann's next point in discussing the image of God is sexual differentiation and community, which is understood to imply that "likeness to God cannot be lived in isolation. It can be lived only in human community" (p. 222). Levinas helps us see that the meaning of "face" has a comparably communal dimension.

9. Moltmann, *God in Creation*, 221–22. Emphasis his.

10. Turner, *Ritual Process*, 83. Emphasis his.

11. Wentz, *The Contemplation of Otherness*, 34. Cf. Michael Theunissen, *The Other: Studies in the Social Ontology of Husserl, Heidegger, Sartre, and Buber*, trans. Christopher Macann (Cambridge: MIT Press, 1984), 326. Cf. Farley, *Good and Evil*, chap. 2, on how "the social" does not collapse into the interhuman.

12. See especially M. K. Taylor, *Remembering Esperanza*, 115–21. See also Miles, *Carnal Knowing*, for example, on the strikingly different ways in which we in the West have symbolized female and male nakedness. See also Smith, *Argument to the Other*, 172. Rosemary Radford Ruether, in *Sexism and God-Talk: Toward a Feminist Theology* (Boston: Beacon Press, 1983), 111ff., warns: "There is no valid biological basis for labeling certain psychic capacities, such as reason, 'masculine' and others, such as intuition, 'feminine.' To put it bluntly, there is no biological connection between male gonads and the capacity to reason. Likewise, there is no biological connection between female sexual organs and the capacity to be intuitive, caring, or nurturing." Yet Ruether does grant a "possible biological basis" for gender differences with respect to identification with and integration of right- and left-brain characteristics. For a range of views here, see Anne Carr, "Theological Anthropology and the Experience of Women," *Chicago Studies* 19 (Spring 1980): 113–28. It would seem that the tendency to absolutize the representative could lead to a denial that sufficient difference exists within, say, either gender to make same gender relationships significant.

13. Farley, *Good and Evil*, 45; cf. 125, 233.
14. Habermas, *The Theory of Communicative Action*, 1:50–51, puts the point in this way: "Thus a linguistically constituted worldview can be identified with the world order itself to such an extent that it cannot be perceived *as* an interpretation of the world that is subject to error and open to criticism. In this respect the confusion of nature and culture takes on the significance of a reification of worldview. . . . As a result the concept of world is dogmatically invested with a specific content that is withdrawn from rational discussion and thus from criticism." Emphasis his. I am indebted to Curtis Thompson for this reference. Miles, *Carnal Knowing*, pp. 9–10, pushes the point of the social location of our knowing very far indeed, citing claims that "the very structure of our minds" (Rom Harre) and "our biology—bones, muscles, sense organs, nerves, brain, lungs, circulation, everything" (Ruth Hubbard)— must be understood to be so affected. I am arguing for a process of reciprocal influence.
15. Theunissen, *The Other*, 286. In his remarkable study Theunissen considers other "dialogical" thinkers such as Rosenzweig and Rosenstock-Hussey. But in these other figures, as in Buber, he finds a "positive categorial elucidation of the I-Thou relationship" only "in a piecemeal fashion" (p. 290).
16. Theunissen, *The Other*, 311. Theunissen does note that for Buber "I and Thou are not imbedded in a totality and, so to speak, neutralized with respect to it" (p. 277). In Levinas's thought, "the temporal dialectic is the dialectic of sociality" in that "temporality, the advent of an *other* instant really other than the present instant (not the extrapolation of the present that thought inevitably posits), can only be produced in relation with an Other" (Smith, *Argument to the Other*, 69).
17. See pp. 40–49 above. To say that the "within" is mysterious is not to claim that it is impenetrable. Already at the microscopic level Bell's theorem suggests a significant relatedness between contemporaries. See Henry P. Stapp, "Einstein Time and Process Time," 264–70, in Griffin, *Physics and the Ultimate Significance of Time*.
18. Søren Kierkegaard, *Either/Or*, trans. David F. Swenson, Lillian M. Swenson, and Walter Lowrie, 2 vols. (Princeton: Princeton University Press, 1944), 1:3. Kierkegaard continued to write, believing that "the misdirection of speculation . . . must not be something accidental, but must lie far deeper in the whole tendency of the time—it must indeed lie in the fact that one had with such great knowledge altogether forgotten what it is to *exist* and what *inwardness* means" (Kierkegaard, *Concluding Unscientific Postscript to the Philosophical Fragments*, trans. David F. Swenson and Walter Lowrie [Princeton: Princeton University Press, 1944], 216). Emphasis his.
19. For a discussion of "privileged access," see Peter Geach, *Mental Acts, Their Content and Their Objects* (London: Routledge & Kegan Paul, 1956).
20. Kierkegaard, *Either/Or*, 2:147.
21. Peukert, *Science, Action and Fundamental Theology*, could be said to be a multi-disciplinary book-length statement of this point.

22. David Kolb, *The Critique of Pure Modernity: Hegel, Heidegger, and After* (Chicago: University of Chicago Press, 1986), 2. One might find the correction that Kolb is calling for in the movement from Kierkegaard's pseudonym Johannes Climacus, who can speak of "the other" as "possibility" (*Postscript*, part 2, chaps. 2 and 3), to Anti-Climacus in *The Sickness Unto Death*, passim, where "the other" contributes to the necessity that meets possibility in freedom.

23. D. W. Winnicott, *Home Is Where We Start From: Essays by a Psychoanalyst* (New York: W. W. Norton & Co., 1986). On Winnicott's understanding of the child's development of a sense of continuity in time, "the fourth dimension in integration," see Madeleine Davis and David Wallbridge, *Boundary and Space: An Introduction to the Work of D. W. Winnicott* (London: Karnac, 1981), 178–80.

24. Davis and Wallbridge, *Boundary and Space*, 63–64. See also the discussion in Catherine Keller, *From a Broken Web: Separation, Sexism, and Self* (Boston: Beacon Press, 1986), 143–45; and Jessica Benjamin, *Bonds of Love: Psychoanalysis, Feminism, and the Problem of Domination* (New York: Pantheon Books, 1988). I think again of Monet's remark (chap. 2, note 60, above) that "the motif is insignificant for me; what I want to reproduce is what lies between the motif and me."

25. D. W. Winnicott, *Collected Papers: Through Paediatrics to Psycho-Analysis* (New York: Basic Books, 1975), 149ff.

26. Winnicott, *Collected Papers*, 212.

27. Winnicott, *Collected Papers*, 245. Emphasis his.

28. Winnicott, *Collected Papers*, 90.

29. Winnicott, *Collected Papers*.

30. This continuity seems best recognized in the "traducianist" view as summarized by Heinrich Schmid, *Doctrinal Theology of the Evangelical Lutheran Church*, trans. Charles A. Hay and Henry E. Jacobs (Philadelphia: Lutheran Publication Society, 1875, 1889, 1899), 3d ed., 166ff. To the question "whether human souls are created daily by God" (the "creationist" view), it is held that, the first human pair aside, human souls "are created, not daily, nor begotten of their parents as the body or souls of brutes, but, *by virtue of the divine blessing, are propagated, per traducem, by their parents.*" Emphasis his. In support of this view Schmid cites many Scripture passages, including Gen. 5:3, as well as the fact that "if it be affirmed that souls are created immediately by God . . . it follows that man does not beget an entire man." While one may pause over Schmid's qualifying remarks, this emphasis seems essentially sound. Within Christendom it is denied not only obviously by "creationist" views but implicitly by views that seek such a "high" view of infant baptism that they virtually sever the unbaptized infant's relationship with God. For a more balanced view, see Margaret Hammer, "Birthing: Perspectives for Theology and Ministry," *Word and World* 4, no. 4 (Fall 1984): 391–400. G. C. Berkouwer's *Man: The Image of God* (Grand Rapids: Wm.

B. Eerdman's Publishing Co., 1962) is a Reformed statement seeking to move beyond the dichotomy of creationism and traducianism. But he is concerned that theological reflection retains "the function of the creationist motif" "as a warning against every sort of secularizing of the question of origins, as a protest against the denigration of the mystery of man's nature, of each individual man's nature" (p. 305).

31. Wolfhart Pannenberg, *Anthropology in Theological Perspective*, trans. Matthew J. O'Connell (Philadelphia: Westminster Press, 1985), 227. Emphasis mine.

32. Pannenberg consistently speaks of God as "the power that determines all experienced reality." See, e.g., Pannenberg, *Anthropology in Theological Perspective*, 280, where he also asserts that "the various claims made regarding God and the gods must be judged by whether and to what extent they illuminate our understanding of experienced reality." Winnicott emphasizes that in the healthy pattern of child development "the fusion allows of experience *apart from the action of opposition* (reaction to frustration)." In the unhealthy patterns where such experience is absent fusion occurs "through the 'erotization' of aggressive elements. Here is the root of compulsive sadistic trends, which can turn round into masochism." See Winnicott, *Collected Papers*, 212–13. Emphasis his. See also Davis and Wallbridge, *Boundary and Space*, 43, where Winnicott stresses that "the ego *initiates* object relating": "With good-enough mothering at the beginning the baby is not subjected to instinctual gratifications except in so far as there is ego-participation. In this respect it is not so much a question of giving the baby satisfaction as of letting the baby find and come to terms with the object."

33. Pannenberg, *Anthropology in Theological Perspective*, 39.

34. Pannenberg, *Anthropology in Theological Perspective*, 62. Emphasis his. As to the matter of "the distinction from other objects," Mary Wallum has pointed out to me that this cannot be taken to mean that a cat cannot tell the difference between a bird in a tree and the tree itself. Whatever discontinuity is to be affirmed, the reality of continuity cannot be dismissed.

35. Pannenberg, *Anthropology in Theological Perspective*, 188–89, 223–24. Moving beyond the individual development of the infant, one is reminded of how family systems theorists, following Gregory Bateson, speak of "feedback stabilizing." See, e.g., Bradford P. Keeney, *Mind and Therapy* (New York: Basic Books, 1985), 44–51; and his article (with Jeffrey M. Ross), "The Dance of Duality," 47–50, in *Family Therapy Networker* 9, no. 3 (May–June, 1985), on the "recursive complementarity of feedback": "Feedback is a method of *stabilizing* a system by recycling into it the *changes* of its past performance." Emphasis his.

36. Winnicott, *Home Is Where We Start From*, 46.

37. See Pannenberg's very rich discussion in *Anthropology in Theological Perspective*, chap. 7.

38. Douglas John Hall speaks of this creaturely condition (as of the experience of limits, temptation, and anxiety) in *God and Human Suffering: An Exercise*

in the Theology of the Cross (Minneapolis: Augsburg Publishing House, 1986), 53–62.

39. See Moltmann's discussion of this point, *God in Creation*, 188. Phyllis Trible, *God and the Rhetoric of Sexuality* (Philadelphia: Fortress Press, 1978), 90ff., suggests that "companion" might be a better translation of *ezer*. For another suggestion, "a power equal to man," see R. David Freedman, "Women, A Power Equal to Man," *Biblical Archaeology Review* 9, no. 1 (January/February 1983): 56–58. I have this reference from Mary Knutsen, who points out that in the imagery of this text it is the male figure who requires the "help" and the female figure who provides it. Margaret Miles points out that in the classical Western Christian tradition, Eve may indeed have been "built by God," but she is "designed and 'built' for procreation, limited in rationality and dangerous to men" (Miles, *Carnal Knowing*, 97; cf. her discussion, 116, 167, of domination). Pannenberg, *Anthropology in Theological Perspective*, 76, connects this exocentric character with the "dominion" theme: "Precisely because human beings reach beyond the given, and therefore ultimately because human exocentricity is characterized by an impulse, inconceivable except in religious terms, to the unconditioned do they have the ability to rule over the objects of their natural world."

40. See David Little, "Calvin and the Prospects for a Christian Theory of Natural Law," 175–98, in *Norm and Context in Christian Ethics*, ed. Gene H. Outka and Paul Ramsey (New York: Charles Scribner's Sons, 1968), for a remarkable discussion (drawing particularly on the work of anthropologist Clyde Kluckhohn, though many other field studies are cited as well) of "cross-cultural 'ethical universals' that are now widely recognized to exist in all societies . . . as simply *a specification and elaboration of the conditions for social cooperation*" (p. 189, emphasis his).

41. Farley, *Good and Evil*, 40.

42. Garrison Keillor, *Happy to Be Here* (New York: Penguin Books, 1983), 88. Emphasis his.

43. Csikszentmihalyi, *Flow: The Psychology of Optimal Experience*, 6, 18.

44. Thus Robert Solomon, *The Passions* (Garden City, N.Y.: Doubleday & Co., Anchor Books, 1976), 279, writes: "Our mythologies synthesize our views as emotional judgments into a coherent dramatic framework, organizing the dull facts of the world into the excitement of personal involvement and meaningfulness." Solomon is not willing to speak of us as merely "suffering" our emotions (p. 428), for: "Subjectivity without objectivity is blind; objectivity without subjectivity is meaningless. The first is madness, the second meaningless" (pp. 64–65). See Farley, *Good and Evil*, chap. 5, on the "elemental passions of personal being." On the role of the body in this, see Moltmann, *God in Creation*, 188ff.

45. Keller, *From a Broken Web*, 136. Emphasis hers. In her major study, Keller draws heavily (though not uncritically) on process metaphysics. Her teacher, John B. Cobb, Jr., has done so as well and has remarked concerning the way

in which this self concept moves toward Buddhist thought. See John B. Cobb, Jr., *Christ in a Pluralistic Age* (Philadelphia: Westminster Press, 1975), chap. 13, "The Perfection of Love."

46. William James, in *The Principles of Psychology* (New York: Henry Holt & Co., 1890), 2:28, emphasized that impressions fall "simultaneously on a mind *which has not yet experienced them separately*." Emphasis his. See the discussion of James's views in Keller, *From a Broken Web*, 177–79. In writing of this matter, I have the benefit of an unpublished paper by Ann Klein of Rice University on "Autonomy and Relatedness" (American Academy of Religion meeting in Anaheim, Calif., November 19, 1989).

47. See Thomas Moore, ed., *A Blue Fire: Selected Writings of James Hillman* (New York: Harper & Row, 1989).

48. See especially Jacques Lacan, *The Language of the Self: The Function of Language in Psychoanalysis*, translated with notes and commentary by Anthony Wilden (Baltimore: Johns Hopkins University Press, 1968). Wilden comments: "Lacan's work has surely resulted in the final demise of the *cogito* that Husserl, Merleau-Ponty, and Sartre once struggled with, besides giving us the wherewithal to brush away the last vestiges of the atomistic, linear, and essentially solipsistic psychology inherited by the modern world, and to replace it by analyses of relationships, dialectical opposition and communication" (pp. 310–11).

49. See Paul Ricoeur, *Time and Narrative*, trans. Kathleen McLaughlin, Kathleen Blaney, and David D. Pellauer, 3 vols. (Chicago: University of Chicago Press, 1984–88).

50. Lewis Thomas, *The Lives of a Cell: Notes of a Biology Watcher* (New York: Bantam Books, 1975), 2, 167.

51. Alfred North Whitehead, *Process and Reality: An Essay in Cosmology*, corrected ed. by David Ray Griffin and Donald W. Sherburne (New York: Free Press, 1978), 35–36; cf. 83–109. I have discussed memory, pattern, and intentionality in *Faith and Process: The Significance of Process Thought for Christian Faith* (Minneapolis: Augsburg Publishing House, 1979), 90–102. For a significant statement on behalf of greater continuity, see Robert Neville, *The Cosmology of Freedom* (New Haven: Yale University Press, 1974). From the vast literature on this topic within the process tradition, two continue to deserve special mention: William J. Gallagher, "Whitehead's Psychological Physiology: A Third View," *Process Studies* 4, no. 4 (Winter 1974): 263–74; and Charles Hartshorne, "Personal Identity from A to Z," *Process Studies* 2, no. 3 (Fall 1972): 209–15.

52. See, e.g., the critique of static conceptions of the "orders of creation" in Wingren, *Creation and Law*, 91–93; and Bonhoeffer, *Ethics*, 207–13. Cf. Pannenberg, *Anthropology in Theological Perspective*, 490. Essentially the same concern is expressed by Gary M. Simpson in *"Theologia Crucis* and the Forensically Fraught World: Engaging Helmut Peukert and Jürgen Habermas," *Journal of the American Academy of Religion* 57, no. 3 (Fall 1989),

through the development of this thesis: "The promotion of the forensically fraught world necessitates the development of fundamental theology as a political *theologia crucis* since on the cross God also submits to and becomes dependent upon the forensically fraught world" (p. 532).

53. The classical statement of this admonition is G. E. Moore, *Principia Ethica* (Cambridge: Cambridge University Press, 1903, 1976).

54. Cahoone, *Dilemma of Modernity*, in the first section of his epilogue, entitled "Jackboots on the Stairs," 267–70, suggests the troubling efficacy of this distinction.

55. Farley, *God and Evil*, 41. Farley formulates the claim as "compassionate obligation," 43ff.

56. See chap. 1, note 59, above.

57. Mary Douglas, *Purity and Danger: An Analysis of Concepts of Pollution and Taboo* (New York: Frederick Praeger, 1966). She writes: "Four kinds of social pollution seem worth distinguishing. The first is danger pressing on external boundaries; the second, danger from transgressing the internal lines of the system; the third, danger in the margins of the lines. The fourth is danger from internal contradiction, when some of the basic postulates are denied by other basic postulates." Margaret Miles offers a book-length documentation of this point. See especially *Carnal Knowing*, chap. 5, "'Carnal Abominations': The Female Body as Grotesque." Cf. pp. 75ff, for her discussion of the "woman as temptation" as central to the male monk's inner dynamic of temptation and resistance.

58. Hannah Arendt, *The Human Condition* (Chicago: University of Chicago Press, 1958, 1969), 237. A very systematic development of this point is represented in the work of Lawrence Kohlberg concerning moral development where an increase in self-determination *and* increase in the reciprocity of relationship are linked in the movement toward internalization and universalization. See Lawrence Kohlberg, *The Philosophy of Moral Development: Moral Stages and the Idea of Justice* (San Francisco: Harper & Row, 1981). Cf. Peukert, *Science, Action and Fundamental Theology*, 180–81. In feminist criticism of Kohlberg the role of the other assumes even greater importance. See Carol Gilligan, *In A Different Voice: Psychological Theory and Women's Development* (Cambridge: Harvard University Press, 1982); and Carol Gilligan, Janie Victoria Ward, and Jill McLean Taylor with Betty Bardige, eds., *Mapping the Moral Domain: A Contribution of Women's Thinking to Psychological Theory and Education* (Cambridge: Harvard University Press, 1988).

59. Peukert, *Science, Action and Fundamental Theology*, 188, discussing the work of Paul Lorenzen. That the claim is not simply collapsed into the gift and task is evident in the matter of "passing life on." While the rhythm of life leaves one no choice, finally, about "passing on" (to employ a popular euphemism), the specificity of claim is sounded in Erik Erikson's account of "generativity," which is "primarily the interest in establishing and guiding the next generation, although there are people who, from misfortune or because

of special and genuine gifts in other directions, do not apply this drive to offspring but to other forms of altruistic concern and of creativity, which may absorb their kind of parental responsibility. The principal thing is to realize that this is a stage of the growth of the healthy personality and that where such enrichment fails altogether, regression from generativity to an obsessive need for pseudo intimacy takes place, often with a pervading sense of stagnation and interpersonal impoverishment. Individuals who do not develop generativity often begin to indulge themselves as if they were their own one and only child" (Erik Erikson, "Growth and Crises of the Healthy Personality," *Psychological Issues* 1, no. 1 [1959]: 97). Cf. Sallie McFague's discussion of "universal parenthood" (Jonathan Schell's term) in *Models of God: Theology for an Ecological, Nuclear Age* (Philadelphia: Fortress Press, 1987), 116–23.

60. Turner, *Ritual Process*, 132. For the broadening of "communitarian" understanding to consider "our entire life a practice in which all entities are engaged . . . in a wide-ranging set of relationships to nature, to other persons, and to one's own work and station," see Douglas Sturm, *Community and Alienation: Essays on Process Thought and Public Life* (Notre Dame, Ind.: University of Notre Dame Press, 1988), 170. Thomas Ogletree, *Hospitality to the Stranger* (Philadelphia: Fortress Press, 1985), 128–30, notes how Synoptic and Pauline social thought relativizes the family in relationship to the eschatological community.

61. Smith's summation of Lovinas in *Argument to the Other*, 78. Cf. pp. 172, 74.

62. Heinz Kohut, *The Analysis of the Self: A Systematic Approach to the Psychoanalytic Treatment of Narcissistic Personality Disorders* (New York: International Universities Press, 1971); and idem, *The Restoration of the Self* (New York: International Universities Press, 1977). See also Cahoone, *Dilemma of Modernity*, 94–96. Benjamin DeMott phrased the point well in saying that the realization of humanness depends "upon my capacity and my desire to make real to myself the inward life, the subjective reality of the lives that are lived beyond me." See Benjamin DeMott, *Supergrow: Essays and Reports on Imagination in America* (New York: E. P. Dutton & Co., 1969), 93. He distinguishes this from *both* the ideal of self-fulfillment and that of ego transcendence.

63. See Volney P. Gay, "Ritual and Self-Esteem in Victor Turner and Heinz Kohut," *Zygon* 18, no. 3 (September 1983): 271–82.

64. Pannenberg, *Anthropology in Theological Perspective*, 109. Pannenberg argues that it is because the self fails to attend to the other as other, but only to itself in the other that "the ego that is shut up in itself is wholly at the mercy of the otherness of the other, whether this is the effect of alcohol or the grind of professional life or the emptiness of distractions." I find this plausible so long as we do not take it to say that the causality of self-hatred or even self-neglect can be reduced to pride.

65. Smith, *Argument to the Other*, 88, 75.

66. See, e.g., Julia Kristeva, *Powers of Horror: An Essay on Abjection*, trans. Leon S. Roudiez (New York: Columbia University Press, 1982), esp. chap. 4, "Semiotics of Biblical Abomination." In my next chapter, I will consider how the Christian may respond to Kristeva's move to implicate the God concept in this offense.

67. Valerie Saiving's classic statement is "The Human Situation: A Feminine View," in *Womanspirit Rising: A Feminist Reader in Religion*, ed. Carol Christ and Judith Plaskow (San Francisco: Harper & Row, 1979). Keller, *From a Broken Web*, 12, summarizes the main point well: that "the traditional notions of sin as pride and self-assertion serve to reinforce the subordination of women, whose temptations *as* women lie in the realm of underdevelopment or negation of the self." Emphasis hers. Drawing on Kierkegaard, Wanda Warren Berry shows how one can sin "either by negating God in defiant 'strength' or by negating the self in weakly refusing to constitute a gathered will." See Wanda Warren Berry, "Images of Sin and Salvation in Feminist Theology," 25–54, *Anglican Theological Review* 60 (January 1978), 46. Robin Morgan, *The Anatomy of Freedom: Feminism, Physics and Global Politics* (Garden City, N.Y.: Doubleday & Co., Anchor Books, 1982, 1984), 203, turns the tables on the traditional emphasis: "If individuation is the piston of life, then racism and sexism are no surprise. Because *the deepest fear would be, not as we have thought politically, of the Other, but of the Same.*" Emphasis hers.

68. Gene H. Outka, *Agape: An Ethical Analysis* (New Haven: Yale University Press, 1972), 277ff.

69. Ogletree, *Hospitality to the Stranger*, 52.

70. David W. Augsburger, *Pastoral Counseling Across Cultures* (Philadelphia: Westminster Press, 1986), 88–89, notes two contrasting cultural paths: "The Western one leads from early autonomy via responsibility-for-self training to identity formation as an individual self whose choices, actions, and behavior are 'his own business' or 'her private responsibility'; the Eastern path leads from infantile dependency to appropriate childhood conformity to adolescent familial responsibility to young adult corporate solidarity with the group." Augsburger goes on to remark concerning how the pathology related to mental distress develops differently on the two paths. As to gender differences here, see the work of Carol Gilligan cited in note 58 above.

71. August Wilson makes this point very well in such plays as *Ma Rainey's Black Bottom* (New York: New American Library, 1985), *Fences* (New York: New American Library, 1986), and, more recently, *Joe Turner's Come and Gone* (New York: New American Library, 1988) and *The Piano Lesson* (New York: Dalton, 1990).

72. Eberhard Jüngel, *God as the Mystery of the World: On the Foundation of the Theology of the Crucified One in the Dispute Between Theism and Atheism*, trans. Darrell L. Guder (Grand Rapids: Wm. B. Eerdmans Publishing Co., 1983), 321–22. Emphasis his. Cf. Ogletree, *Hospitality to the Stranger*, 57,

on the "dialectic of desire and need for the other": "On the one hand, need grounds desire, giving it both its fundamental impulse and also its necessity in human life processes. On the other hand, desire transcends need, yet without wholly losing its rootage in the dynamics of need. Indeed, in its transcendence of need, it actually contributes to the realization of the relation which is the proper object of the need in the first place."

73. Theunissen, *The Other*, 383. He adds: "Presumably, that reality that the dialogic of the between shows itself to be from a theological viewpoint is *the* side of the kingdom of God that philosophically can be taken account of at all: the side not of 'grace,' but of the 'will.' The will to dialogical self-becoming belongs to the striving after the kingdom of God in such a way that its future is promised in the present love of human beings for one another." Emphasis his. In chap. 5, I will return to the matter of what can be said to be promised.

74. See the remarkable study by Juan Luis Segundo, *Evolution and Guilt* (Maryknoll, N.Y.: Orbis Books, 1974).

75. Arendt, *Human Condition*, 237.

76. Arendt, *Human Condition*.

77. Kierkegaard, *The Sickness Unto Death*, 122.

78. I am particularly grateful to Kirsten Mickelson for pressing this question.

79. Peukert, *Science, Action and Fundamental Theology*, 69. Simpson, "*Theologia Crucis*," 529ff., argues that Peukert's move to the resurrection as the resolution of this challenge leaps over the cross and therewith the need for "reflexive critique and repentance." I return to this issue in chaps. 5 and 6.

80. On the Holocaust as a confidence shattering *caesura*, see Arthur Cohen, *The Tremendum: A Theological Interpretation of the Holocaust* (New York: Crossroad, 1981). M. Scott Peck, *People of the Lie: The Hope for Healing Human Evil* (New York: Simon & Schuster, 1983), offers a psychiatric sketch of radical evil. Paul Ricoeur's *The Symbolism of Evil*, trans. Emerson Buchanan (Boston: Beacon Press, 1967) remains a powerful phenomenological statement of the theological category of "the bondage of the will."

81. See James Baldwin, *Another Country* (New York: Dell Publishing Co., 1960, 1962).

Chapter 4. Life "Before" the Other

1. Moltmann, *God in Creation*, 182.

2. Charles Hartshorne and William L. Reese, eds., *Philosophers Speak of God* (Chicago: University of Chicago Press, 1953), 7.

3. Ludwig Wittgenstein, *Tractatus Logico-Politicus* (London: Kegan Paul, 1922–1947), statement 6.54 (p. 189). Yet it may be too much to say that "what is hidden . . . is of no interest to us"; see idem, *Philosophical Investigations*, trans. G. E. M. Anscombe (New York: Macmillan Co., 1953), 50e.

4. I have taken this particular listing from Schmid, *Doctrinal Theology of the Evangelical Lutheran Church*, 118ff. Schmid lists the following "positive"

attributes: life, knowledge, wisdom, holiness, justice, truth, power, goodness, perfection.

5. See Rudolf Otto, *The Idea of the Holy*, trans. John W. Harvey, 9th ed. (London: Oxford University Press, 1928). Cf. John G. Gammie, *Holiness in Israel* (Minneapolis: Augsburg Fortress, 1989), where Otto's analysis constitutes "a starting point and constant frame of reference" (p. 6). It is striking that as an expression of the "mystery" theme Gammie offers Exod. 19:9a: "Lo, *I am going to come to you* in a dense cloud." Emphasis mine. He does note that while "Otto amply documented the notion of unapproachability," he does not "sufficiently probe the notion that the holy calls for purity, cleanness" (pp. 7–8).

6. Ann and Barry Ulanov, *Primary Speech: A Psychology of Prayer* (Atlanta, Ga.: John Knox Press, 1982), 124–25.

7. C. S. Lewis, *Till We Have Faces* (Grand Rapids: Wm. B. Eerdmans Publishing Co., 1977), 308. Emphasis his.

8. See pp. 5–16 above.

9. Walter Beyerlin, ed., *Near Eastern Religious Texts Relating to the Old Testament* (Philadelphia: Westminster, 1978), 22. cf. Terence Fretheim, who includes many other such references in his "Nature's Praise of God in the Psalms," *Ex Auditu* 3 (1988): 16–30.

10. Russell, "Cosmology, Creation, and Contingency," 177–210, in Peters, *Cosmos as Creation*, 184. Russell adds: "The ages of each system under study nest properly: the geological age of the earth is consistent with the age of the sun. Physical cosmology gives a unified interpretative scenario through which the universe developed from an embryonic fireball into the present composition. Recent work in high energy physics when projected back to the temperatures of the earliest epoch of the universe suggest even more unified scenarios for all of fundamental physics" (184–85). Cf. comments about the prospects for a "new natural theology" in Toulmin, *The Return to Cosmology*, 235.

11. Barbour, "Creation and Cosmology," 115–51, in Peters, *Cosmos as Creation*, 121.

12. Thus elements of the Big Bang theory are being questioned. See *Nature*, January 1991, for an analysis by Dr. Will Saunders of Oxford University of a galactic survey by the Infrared Astronomical Satellite which shows the universe to be full of superstructures and companion supervoids far too vast to have formed since the Big Bang.

13. Ernan McMullin, "How Should Cosmology Relate to Theology?" 39–52, in *The Sciences and Theology in the Twentieth Century*, ed. Arthur R. Peacocke (Notre Dame, Ind.: University of Notre Dame Press, 1981), 38. Emphasis his. Cf. Russell's discussion in Peters, *Cosmos as Creation*, 184–96, where a helpful complexity is introduced.

14. Barbour, in Peters, *Cosmos as Creation*, 130.

15. Barbour, in Peters, *Cosmos as Creation*, 132. Barbour describes several ways in which many worlds could occur: successive cycles of an oscillating universe,

multiple isolated domains, many-worlds quantum theory and quantum vacuum fluctuations.

16. Barbour suggests that one could interpret many-worlds hypotheses *theistically* by holding "that God created many universes in order that life and thought would occur in this one" (in Peters, *Cosmos as Creation*, 133–34). This discussion is reminiscent of the conversation concerning the place of a notion of God in the Whiteheadian interpretation of order and novelty. I have summarized this discussion, including Donald Sherburne's proposal of a "Whitehead without God," in *Faith and Process,* chap. 2.

17. Loren Eiseley, *All the Strange Hours* (New York: Charles Scribner's Sons, 1975), 242.

18. Moltmann, *God in Creation*, 185ff., cites Pierre Teilhard de Chardin's comment that in "three successive steps (astronomy, biology, psychoanalysis) . . . man has seemed definitely to redissolve in the common ground of things." He wisely proposes that Christian anthropology "start with the complexes and milieus in which human beings appear and from which they live" so that we do not introduce the God relationship as an arbitrary appeal. For a brief discussion of the "ontological," "cosmological," "teleological," and "moral" arguments as arguments, not proofs, see my comments in "The Knowledge of God," in Braaten and Jenson, *Christian Dogmatics*, 1:197–268, 236–41. Michael D. Beaty, "God Among the Philosophers," *Christian Century* 108 (June 12–19, 1991): 620–23, provides a helpful summary of recent attempts to defend traditional theism within the contexts of analytic philosophy.

19. Gustafson, *Ethics from a Theocentric Perspective*, 1:32.

20. This epistemological status fits the hypothesis. But such internal coherence should not be offered as itself an argument for faith's claims. One way of doing that may be to contend that religious belief is justified as "basic" to a whole framework of thought. I agree with Nancy Frankenberry's critique of such "basicalism" in *Religion and Radical Empiricism* (Albany: State University of New York Press, 1988). See also Keith Parsons, *God and the Burden of Proof: Plantinga, Swinburne, and the Analytic Defense of Theism* (Buffalo, N.Y.: Prometheus Books, 1989). In my *God—The Question and the Quest* (Philadelphia: Fortress Press, 1985), I have argued that the believer does bear a relatively greater "burden of proof," a position underlying my discussion in chap. 6 of "claiming the connection" with unfaith.

21. As a sampling one might consider Charles Hartshorne's appeal in *Anselm's Discovery: A Re-examination of the Ontological Proof for God's Existence* (La Salle, Ill.: Open Court, 1965) to necessity in that the existence of God does not compete with other possibilities (this being the meaning of contingency) or Robert Neville's evocation of the indeterminate in that anything determinate is created in the ontological sense. Neville has continued to champion this view, stated rather fully as early as 1968 in his *God the Creator: On the Transcendence and Presence of God* (Chicago: University of Chicago Press). Frederick Sontag, *Divine Perfection: Possible Ideas of God* (New

York: Harper & Row, 1962), usefully gathers the discussion of such classical notions as simplicity and self-sufficiency.

22. See Philip Hefner's discussion in "The Creation," in Braaten and Jenson, *Christian Dogmatics*, 1:269–362, 325–28. Hefner clearly does not understand the recognition of human creativity as compromising the unique divine creativity. Indeed, he can write (p. 312): "There is scarcely a more offensive idea for the Christian than one that holds God in some way responsible for evil. Perhaps the only idea more repugnant is the alternative we mentioned— that God is limited in power over anything, including evil." While I trust it will be clear that I do hold that "more repugnant" idea, I hope to show that the transcendence of God that Hefner is articulating can be adequately formulated in other terms.

23. This is H. P. Owen's statement of the classical theistic understanding: "Whereas creatures exist *per se* ('by or in themselves'), only the Creator exists *a se* ('from or of himself'). To say that creatures exist *per se* is to affirm (against monism) that each of them is real, distinct and autonomous. Yet their autonomy is limited; and the principal form of limitation is their dependence on external factors" (H. P. Owen, *Concepts of Deity* [New York: Herder & Herder, 1971], 14). I seek to retain a notion of aseity, but I recognize that careful formulation is necessary if I am not to follow Owen in his claim that, for example, immutability and impassibility are entailed by aseity (p. 17). That God exists *a se* need not entail that such "total independence of external factors" characterizes the life of God. Cf. Keith Ward's revised statement of classical theism in his discussion of divine freedom and necessity in *Divine Action* (London: Collins, 1990), 21ff.

24. See John Bright, *A History of Israel*, 2d ed. (Philadelphia: Westminster Press, 1972), 140ff. Bright's conclusion is that "henotheism is clearly an insufficient description of the faith of early Israel" (p. 141). My point is that theoretical monotheism is dependent (logically, whether or not also chronologically) on the claim that Israel is to *worship* no other God.

25. William Hasker, *God, Time and Knowledge* (Ithaca, N.Y.: Cornell University Press, 1989), 151, suggests that one "might hesitate to say that God 'deliberates,' since this implies a period of time during which God does not yet know what he will do. The same might be said of 'decides,' which suggests that the decision is preceded by a state of indecision. It may be that God *wills* and *does* certain things, but that he never *decided* to do them." Yet Hasker immediately adds the point I am making: "Though, certainly, whatever he will, he wills decisively." Emphasis his. In the next section, I discuss whether "the other" in some sense may be a requirement in whatever God wills, perhaps for the very notion of willing.

26. Bernard J. Cooke, *The Distancing of God: The Ambiguity of Symbol in History and Theology* (Minneapolis: Augsburg Fortress, 1990). Cooke speaks as well of the distancing effects of ecclesiastical structures, of the Eucharist as a spectacle performed by clergy, and of monasticism and celibacy as paradigms for Christian discipleship.

27. Cf. the suggestions of Jüngel and Moltmann as to how traditional theism leads to atheism, in Jüngel, *God as the Mystery of the World;* and *The Crucified God* (New York: Harper & Row, 1974).

28. Søren Kierkegaard, *Christian Discourses*, trans. Walter Lowrie (London: Oxford University Press, 1939), 132–33. For Kierkegaard's theme that between God and us there is "an infinite difference of quality," see, among many references, Kierkegaard, *Training in Christianity*, trans. Walter Lowrie (London: Oxford University Press), 31.

29. Karl Barth, *Evangelical Theology: An Introduction*, trans. Grover Foley (New York: Holt, Rinehart & Winston, 1963), 24. Of many such Barthian passages, I add only one (Karl Barth, *Church Dogmatics*, trans. G. W. Bromiley, 4 vols. in 13 [Edinburgh: T. & T. Clark, 1936–69]): "We may believe that God can and must only be absolute in contrast to all that is relative, exalted in contrast to all that is lowly, active in contrast to all suffering, inviolable in contrast to all temptation, transcendent in contrast to all immanence, and therefore divine in contrast to everything human, in short that He can and must be only the 'Wholly Other.' But such beliefs are shown to be quite untenable, and corrupt and pagan, by the fact that God does in fact be and do this in Jesus Christ. We cannot make them the standard by which to measure what God can or cannot do, or the basis of the judgment that in doing this He brings Himself into self-contradiction. By doing this God proves to us that He can do it, that to do it is within His nature. And He shows Himself to be more great and rich and sovereign than we had ever imagined. And our ideas of His nature must be guided by this, and not *vice versa*" (*Church Dogmatics*, 4 (1): 186.

30. Dietrich Bonhoeffer, *Act and Being*, trans. Bernard Noble (New York: Harper & Brothers, 1956), 90f. Emphasis his. Bonhoeffer, of course, understood himself to be writing in criticism of Barth. See James H. Burtness, "As Though God Were Not Given: Barth, Bonhoeffer, and the *Finitum Capax Infiniti*," *dialog* 19, no. 4 (Fall, 1980): 249–55.

31. Richard A. Creel, *Divine Impassibility: An Essay in Philosophical Theology* (Cambridge: Cambridge University Press, 1986), 14–34.

32. Shirley MacLaine, *Dancing in the Light* (New York: Bantam Books, 1985), 404–5. Emphasis hers.

33. Sheila Greeve Davaney, *Divine Power: A Study of Karl Barth and Charles Hartshorne* (Philadelphia: Fortress Press, 1986), 239.

34. See Jüngel's sketch for such a theology in "response to Josef Blank," 297–304, in *Paradigm Change in Theology*, ed. Hans Küng and David Tracy, 303. Emphasis his. I am clear that one needs to recognize that all our theological work remains ours; it does not becomes God's self-description. I am less clear about the degree to which this recognition of the *how* of our speaking can guide discriminating decisions within theological speech regarding *what* we shall say of God. James Gustafson agonizes over this (*Ethics from a Theocentric Perspective*, 1:271: "One can acknowledge dependence on ordering powers that sustain life and bear down upon it without conceiving these

powers as gifted with intelligence and arbitrary will. One can be grateful for the divine governance, for all that it sustains and makes possible, without conceptually personalizing the Governor. The language of piety may well use personalized symbols: they have some warrants from our perception and construal of the divine purposes and from their expressive appropriateness for religious affectivity. But they do not warrant the theological construction of an anthropomorphic divine agency. In this way I agree with Tillich that we can be personally related to the divine governance without conceiving of God as a person." This seems to know, as it were, at once too much and too little. In my discussion I am trying rather to hold to the dialectic of saying that we have the treasure in earthen vessels, but the vessels are not empty.

35. I have this reference from my colleague, Terence Fretheim, who contrasts such plastic images with the biblical references to Jesus as the image of God (Col. 1:15).

36. Peter C. Hodgson, *God in History: Shapes of Freedom* (Nashville: Abingdon Press, 1989), 108. Emphasis his.

37. Cf. Jüngel, in Küng and Tracy, *Paradigm Change in Theology*, 301: "The paradigm constituted by the ontology of event, relation and subject has not only made possible a clearer understanding of the *historicity of the claim to truth of the biblical texts*. It has also enabled us to arrive at a stricter understanding of *the historicity of the God* who (according to these texts) has come to the world." Emphasis his.

38. Jüngel, *God as the Mystery of the World*, 384.

39. Robert W. Jenson, *The Triune Identity: God According to the Gospel* (Philadelphia: Fortress Press, 1982), 85. Emphasis his.

40. Paul S. Fiddes, *The Creative Suffering of God* (Oxford: Clarendon Press; New York: Oxford University Press, 1988), 68–76. Fiddes places Moltmann in the "desire" camp, but Moltmann is specifically critical of emanation doctrines in which "the differentiations between God and the world have to be ascribed, not to creation but to 'the Fall' " (Moltmann, *God in Creation*, 84). He tries to find a middle way here by appropriating the Reformed doctrine of "essential decree." In filling this out, Moltmann employs the kabbalistic doctrine of *zimsum*, self-limitation: "God makes room for his creation by withdrawing his presence. What comes into being is a *nihil* which does not contain the negation of a creaturely being (since creation is not yet existent), but which represents the partial negation of the divine Being, inasmuch as God is not yet Creator. . . . In this sense God's self-humiliation does not begin merely with creation, inasmuch as God commits himself to this world: it begins beforehand, and is the presupposition that makes creation possible. . . . This self-restrictive love is the beginning of that self-emptying of God which Philippians 2 sees as the divine mystery of the Messiah" (pp. 88–89; cf. 156). A less picturesque effort to find a middle way is represented by Keith Ward in *Rational Theology and the Creativity of God* (New York: Pilgrim Press, 1982), in his effort to hold together freedom and love in God's "rational choice" (p. 145) to create.

41. Fiddes, *Creative Suffering*, 74.
42. Fiddes, *Creative Suffering*, 75.
43. Whitehead, working as an empirical philosopher, can come as far as to say that God "at once exemplifies and establishes the categoreal conditions"; see the discussion in Whitehead's *Process and Reality*, 344. This involves locating God "within the metaphysical ultimate" of creativity as "its primordial, nontemporal accident" (p. 7)—a step for which he has been duly criticized by such authors as Robert Neville (see especially *Creativity and God: A Challenge to Process Theology* [New York: Seabury Press, 1980]); and Langdon Gilkey (see especially *Reaping the Whirlwind* [New York: Seabury Press, 1976]). Mortimer Adler, *How to Think About God: A Guide for the 20th Century Pagan* (New York: Macmillan Co., 1980), proceeds differently, utilizing two steps: (1) assuming an everlasting but radically contingent cosmos and positing God as the "exnihilating" cause of its continued existence, and (2) given such a sufficient reason (though not a necessary proof, Adler grants) to affirm God's existence, turning to the "more likely assumption of a created cosmos." Throughout my discussion here I am moving toward the point that, in any case, the universe is *not now nothing*. If that is granted in understanding the faith, we clearly need to find some way to speak of God's transcendence in relationship. But it does not follow that the claim that the transcendent love experienced in relationship is the fruit of God's freedom contributes nothing to the relationship experienced. Jon D. Levenson's *Creation and the Persistence of Evil: The Jewish Drama of Divine Omnipotence* (San Francisco: Harper & Row, 1988) is an interesting discussion of how the biblical texts deal "with the question of how to neutralize the powerful and ongoing threat of chaos" (p. xiv).
44. See, e.g., Jenson, *The Triune Identity;* and Karl Rahner, *The Trinity*, trans. Joseph Conceel (New York: Seabury Press, 1974).
45. See Fiddes's (*Creative Suffering*, 69) gathering of several of Karl Barth's statements at this point: "The choosing of the world by God is indeed a 'free overflowing' of his goodness, an 'expression and application of the love in which He is God,' but God does not 'need His being' in order to be who he is or to make the choices he does. His own being, like his activity in the world, is a matter of his free will and determination. God in himself is an act or event in which he posits his own reality: in short, 'God is His own decision.'" And again: "God necessarily decides to be the one who loves himself in the fellowship of the Trinity, but he need not have chosen to love *us*. God's loving is necessary, for it is the being, the essence, and the nature of God. But for this very reason it is also free from every necessity in respect of its object" (p. 70). Emphasis his.
46. Jüngel, *God as the Mystery of the World*, 328. Emphasis his.
47. Cf. Ward, *Divine Action*, 21–26. In the next section, I will discuss how divine suffering and joy can be integrated with talk of an impassible God.
48. See chap. 2, note 10, above.

49. Charles Birch and John B. Cobb, Jr., *The Liberation of Life: From the Cell to the Community* (Cambridge, Mass.: Cambridge University Press, 1981), 197.

50. H. Richard Niebuhr, in collaboration with Daniel Day Williams and James M. Gustafson, *The Purpose of the Church and Its Ministry: Reflection on the Aims of Theological Education* (New York: Harper & Brothers, 1956), 35.

51. Cohen, *The Tremendum*, 83–84. Emphasis his.

52. Such continuity in evil could lead one to adopt a "theogonic" understanding, where God struggles eternally with opposition. See the magisterial discussion of "the Adamic," "the tragic," and "the theogonic" myths in Ricoeur, *The Symbolism of Evil*. I am arguing that with the gift of freedom, God gives the reality of consequence—for us and for God as well.

53. Gilkey, *Reaping the Whirlwind*, 247–48.

54. Gilkey, *Reaping the Whirlwind*. Emphasis his.

55. Schmid, *Doctrinal Theology*, part 1, chap. 4.

56. Terence E. Fretheim, *The Suffering of God: An Old Testament Perspective* (Philadelphia: Fortress Press, 1984), 51–52. See especially the discussion of "The Divine Perhaps," "The Divine If," "The Divine Consultation," and "The Divine Question" in chap. 4. Cf. Fretheim, "The Repentance of God: A Key to Evaluating Old Testament God-Talk," 47–70, in *Horizons in Biblical Theology* 10, no. 1 (June 1988): 47–70: "Given God's faithfulness and the constancy of God's loving purposes, it may be that God will have to forsake God's own past in order to be true to those purposes, indeed for the sake of God's own name (p. 60). Fretheim emphasizes that "it is thus clear that this confession [that God is a God who repents] stands in sharpest contrast to any arbitrariness of divine action" (p. 61).

57. Arland J. Hultgren, *Christ and His Benefits: Christology and Redemption in the New Testament* (Philadelphia: Fortress Press, 1987), 175. See p. 42 for the distinction between the "theopractic" and the "christopractic."

58. Herbert W. Richardson, *Toward an American Theology* (New York: Harper & Row, 1967), 130.

59. Richardson, *Toward an American Theology*. Richardson does "suspect that the strong Reformation emphasis on the total corruption of man without a corresponding emphasis upon his dignity has actually undercut what it was intended to support: namely, man's sense that he needs a redeemer. The world agrees that all men are sinners, but it does not see that the redemption of sinners is worth caring about. The relative failure of Christianity to be an effective redemptive force in the world arises in large part from this failure to affirm clearly the spiritual dignity of human life." I find Richardson critiquing here what I have above (in the preceding section of this chapter) called the "logic of disjunction." Cf. Eugene TeSelle, *Christ in Context: Divine Purpose and Human Possibility* (Philadelphia: Fortress Press, 1975), for a "participationist" attempt to combine the "Scotist" stress on the "world transcending, coherent" purposes of God (according to which the sending of

Christ cannot be made contingent on the human happening of sin) and the "Thomists' healthy respect for the place of finite freedom, and secondary causes generally, in the course of events" (p. 45).

60. Cf. Carl Braaten, "The Person of Jesus Christ," 469–569, in Braaten and Jenson, *Christian Dogmatics*, on the Creed of Chalcedon calling Mary *theotokos*, the mother of God: "The advantage of the *theotokos* formula is that it underscored that the subject of the incarnation was actually God—God the Son. . . . The gospel narrative of God becoming one with humanity in Jesus the Christ conflicts sharply with an ontology of divine immutability in which God simply is what he is in static identity. An absolutely immutable God is not able to become the subject of incarnational predicates, making the history of human existence his own history and assuming the reality of the world's becoming into his own reality as the Logos of God. An ontology constructed in the light of faith in the gospel will speak not of the utter impassibility and immutability of God but rather of the historicity of God and God's coming-to-be in the humanity of Jesus the Christ." Lutherans express their commitment to the emphatic character of the togetherness of the divine and the human by speaking of the *communicatio idiomata*, the "communication of attributes," characterizing the person of Jesus. See Braaten's discussion of this (*Christian Dogmatics*, 1:507–11), including the "*majestatic*" genus by which divine qualities are attributed to the human nature and (in the kenotic Lutheran Christology of the nineteenth century) the "*tapeinotic*" genus, by which human attributes are communicated to the divine nature. Cf. Richardson's comment on the language of II Constantinople, that "God the Word was twice begotten": "By binding together the two beginnings of the Son, the formula . . . explains who the very *person* begotten of Mary is. The person begotten of Mary is one and the same as the person begotten of the Father. . . . *Who* is Jesus, the Babe of Mary? He is God in person!" (Richardson, *Toward an American Theology*, 138). Emphasis his. John B. Cobb, Jr.'s *Christ in a Pluralistic Age* is a helpful contemporary effort to speak of how the divine and the human are "co-constitutive" of the person of Jesus.

61. Kierkegaard, *Philosophical Fragments*, 44.

62. See p. 97 above, for this theme from *The Sickness Unto Death*.

63. A classic statement is in Abraham J. Heschel, *The Prophets*, 2 vols. (New York: Harper Torchbook, 1962), 2:63: "Pathos includes love, but goes beyond it. God's relation to man is not an indiscriminate outpouring of goodness, . . . but an intimate accessibility, manifesting itself in His sensitive and manifold reactions. . . . God's concern is the prerequisite and source of his anger. It is because He cares for man that His anger may be kindled against man."

64. Kierkegaard, *The Sickness Unto Death*, 100.

65. Brock, *Journeys by Heart*, 52.

66. Friedrich Mildenberger, *Theology of the Lutheran Confessions*, trans. Erwin L. Lueker, ed. Robert C. Schultz (Philadelphia: Fortress Press, 1986), 42. Emphasis mine. Cf. Hultgren, *Christ and His Benefits*, 176, for a critique of

a "Christ elect" position, that the earliest redemptive christology looked solely to the future and that later there came to be a looking back to the cross: "Rather, from the outset and then in all types of redemptive christology, the cross and resurrection—taken together as a unity—are seen to be the event in which redemption is achieved . . . or made possible."

67. See Richardson, *Toward an American Theology*, esp. 141ff. Richardson contends (p. 132) that "to assert . . . that sanctification is the chief reason for the incarnation is not to undercut redemption, but to affirm the sole condition that gives it any meaning." The same concern may be found in Dietrich Ritschl's effort in *Memory and Hope: An Inquiry Concerning the Presence of Christ* (New York: Macmillan Co., 1967) to speak of the Holy Spirit as the presence of Christ in a view that is "broader than the traditional concentration on justification or the modern exposition of the analysis of self-understanding" (p. 224).

68. Brock, *Journeys by Heart*, 150–156; and M. K. Taylor, *Remembering Esperanza*, 168–75. Brock and Taylor are very much to the point in their critique of Christologies of the particularity of Jesus which leave him a metaphysical miracle without any actual effect in history. See also chap. 5, notes 60, 61, 66, below, for the discussion by F. W. Dillistone and George Rupp of other efforts that represent a "prospective" or "process realism" approach to Christ's efficacy.

69. Hodgson, *God in History*, 105.

70. Hultgren, *Christ and His Benefits*, 198.

71. One finds this tendency in strange places. Thus in *Models of God*, Sallie McFague, who has written so helpfully in criticism of imperialistic and triumphalist metaphors for God as "opposed to life, its continuation and fulfillment" (p. ix), can so stress the "is not" of metaphor over the "is" as to leave the door open to undercutting her contribution: "Models of God are not definitions of God, but likely accounts of experiences of relating to God with the help of relationships we know and understand. . . . In other words, how language, any language, applies to God we do not know. . . . Metaphors (and all languages about God) are principally adverbial, having to do with how we relate to God, rather than defining the nature of God" (p. 39).

72. See Martinson, *A Theology of World Religions*, 175–82, for a discussion of how "the Western ethos, incarnate in Christianity and Marxism, introduced a new and momentous experience of time" (p. 175). Martinson is careful not to overdraw the contrast between West and East. In this connection, see Masao Abe, *Zen and Western Thought*, ed. William R. LaFleur (Honolulu: University of Hawaii Press, 1985), 248, for a haunting suggestion of the challenge his Buddhist faith faces: "The crucial task for Buddhism is this: How can Buddhism on the basis of 'without why' as its ultimate ground formulate a *positive direction* through which ethics and history can develop? In other words, how can a *new teleology* be established on the ground of 'suchness,' which is neither teleological nor mechanical?" Emphasis his.

73. This understanding of God seems to be finally controlling in the complex writings of Wolfhart Pannenberg. Thus, while Pannenberg's *Anthropology in Theological Perspective* represents a rich affirmation of human thought and action in the setting of an emphasis on genuine historical development, the last word (p. 525) seems to be that "it is *from* the future that the abiding essence of things discloses itself." Emphasis mine. For a probing of this issue in Pannenberg, see David P. Polk, "The All-Determining God and the Peril of Determinism," 152–68, in *The Theology of Wolfhart Pannenberg*, ed. Carl E. Braaten and Philip Clayton (Minneapolis: Augsburg Publishing House, 1988). For a helpful brief summary of the "paradox of two agents," see Robert H. King, *The Meaning of God* (Philadelphia: Fortress Press, 1973), 73ff.

74. This is the distinction David Ray Griffin uses in "Process Theism: A Response to Robert Neville" (Paper available from the Center for Process Studies, Claremont, Calif.), in considering Robert Neville's critique of process theism in *Creativity and God* (and elsewhere). That persons working in the process materials can join Jüngians (and others) by opting to locate God beyond the distinction between good and evil is well illustrated by Bernard Loomer, *The Size of God: The Theology of Bernard Loomer in Context*, ed. William Dean and Larry E. Axel (Macon, Ga.: Mercer University Press, 1987), 16: "The thesis of my essay is that God should be identified with the totality of the world, with whatever unity the totality possesses." Marvin Shaw, "The Romantic Love of Evil: Loomer's Proposal of a Reorientation in Religious Naturalism," *American Journal of Theology and Philosophy* 10, no. 1 (January, 1989): 33–48), questions how Loomer can then justify "an ethical selection from the rich ambiguity of nature."

75. *Webster's Third New International Dictionary of the English Language, Unabridged*, ed. Philip Babcock Gove (Springfield, Mass.: G. & C. Merriam Co., 1961), 197.

76. Ruth Page, *Ambiguity and the Presence of God* (London: SCM Press, 1985), 140–41.

77. Page, *Ambiguity and the Presence of God*. Emphasis hers.

78. John Smith, *Experience and God* (New York: Oxford University Press, 1968), 52–53: "Absolute immediacy can never deliver what it promises because some form of mediation—concepts, language, symbols—always intervenes and makes it impossible to pass from the experience to the reality of God; inference does not suffice because it always takes the form of necessity." Hence Smith argues for experience and mediation together, reflecting "the peculiar character of the reality of God."

79. Kierkegaard, *Concluding Unscientific Postscript to the Philosophical Fragments*, 1944), 35. Or one might speak, with Jüngel (*God as the Mystery of the World*, 165, 182, 349), of God "present as absent." Pannenberg has particularly emphasized that even though God is the author of revelation, God is not the content. See Wolfhart Pannenberg, *Systematische Theologie* (Göttingen: Vandenhoeck & Ruprecht, 1988), 1:264–67. One is reminded of Luther's critique of "enthusiasm."

80. I have discussed such "incognitos" in Braaten and Jenson, *Christian Dogmatics*, 1:229–236. On religion's commitment to "the real," see Clifford Geertz, *Islam Observed: Religious Development in Morocco and Indonesia* (New Haven: Yale University Press, 1968), 97. Gunn, *Interpretation of Otherness*, remains a helpful study of the expression of the liminal in literature (see esp. 78ff., 223ff.).

81. See Whitehead, *Process and Reality*, 4–7, on the difficulty of discerning universals by the method of difference. Cf. Kierkegaard, *Concluding Unscientific Postscript*, 204–5, on the correlation of the omnipresence and the hiddenness of God.

82. Some Christian talk of the hiddenness of God does seem to impose a limitation or barrier to knowledge other than that to be drawn from the analogy to interpersonal knowing. Yet this theme is not necessarily to be understood as undercutting fundamental clarity of revelation, though it may entail a rather severe narrowing of focus. See the much-cited article of Brian Gerrish, "To the Unknown God," *The Journal of Religion* 53 (July, 1973): 268–93. Gerrish writes of Luther in these terms: "In Christ, God works in a paradoxical mode *sub contrariis*. His wisdom is hidden under folly, his strength under abject weakness" (p. 268). Nonetheless, he limits this point: "It was not, of course, his intention to admit that faith is fancy, inventing a God for its own comfort other than he is in himself. On the contrary, he insists that faith in Christ *is* knowledge of the Hidden God." He cites Luther as follows: "Begin from below, from the Incarnate Son . . . Christ will bring you to the Hidden God. . . . If you take the Revealed God, he will bring you to the Hidden God at the same time" (pp. 278–79). Emphasis his. For an exploration of the darker possibility resident in the ambiguity of claimed revelation, see Robert Mesle, "A Friend's Love: Why Does Process Theism Matter?" *Christian Century* 104 (15–17 July 1987) 622–24, and Mesle's further reservations in "Does Process Theism Matter?" (Lecture available from the Center for Process Studies, Claremont, Calif.). Mesle is particularly responding to the notion of "epistemic distance" as presented by John Hick in *Evil and the God of Love* (New York: Harper & Row, 1966, 1968), 317. Page, *Ambiguity and the Presence of God*, represents a full-length probing of the issue. See also Daniel Taylor, *The Myth of Certainty: The Reflective Christian and the Risk of Commitment* (Waco, Tex.: Word Books, 1986).

83. For a critique of such "paradoxes," see Don Cupitt, *Taking Leave of God* (London: SCM Press, 1980).

84. Kathryn Tanner, *God and Creation in Christian Theology: Tyranny or Empowerment?* (Oxford: Basil Blackwell, 1988), 47.

85. Kierkegaard, *Christian Discourses*, 133; cf. Ward, *Divine Action*, 77. For a similar reading of the way in which in the Book of Exodus the "suffering God" metaphor "norms" the motif of the sovereignty of God, see Terence Fretheim, "Suffering God and Sovereign God in Exodus: A Collison of Images," *Horizons in Biblical Theology* 11 (1989): 31–56.

86. Ward, *Divine Action*, 21–37.
87. Anders Nygren's *Agape and Eros*, trans. Philip S. Watson, (London: SPCK, 1973) can be read in this way. For a response, see Daniel Day Williams, *The Spirit and the Forms of Love* (New York: Harper and Row, 1968), 38.
88. Owen, *Concepts of Deity*, 24.
89. Thus in Schmid, *Doctrinal Theology*, 313, the properties of the two natures are said to be ascribed "*only to the person*" they characterize, but not to each other, "for the two natures are not in substance changed by the personal union." Emphasis his. How do we know this? John Gerhard provides the answer: "From the nature of Deity. Deity is incapable of suffering, or of change, and interchange; therefore suffering cannot be ascribed to it. Deity pertains to the entire Trinity; . . . but if, therefore, Deity in itself were said to have suffered, the entire Trinity would have suffered, and the error of the Sabellians and Patripassians would be reproduced in the Church" (pp. 324–25). If all suffering must be denied to God, no consideration will be given to making distinctions in suffering within the triune life.
90. Braaten and Jenson, *Christian Dogmatics*, 1:532–33.
91. Hall, *God and Human Suffering*, 106.
92. Braaten and Jenson, *Christian Dogmatics*, 1:533.
93. G. L. Prestige, *God in Patristic Thought* (London: SPCK, 1952), 6–7.
94. Owen, *Concepts of Deity*, 17.
95. Moltmann, *The Crucified God*, 229–30. Charles Taliaferro, in a more recent phase of the discussion in "The Passibility of God," *Religious Studies* 25 (1989): 217–24, provides a detailed response to Richard Creel's *Divine Impassibility*.
96. Paul Tillich, *Systematic Theology*, 3 vols. (Chicago: University of Chicago Press, 1951–63), 1:147–53.
97. Cf. Tanner, *God and Creation*.
98. Hodgson, *God in History*, 198–205. What I have called here "the categorical difference" seems to lead Hodgson to hold that "the guiding gestalt is not a person or personal agent, but a transpersonal structure of praxis that grounds personal existence and builds interpersonal relations." Yet he wants to hold that "it itself is intrinsically relational, social communicative in character." Barbour, in *Religion in an Age of Science*, chap. 9, displays an even fuller list of "models of God's role in nature."
99. This objection has been voiced by writers otherwise sympathetic to the process orientation in which such access plays a major role. (The notion of God's noncoercive prevenient action is certainly not limited to process thinkers, though they display the notion very directly and fully). See Page, *Ambiguity and the Presence of God*, 132, on the "coercive" character of such divine guidance. Cf. David A. Pailin, *God and the Processes of Reality: Foundations of a Credible Theism* (London: Routledge & Kegan Paul, 1989), 145: "In practice a sufficiently attractive 'lure' may be as compelling, perhaps even more compelling, than coercive might." Such objections seem to underestimate

the genuine reality of that which is other than God. But process thought, in recognizing that reality, suggests a conception of power-in-relation which respects and risks the freedom of the other. See John B. Cobb, Jr., *God and the World* (Philadelphia: Westminster Press, 1969), 89–90; and Bernard Loomer, "Two Conceptions of Power," *Process Studies* 6 (1976): 5–32.

100. See the letter of 16 July, 1944 in Dietrich Bonhoeffer, *Letters and Papers from Prison*, ed. Eberhard Bethge, trans. Reginald Fuller (London: SCM Press, 1953, 1967), 188. Cf. Fretheim, *The Suffering of God*, chaps. 7–9, for distinctions between God suffering "because," "with," and "for."

101. Ward, *Divine Action*, 115. Cf. p. 113 ("the intersections") and p. 121 ("the constraints"). Ward distinguishes between "five distinct types of Divine action": (1) the originative act of creating this universe, (2) particular acts of imaginative development shaping this universe in contingent ways, (3) acts in response to the "chance" permutations of natural forces and to the free choices of rational creatures, (4) acts by which God relates in a personal way to persons, "inspiring or impeding their actions . . . and responding to their prayers," and (5) acts of the redemptive shaping of good out of evil or of the destruction of evil. My emphasis on the overarching category of relationship stresses the unity among the types.

102. Stephen T. Davis, *Logic and the Nature of God* (Grand Rapids: Wm. B. Eerdmans Publishing Co., 1983), argues that foreknowledge need not entail a human-freedom-denying predetermination. But how much comfort is gained? See Hasker, *God, Time and Knowledge*, for a development of the argument that *"whether or not there are creatures endowed with libertarian free will, it is impossible that God should use a foreknowledge derived from the actual occurrence of future events to determine his own prior actions in the providential governance of the world"* (p. 63). Emphasis his. Hasker is stressing that foreknowledge of any concrete future involves "the entirety of the causally relevant past history of the universe," so that "none of it is left to be decided by God" on the basis of God's foreknowledge (pp. 61–62). In any case, the "newness" of life would be denied the all-knowing God, and that is a great price for the believer to pay.

103. Rowan Williams, *Resurrection: Interpreting the Easter Gospel* (London: Darton, Longman & Todd, 1982), 23.

104. See chap. 2 above. To cite Keith Ward once more in *Rational Theology and the Creativity of God*, 208: "What could perhaps be true, consistently with human freedom and the general evolutionary character of the cosmos, is that God could guide, sustain and inspire the efforts of creatures . . . to an extent that does not undermine the general structure of reality. There might be providential Divine guidance, and particular 'miraculous' salvific acts, which would not undermine the structure of law and human autonomy, but might point to a fulfilment of that structure and autonomy in a wider context of relation to the Divine." I take up the theme of such fulfillment in the next chapter.

Chapter 5. To Become Other in Faith

1. Moltmann, *God in Creation*, 227. Emphasis his.
2. Moltmann, *God in Creation*, 227.
3. This is clearly the conclusion, e.g., of a study conducted by the Minneapolis-based Search Institute and funded by the Lilly Endowment. See Peter Benson and Carolyn H. Eklin, *Effective Christian Education: A National Study of Protestant Congregations—A Summary Report on Faith, Loyalty, and Congregational Life* (Minneapolis: Search Institute, 1990). For comment and a listing of the "eight dimensions of mature faith," see Eugene C. Roehlkepartain, "What Makes Faith Mature?" *Christian Century* 107 (9 May 1990): 496–99. I do not think Christian leaders do well to appeal to essentially endless debate about criteria instead of facing findings such as this: "Only a minority of Protestant adults evidence the kind of integrated, vibrant, and life-encompassing faith congregations seek to develop." The authors of the study may be right in claiming that "nothing matters more than Christian education," but that point needs to be understood to apply not only to the formal programming of the churches and to involve the "how" *and the* "what" of the teaching.
4. I take this passage from Luther's sermon "Two Kinds of Righteousness" (1519) as found in John Dillenberger, ed., *Martin Luther: Selections from His Writings* (Garden City, N.Y.: Doubleday & Co., Anchor Books, 1961), 88. For a fuller and very accessible secondary account, see Eberhard Jüngel, *The Freedom of a Christian*, trans. Roy A. Harrisville (Minneapolis: Augsburg Publishing House, 1988). Jüngel makes the point that "to be justified means to be unconditionally distinguished from God *for one's own good*" (p. 26, emphasis mine) and that "humanity is the creature on whom God is doing construction" (p. 46). Accordingly, Luther writes that Christ must be preached in such a fashion "that he may not only be Christ, but be Christ for you and me, and that what is said of him and is denoted in his name may be effectual in us" (p. 66). For another formulation, see Paul Althaus, *The Theology of Martin Luther*, trans. Robert Schultz (Philadelphia: Fortress Press Press, 1966), 244–45: "Righteous man and sinner are here not total but partial dimensions of man. . . . On the one hand, the Christian is involved in a daily renewed surrender of himself in faith to God's totally merciful judgment of life and death as a daily new reception of judgment and of the grace of justification. On the other hand, the constant renewal of my surrender to God's working in me results in the progressive death of the old man and the resurrection of the new man. The former is total; the latter is only partial."
5. Dillenberger, *Martin Luther: Selections*. Cf. Jose Miguez Bonino, "The Biblical Roots of Justice," *Word and World* 7, no. 1 (Winter 1987): 12–21, for a discussion of how "in the perspective of the covenant, God's action is understood as 'enabling,' as constituting a human subject (personally and communally) who participates meaningfully and effectively in God's work" (p. 19).

6. See Anne Carr, *Transforming Grace: Christian Tradition and Women's Experience* (San Francisco: Harper & Row, 1988), and Cobb, *Christ in a Pluralistic Age*, 122. Carr and Cobb remind one of Schleiermacher's efforts to speak of Christ generatively as *Urbild* rather than merely as an exemplary *Vorbild*. See Friedrich Schleiermacher, *The Christian Faith*, trans. H. R. Mackintosh and J. S. Stewart, 2d German ed. (Edinburgh: T. & T. Clark, 1928), 438ff. James Gustafson's *Christ and the Moral Life* (New York: Harper & Row, 1968) remains a helpful survey of options. Lutherans themselves do not speak with a single voice at this point. For a discussion of Melanchthon's forensic emphasis and Luther's Christ mysticism, see Steven Haggmark's unpublished doctoral dissertation, "The Possibility of a Metaphysic in Lutheran Theology with Special Reference to Boehme" (Luther Northwestern Theological Seminary, 1992), chap. 2. Gerhard O. Forde, *Justification by Faith—A Matter of Death and Life* (Philadelphia: Fortress Press, 1982), has made the point that the legal metaphor of justification needs to be coupled with a death-life dynamic in order to bear the full explosive power of the gospel.
7. *Come Holy Spirit, Renew the Whole Creation*, Six Bible Studies on the Theme of the Seventh Assembly of the World Council of Churches (Geneva: World Council of Churches Publications, 1989), 8.
8. See pp. 83–85 above.
9. Walter Altmann, "Interpreting the Doctrine of the Two Kingdoms: God's Kingship in the Church and in Politics," *Word and World* 7, no. 1 (Winter 1987): 43–58, 47. Yet Lutherans are notoriously nervous when that unity is seen to compromise crucial distinctions. This is nicely illustrated by Robert Benne's response to "A Postcommunist Manifesto" by Max L. Stackhouse and Dennis P. McCann, *Christian Century* 108 (16 January 1991): 1, 44–47. Benne appreciates the call for "a renewed *public* relevance of Christian religious and moral claims for the evolving system of democratic capitalism" but emphasizes that "we do not betray the gospel when our parishes do not foster a constructive engagement with the marketplace," concluding, "This Calvinist and Catholic enthusiasm invites a dash of Lutheran diffidence" (*Christian Century* 108 [23 January 1991]: 77–79). Emphasis his.
10. Dorothee Soelle, *Political Theology*, trans. John Shelley (Philadelphia: Fortress Press, 1971), 60. For a contemporary churchly statement with a similarly inclusive sense of what and who "salvation" talk is about, see *I Have Heard the Cry of My People*, the study book of the Lutheran World Federation's eighth assembly, Curitiba, Brazil (Geneva: Lutheran World Federation, 1989), 20, 30.
11. See pp. 95–96 above. For a discussion of how, in any case, the work of God in Christ is understood by Luther as the Creator God continuing to lay claim to creation, see David Lofgren, *Die Theologie der Schöpfung bei Luther* (Göttingen: Vandenhoeck & Ruprecht, 1960), 177–81.
12. See chap. 4, pp. 97–98 above.

13. In like manner, Moltmann, *God in Creation*, argues for distinguishing between the divine Spirit's cosmic, reconciling and redeeming "indwelling" (p. 12).
14. See pp. 104–109 above.
15. Lutherans have particularly agonized over this point. See Ekehard Muhlenberg, "*Synergia* and Justification by Faith," 15–37, in *Discord, Dialogue and Concord*, ed. Lewis Spitz (Philadelphia: Fortress Press, 1977), 34. Cf. Eugene Fevold's historical summary in "The Theological Scene," 305–28, in E. Clifford Nelson, *The Lutherans in North America* (Philadelphia: Fortress Press, 1975). Cf. Carl E. Braaten, *Justification: The Article by Which the Church Stands or Falls* (Minneapolis: Fortress Press, 1990), esp. chap. 2; and Robert W. Bertram, "Liberation by Faith: Segundo and Luther in Mutual Criticism," *dialog* 27, no. 4 (Fall 1988): 268–76. For an indication that it is not only Lutherans who seek to speak about how God's "redemptive gestalt" "transfigures and empowers the human emancipatory project," see Hodgson, *God in History*, 48–49 and passim.
16. See Terence Fretheim, "The Reclamation of Creation, Redemption and Law in Exodus," *Interpretation* 45 (October 1991): 354–64, for a statement of how the original creation was not without law, in that creational life needed to be both preserved and developed.
17. See pp. 93–94, 185 n. 61, above.
18. It is worth noting that Lutherans, while traditionally linked with the view that "the powers that be are ordained by God" (Romans 13), recognize that the sense of mutability is crucial. See *Lutheran Church—Salt or Mirror of Society, Case Studies on the Theory and Practice of the Two Kingdoms Doctrine*, ed. Ulrich Duchrow (Geneva: Lutheran World Federation, 1977). In a closing comment (p. 293), Duchrow writes: "The history of the tradition provides a shocking example of naivete and ideological self-deception. . . . The 'Old Adam' who is still at work in the *corpus permixtum* that is the church tends more and more—consciously or unconsciously—to declare those laws immutable which serve the interests of the powers that be; for only then can he live undisturbed by the existing powers, and even enjoy their support!" Old Testament scholars recognize this mutability. See, e.g., H. J. Hermission, "Observations on the Creation Theology in Wisdom," 118–34, in *Creation in the Old Testament*, ed. B. W. Anderson (Philadelphia: Fortress Press, 1984), 122: "Creation did not only happen at the beginning of the world, but takes place continuously; therefore, the orders have not become rigid, but necessarily remain flexible."
19. Sharon D. Welch, *A Feminist Ethic of Risk* (Minneapolis: Fortress Press, 1990), 3. For further development of Welch's opposing view, which warrants the "Risk" in her title, cf. pp. 32, 35, 47, 97, 99.
20. On p. 100 above, I have used the contemporary language of process thought to make this point. But it is available in other frameworks. Thus in commenting on Luther's *The Freedom of a Christian*, Jüngel builds on the point that "to be justified means to be unconditionally distinguished from God" (see note

4 above) by appropriating Luther's distinction between "inner" and "outer" in order to "preserve the connection which must be maintained between God, humanity, and the world from being misunderstood and misused as a connection *without a direction*" Jüngel, *Freedom of a Christian*, 80–81. Emphasis his.

21. The traditional corporal works of mercy are these: feeding the hungry, giving drink to the thirsty, clothing the naked, harboring the stranger, visiting the sick, ministering to the prisoner, burying the dead. For a discussion of how these works were understood in the early church, see Robert L. Wilken, *The Christians as the Romans Saw Them* (New Haven, Conn.: Yale University Press, 1984). For a contemporary statement in, once again, a very different setting, consider Beverly Wildung Harrison, *Making the Connections: Essays in Feminist Social Ethics*, ed. Carol S. Robb (Boston: Beacon Press, 1985), 177: "The people of God live under a stringent expectation of communal right relationships in which the meaning of justice is discerned particularly by the way the community deals with those who are most marginated or are not well placed to defend their own needs and interests." For further analysis, Harrison appropriately refers her readers to the writings of Gustavo Gutiérrez.

22. *Come Holy Spirit* (Canberra), 10.

23. Parker Palmer, *The Company of Strangers: Christians and the Renewal of America's Public Life* (New York: Crossroad, 1981), 64–65.

24. See pp. 17–18 above.

25. For a development of this theme, see Michael Welker, "Security of Expectations: Reformulating the Theology of Law and Gospel," 237–60, in *Journal of Religion* 66 (1986): 237–60.

26. Thus Mihaly Csikszentmihalyi (chap. 2, notes 49, 66, and 83, above) urges that we replace "brotherhood" with "beinghood" in our ethical reflection.

27. Michael Foucault, *The Archeology of Knowledge*, trans. A. M. Sheridan Smith (New York: Pantheon Books, 1972), 131, writes that the lesson of history "establishes that *we are difference*, that our reason is the difference of discourses, our history the difference of times, our selves the difference of masks." Emphasis mine. The specific analyses may be found in Michael Foucault, *Madness and Civilization: A History of Insanity in the Age of Reason*, trans. Richard Howard (New York: Random House, 1965); idem, *The Birth of the Clinic: An Archaeology of Medical Perception*, trans. A. M. Sheridan Smith (New York: Random House, 1975); idem, *Discipline and Punish: The Birth of the Prison*, trans. Alan Sheridan (New York: Random House, 1979); and idem, *The History of Sexuality*, trans. Robert Hurley (New York: Random House, 1978, 1985).

28. Palmer, in *Company of Strangers*, 30–31, comments: "The private has grown out of proportion in our society, and the inward journey has been perverted into narcissism, partly because we have failed to identify their public counterweight. . . . Public life alone has too much centrifugal force; it spins us away from our center and can cause personal fragmentation. It needs to be

balanced by the centripetal spin of inward experience. . . . Conversely, problems we regard as strictly private almost always have important public dimensions in their solutions."

29. Robert T. Hoeferkamp, "The Viability of Luther Today," 32–42, *Word and World* 7, no. 1:1 (Winter 1987): 40. Cf. Hall, *Imaging God* passim.

30. Luther, *The Freedom of a Christian*, trans. by W. A. Lambert and revised by Harold J. Grimm, *Luther's Works* (Philadelphia: Muhlenberg Press, 1957), 31:371.

31. See pp. 70–71 above.

32. Michael J. Sandel, *Liberalism and the Limits of Justice* (Cambridge: Cambridge University Press, 1982), 92.

33. Elizabeth Bettenhausen, "Dependence, Liberation, and Justification," 59–69, *Word and World* 7, no. 1 (Winter 1987): 63.

34. Sandel, *Liberalism and the Limits of Justice*, 149. Emphasis his.

35. Bettenhausen, "Dependence, Liberation, and Justification," 67.

36. Welch, *Feminist Ethic of Risk*, 162. Cf. the discussion of whether the movement to transcendence is "upward, outward, or downward" in Gunn, *Interpretation of Otherness*, chap. 5.

37. I cite once more the noteworthy collection of articles collected under the theme "Justification and Justice" in *Word and World* 7, no. 1 (Winter 1987): 22–31. This warning is from Gerhard O. Forde, "The Viability of Luther Today: A North American Perspective," 29.

38. Hodgson, *God in History*, 46.

39. Jüngel, *Freedom of a Christian*, 317–18.

40. See Delwin Brown, *To Set at Liberty: Christian Faith and Human Freedom* (Maryknoll, N.Y.: Orbis Books, 1981), 79ff., on how the denial of freedom is "structured into the fabric of our lives."

41. Sandel, *Liberalism and the Limits of Justice*, 66.

42. Jay B. McDaniel, *Of God and Pelicans: A Theology of Reverence for Life* (Louisville, Ky.: Westminster/John Knox Press, 1989), 80–81, employs the categories of harmony ("a general feeling of attunement, balance, accord, and affinity") and intensity ("zest or energetic vitality in relation to other beings"). Cf. Marjorie Hewitt Suchocki's discussion of three levels of "well-being" ("physical," "self-naming and dignity in community," "diversity of communities") in "In Search of Justice," 149–61, in *The Myth of Christian Uniqueness: Toward a Pluralistic Theology of Religions*, ed. John Hick and Paul F. Knitter (Maryknoll, N.Y.: Orbis Books, 1987).

43. A recent instance is the contention that the condemnation of the social policy of apartheid merits "confessional status" (*status confessionis*) because such policy denies the equality of diverse races before God. Earlier in this century the Barmen Declaration of the Confessional Church represented such resistance against the Nazi attack on particular human diversity.

44. Jonathan Schell, *The Fate of the Earth* (New York: Alfred A. Knopf, 1982), 174: "Formerly, the future was simply given to us; now it must be

achieved. . . . If we do not plant and cultivate the future years of human life, we will never reap them."

45. I realize that I am using Bonhoeffer's powerful phrase in a broader sense than that which provides the focus of *Life Together*, trans. John W. Doberstein (New York: Harper & Brothers, 1954). I am encouraged to do so by the fact that in writing of "The Day with Others," Bonhoeffer is concerned to relate prayer and work.

46. See the discussion of Luce Irigaray in M. K. Taylor, *Remembering Esperanza*, 200. Taylor sharpens the point: "Affirmation entails affirming not just the difference of 'the other,' but also the differential traits of the one(s) who claim to identify and encounter 'the others' " (pp. 199–200).

47. M. K. Taylor, *Remembering Esperanza*, 200.

48. Brock, *Journeys by Heart*, 17. It must be said that Brock recognizes that "we are broken by the world of our relationships before we are able to defend ourselves. . . . Those who damage us do not have the power to heal us, for they themselves are not healed" (p. 16). The critical question then becomes just how "the terrifying and destructive factors of life" are "taken into the self" and healed.

49. I have this quotation from Alfie Kohn, *The Brighter Side of Human Nature: Altruism and Empathy in Everyday Life* (New York: Basic Books, 1990), 119.

50. Kohn, *Brighter Side of Human Nature*, 219, 261. Cf. 218.

51. M. K. Taylor, *Remembering Esperanza*, 202–3, makes very effective use of Rabinow's emphasis on questioning, the mutual construction of the liminal world, and the shared and yet tenuous character of that world.

52. M. K. Taylor, *Remembering Esperanza*, 207.

53. See pp. 101–10 above.

54. Jüngel, *Freedom of a Christian*, 74. Emphasis his. He adds: "Whoever interpreted Christian faith to mean that bodily death no longer existed for the believer could only maintain faith as an absurdity." Jüngel effectively juxtaposes this understanding to the following statement by Ernst Bloch: "We do not know who we are. We do not know where we come from and where we are going" (p. 44).

55. Luther, *The Freedom of a Christian*, in *Luther's Works*, 31:344.

56. Gustafson, *Ethics from a Theocentric Perspective*, 1:129ff. Cf. Gustafson's discussion in *Can Ethics Be Christian?* (Chicago: University of Chicago Press, 1975), chap. 4.

57. Ann Belford Ulanov, "What Do We Think People Are Doing When They Pray?" 387–98, *Anglican Theological Review* 60, no. 4 (1978): 388. She adds: "We do not reach this glimpse of the essential self except by sorting through all the feelings, ambitions, and needs that preoccupy us in our days with which we tend to identify ourselves. In this sorting process we identify to ourselves the kinds of reactions that have captured our attention and we stand aside from them, disidentifying them as central marks of who and what we are. We can then discover the 'false gods.' " In personal conversation

Jonathan Strandjord has employed Whiteheadian categories to speak of God as our "counterpart," a "logos-eccentric" [sic] God who de-absolutizes absolute claims made for finite purposes. For a biblical viewpoint, see Levenson, *Creation and the Persistence of Evil*, 172: "It is through the cult that we are enabled to cope with evil, for it is the cult that builds and maintains order, transforms chaos into creation, ennobles humanity, and realizes the kingship of the God who has ordained the cult and commanded that it be guarded and practiced." I am emphasizing that the power of the God relationship, as realized in prayer and cult, is precisely such that it moves to affect the believer's other relationships.

58. David Tracy, "Hermeneutical Reflections in the new Paradigm," 34–62, in Küng and Tracy, *Paradigm Change in Theology*, 49. Similarly, though from a different perspective, Douglas John Hall, in *Thinking the Faith*, 13, writes of how the word of the cross "must become new and unheard of." On the limits of interpretation, see the *dialog* issue "Texts and the Limits of Interpretation," 28, no. 4 (Autumn 1989).

59. Chopp, *The Power to Speak*, 65–66. Chopp emphasizes that the text breaks us open to hear other voices—voices often silenced in our world. Cf. Taylor, *Remembering Esperanza*, 58ff., on how understanding and application are together in reading the text so that one is in conversation with the "Thou" of the text *and* with other "Thou(s)" in the present.

60. F. W. Dillistone, *The Christian Understanding of the Atonement* (Philadelphia: Westminster Press, 1968), 291. This work remains an excellent analysis of eight options.

61. George Rupp, *Christologies and Cultures: Toward a Typology of Religious Worldviews* (The Hague: Mouton, 1974), 163, 47, 193–94.

62. See pp. 94–98 above. Cf. Moltmann, *God in Creation*, 90: "God's adherence to his resolve *to create* also means a resolve *to save*." Emphasis his.

63. See pp. 62–66 above. Stanley Hauerwas, who as much as anyone has emphasized Christian community in ethical reflection, himself makes the descriptive connection in writing of "how my mind has changed." See Hauerwas, "The Testament of Friends," in *Christian Century* 107, no. 7 (28 February, 1990): 212–15: "I have increasingly come to distrust the moral psychology that maintains the existence of such an (isolated) 'I.' The 'self' of self-agency, assumed in my early work, still owed too much to the self abstracted from any narrative—something Derrida and Foucault have rightly questioned. . . . I now think I understand much better how a narrative is necessary for character—or to put it theologically, why sin and forgiveness are necessary for us to be 'selves'—and as an alternative to Descartes and Kant as well as their genealogical critics" (p. 215).

64. See Welch, *Feminist Ethic of Risk*, 111.

65. Shirley C. Guthrie, Jr., *Diversity in Faith: Unity in Christ* (Philadelphia: Westminster Press, 1986), 20.

66. Larry Rasmussen, "A Community of the Cross," 150–62, *dialog* 30, no. 2 (Spring 1991).

67. Cf. Lee E. Snook, "Ecumenical Vision and Evangelical Imagination," *Word and World* 10, no. 3 (Summer 1990): 216–28.

68. Cf. Harrison, *Making the Connections*, xix.

69. See note 43 above.

70. Charles E. Winquist, "Theology, Deconstruction, and Ritual Process," 295–309, *Zygon* 18, no. 3 (September 1983): 301.

71. Dorothee Soelle, *Suffering*, trans. Everett R. Kalin (Philadelphia: Fortress Press, 1975), 74.

72. Cf. McDaniel, *Of God and Pelicans*, 115–16. Brock, in *Journeys by Heart*, 34–35, insightfully critiques those process thinkers who have attempted to replace coercive power with persuasive power: "Persuasion still connotes possession of power by an actor who attempts to get his or her own way. We must move from seeing power as a commodity possessed by a self toward seeing it as the bonds which create and sustain, and are recreated and sustained by relational selves." Cf. Joan Chittister's use of Rollo May's categories (exploitative, competitive, manipulative, nurturant, and integrative) in *Job's Daughters: Women and Power* (New York: Paulist Press, 1990). Farley, *Good and Evil*, 181, also writes of how transforming vitality is not dominated by the "either-or between the self and what is other."

73. See Loomer, "Two Conceptions of power," 17; and chap. 4, note 99, above.

74. David Tracy, *Plurality and Ambiguity: Hermeneutics, Religion, Hope* (San Francisco: Harper & Row, 1987), 79.

75. Hall, *God and Human Suffering*, 113. Emphasis his. Cf. his critique of "ransom" and substitutionary atonement theories, 134–36.

76. Cf. Welch, *Feminist Ethic of Risk*, 86. See Toulmin, *Cosmopolis*, 197–98, 209, on the effectiveness of Jonathan Swift's image of Lilliput in Robinson Crusoe: "Stalin failed to see that the military triviality of the Pope's Swiss Guard increases his claim to a hearing, rather than undermining it; while Amnesty International's moral authority is that much the greater, just because it is a Lilliputian institution."

77. Sandel, *Liberalism and the Limits of Justice*, 172. See his earlier discussion of "intersubjective and intrasubjective" conceptions of self: "Intersubjective conceptions allow that in certain moral circumstances, the relevant description of the self may embrace more than a single, individual human being, as when we attribute responsibility or affirm an obligation to a family or community or class or nation rather than to some particular human being. . . . Intrasubjective conceptions, on the other hand, allow that for certain purposes, the appropriate description of the moral subject may refer to a plurality of selves within a single, individual human being, as when we account for inner deliberation in terms of the pull of competing identities, or moments of introspection in terms of occluded self-knowledge, or when we absolve someone from responsibility for the heretical beliefs 'he' held before his religious conversion" (pp. 62–63). Cf. Julia Kristeva, *Strangers to Ourselves*, trans. Leon S. Roudiez (New York: Columbia University Press, 1991).

78. Sandel, *Liberalism and the Limits of Justice*, 172–3.

79. John Berryman, "Surveillance," *Ohio Review* 15 (Winter 1974): 45. Emphasis his.

80. See Peukert's fuller statement quoted on pp. 73–74 above, and the discussion there.

81. Ward, *Rational Theology and the Creativity of God*, 196. A fuller statement is available in chaps. 3–8 of Ward *Divine Action*.

82. See p. 135 above. Pierre Bayle's "Paulicans" in *Historical and Critical Dictionary* (London: Printed for C. Harper, 1710) is a strong classical critique of "the free will defense."

83. See p. 37 above.

84. Westermann, *Creation*, 22. I have discussed "metaphysical and natural evil" in 433–46 of my locus on "Sin and Evil," in Braaten and Jenson, *Christian Dogmatics*, 1:359–468.

85. Hans Walter Wolff, *Anthropology of the Old Testament*, trans. Margaret Kohl (Philadelphia: Fortress Press, 1974), 102ff., makes the point that death, while "natural," does not cease to be regarded as evil. Wolfhart Pannenberg has pointed to broad expressions of human hope. See, e.g., his discussion of "the incompleteness of history and the presence of truth" in *Anthropology in Theological Perspective*, 515–21.

86. Cf. Farley's discussion of "the tragic" and "benign alienation" in *Good and Evil*, 29, 45, 109.

87. Hodgson, *God in History*, 250.

88. I am citing here Ogletree's summation in *Hospitality to the Stranger*, 77–78, of Ricoeur's discussion in *Freedom and Nature: The Voluntary and the Involuntary*, trans. Erazim V. Kohak (Evanston, Ill.: Northwestern University Press, 1966).

89. See pp. 97–98 above.

90. See chap. 4, note 73, above.

91. Cf. my discussion in *God—The Question and the Quest* (Philadelphia: Fortress Press, 1985), 35–43.

92. Thomas F. Torrance, *Space, Time and Resurrection* (Grand Rapids: Wm. B. Eerdmans Publishing Co., 1976), 180. Cf. chap. 2, note 29, above.

93. Eulalio R. Baltazar, *God Within Process* (Paramus, N.J.: Newman Press, 1970). "Amateur" is Baltazar's characterization (p. 3).

94. Baltazar, *God Within Process*, 119–22.

95. Frank J. Tipler, "The Omega Point as *Eschaton*: Answers to Pannenberg's Questions for Scientists," an unpublished paper presented at the Pannenberg Conference, Lutheran School of Theology at Chicago, November 1988, 22.

96. Hodgson, *God in History*, 231ff., makes this point, citing particularly the work of Rosemary Radford Ruether.

97. Whitehead, *Process and Reality*, 209.

98. Whitehead, *Process and Reality*, 350.

99. Cf. my summary discussion in *Faith and Process*, 125–30.

100. Marjorie Hewitt Suchocki, *The End of Evil: Process Eschatology in Historical Context* (Albany: State University of New York Press, 1988). See the exchange between Suchocki and David Ray Griffin in *Process Studies* 18, no. 1 (Spring 1989): 57–68. In process language Suchocki interposes between "concrescence" and "transition" a third mode of creativity to be called "enjoyment," so that "immediacy" is retained in "satisfaction" (p. 111). God, who—unlike all finite entities—"prehends" without negative prehensions, "prehends the satisfaction's entirety, and hence its subjectivity" (p. 90).

101. Suchocki, *The End of Evil*, 108. Emphasis hers.

102. See Suchocki, *The End of Evil*, chap. 7, "Freedom and Temporal Redemption: The Historical Community."

103. Ward, *Divine Action*, 266.

104. See the reference to "the transformation of all epochs of human history through the fire of the divine judgment" in Wolfhart Pannenberg, *The Apostles' Creed in the Light of Today's Questions* (Philadelphia: Westminster Press, 1972), 178.

105. Arland J. Hultgren, *Paul's Gospel and Mission: The Outlook from His Letter to the Romans* (Philadelphia: Fortress Press, 1985), 113 (see esp. 98–115). Hultgren cites, among others, Karl Barth's version of the *apokatastasis* or universal reconciliation (God's compassion should not fail), but could have cited as well the forceful reasoning of Langdon Gilkey. Gilkey, *Reaping the Whirlwind*, 298, states the logic of hope most pointedly: "There can be no dual destiny in this hope, if there is to be hope at all. No ultimate division between persons who are sheep and persons who are goats, those who participate in God and those who are condemned to hell, is admissible if the divine power is to be ultimately sovereign and the divine love the ultimate quality of that power. . . . However we argue, so long as there is a dual destiny, faith is a merit that saves." I am arguing that the logic of a true telos also calls for some element of continuity —including moral continuity. That it is clear that coherence is strained in meeting these demands points once again to the pressing need for fresh and fundamental theological work on the telos of faith. Suchocki's formulations may represent a beginning.

106. Moltmann, *God in Creation*, 103.

107. Moltmann, *God in Creation*, 103.

108. Cf. Torrance, *Space, Time and Resurrection*; and Pannenberg, *Anthropology in Theological Perspective*, 106.

109. Fiddes, *Creative Suffering*, 105. Emphasis his. Cf. 144.

Chapter 6. To Be with the Others in Faith

1. Stephen Toulmin, in *Cosmopolis* [167–68, 330] sketches an analogous development on the collective level: a three-century trajectory in the shape of an Omega: "We are back close to our starting point. Natural scientists no longer separate the 'observer' from the 'world observed.' . . . Sovereign nation-states find their independence circumscribed; and Descartes' *foundational* ambitions are discredited, taking philosophy back to the skepticism of

Montaigne. In neither intellectual nor practical respects are things still systemic or self-contained. . . . Doctrinally, then, the trajectory of Modernity has closed back on itself into an Omega; but experientially it has headed broadly upward. As people in Europe and North America have learned from the experience of modernity, and have attacked the inequalities built into the 'modern' scaffolding, they have developed a discriminating care for human interests." Emphasis his. I agree that it is a time of moment, but I see both promise and peril in this.

2. The message from the Eighth Assembly of the Lutheran World Federation in Curitiba, Brazil, 30 January–8 February, 1990, 44 (Geneva: *Lutheran World Information*), release of 19 February 1990. Emphasis mine.

3. Paul Varo Martinson, "What Then Shall We Do?" 174–97, in *Lutherans and the Challenge of Religious Pluralism*, ed. Frank W. Klos, C. Lynn Nakamura and Daniel F. Martensen (Minneapolis: Augsburg Publishing House, 1990), 179.

4. See Fritjof Schuon, *The Transcendent Unity of Religions*, trans. Peter Townsend (New York: Harper & Row, 1975). Langdon Gilkey, "Plurality and Its Theological Implications," 37–50, in Hick and Knitter, *Myth of Christian Uniqueness*, warns against this effort to absolutize a mystical inner core and against what might be termed the opposite error: "Each system of religious symbols forms a coherent, interrelated whole; and each *Gestalt* of symbols is particular, at variance with, other *Gestalten*. . . . No one doctrine . . . (. . . for example, God or human being) can be abstracted out and be established as universal in all religions, a point of unity with other religious traditions" (p. 41).

5. Cobb, *Christ in a Pluralistic Age,* 19. Cf. Cobb, *Beyond Dialogue: Towards a Mutual Transformation of Christianity and Buddhism* (Philadelphia: Fortress Press, 1982). Cf. Cobb's discussion in "Beyond 'Pluralism,' " 81–95, in Gavin D'Costa, *Christian Uniqueness Reconsidered: The Myth of a Pluralistic Theology of Religions* (Maryknoll, N.Y.: Orbis Books, 1990). This critical point is a frequent theme in the essays in this volume. For an account of early Christian critical recognition of difference, see Robert L. Wilken, "Religious Pluralism and Early Christian Theology," *Interpretation* 40, no. 4 (October 1986): 379–91.

6. Faced with "the theoretical dilemma" that "there seems no consistent theological way to relativize and yet to assert our own symbols," Gilkey, "Plurality and Its Theological Implications," 46ff, refers us to the "venerable" American tradition of *"intelligent practice."* Emphasis his. Cf. Charles W. Allen, "The Primacy of *Phronesis*: A Proposal for Avoiding Frustrating Tendencies in Our Conceptions of Rationality," *Journal of Religion* 69, no. 3 (July 1989): 359–74. Cf. the last section of this chapter, "Living Faithfully and Fruitfully."

7. See pp. 76–86 above.

8. See "Religious Plurality: Theological Perspectives and Affirmations," a document prepared by an ecumenical consultation called by the Dialogue subunit

of the World Council of Churches, Baar, Switzerland, January 1990, *Buddhist-Christian Studies* 11 (1991): 297–301, para. 8. For a report on the consultation, see Diana L. Eck, "On Seeking and Finding in the World's Religions," *Christian Century* 107 (2 May 1990): 454–56.

9. See the report of Section III, "Spirit of Unity—Reconcile Your People!" Seventh Assembly of the World Council of Churches, Canberra, 1991. Emphasis mine.

10. Paul Althaus, e.g., distinguishes between *Uroffenbarung* (primordial revelation), *Wortoffenbarung* (Israel's history in the Hebrew scripture), and *Christusoffenbarung*. Cf. the discussion in Paul F. Knitter, *Towards a Protestant Theology of Religions: A Case Study of Paul Althaus and Contemporary Attitudes* (Marburg: N. G. Elwert Verlag, 1974); and in Paul Varo Martinson in "Salvation and the Religions: From *Sola* to *Simul*," forthcoming from the Lutheran World Federation (Geneva).

11. Lesslie Newbigin, *The Gospel in a Pluralist Society* (Grand Rapids: Wm. B. Eerdmans Publishing Co., 1989), 38. It is worthy of note that Newbigin remarks that the lenses are to be used to look at the *world,* not simply at God. That this recognition of the human element does not paralyze Newbigin is evident by, among many other things, his prominence in the "The Gospel and Our Culture" newsletter, a publication of a British Council of Churches' group with an admirably broad agenda represented by their four themes: human rights, artificial intelligence, underlying issues for chemists and physicists, and the presuppositions of interfaith dialogue.

12. For a thorough statement of this kind of internal Christian multiplicity, see Lamin Sanneh, *Translating the Message: The Missionary Impact on Culture* (Maryknoll, N.Y.: Orbis Books, 1989). Sanneh observes that "muslims ascribe to Arabic the status of a revealed language," whereas "Christianity has no single revealed language" (pp. 212–14).

13. See pp. 102–103 above.

14. Wolfhart Pannenberg has been particularly clear about stressing that the revelation of God is in and through history, i.e., it is "clothed." In that sense it is not a direct self-revelation of God. See Pannenberg, *Systematische Theologie*, 1:251. This emphasis can be found also in his early work, as in the pioneering work *Revelation as History*, trans. David Granskon (New York: Macmillan Co., 1968).

15. Despite the warning that Langdon Gilkey wisely makes concerning the system-embeddedness of all symbols (n. 4, above), it does not follow that no connections between such systems exist. For an attempt to reflect on the other religions in the light of one central Christian category, see Theodore M. Ludwig, "Revelation in the Religions: Divine Origin and Human Experience," forthcoming from the Lutheran World Federation (Geneva). While attentive to particular differences, Ludwig can write: "There is in all the religions a complex interplay between human experience and the divine origin of revelatory truth" (p. 20). This certainly would not deny that in some religions,

perhaps in Buddhism, the relationship in which revelation occurs would be understood as an internal relationship.

16. See, e.g., the comparative remarks by Stephen Toulmin in "The Historicization of Natural Science: Its Implications for Theology," 233–41, in Küng and Tracy, *Paradigm Change in Theology.*

17. Here I go against the counsel of John Hick, who is fond of quoting Thomas Aquinas's remark that "the thing known is in the knower according to the mode of the knower" (*Summa Theologica* II/II, Q.1, art. 2), and can go on to speak of our capacity for self-deception. Yet Hick argues that it is "very hard, if not impossible, to make global moral judgments" about "the religious totalities." His conclusion is "that the project of a comparative ethical assessment of the great religious totalities leads into an impossible morass from which nothing useful can emerge." See John Hick, *God Has Many Names* (Philadelphia: Westminster Press, 1980, 1982), 48–56. It will be clear, I trust, that I grant the difficulty of the task but find that the very power of religion is such that it requires some kind of moral judgment. Hick himself has offered very discerning moral criticism of the several "great" religious traditions (as, Hinduism: the validating of caste, the cruel persecution of brides with insufficient dowries; Buddhism: indifference to social injustice; Islam: the sanctioning of holy wars and fanatical intolerance; Christianity: the persecution of heretics, the fostering of anti-Semitic attitudes and activities, etc.), in "The Non-Absoluteness of Christianity," 16–36, in Hick and Knitter, *Myth of Christian Uniqueness*, 29–30. If such specific criticism can be (well) offered, I do not see how at least tentative more summary judgments must or even can be avoided.

18. Baar document, para. 14. Cf. Curitiba document, para. 54.

19. Curitiba document, para. 62.

20. Carl E. Braaten, "The Problem of the Absoluteness of Christianity," 341–53, in *Interpretation* 40, no. 4 (October 1986): 353. See also Wolfhart Pannenberg, "Religious Pluralism and Conflicting Truth Claims," 96–106, in D'Costa, *Christian Uniqueness Reconsidered.*

21. Baar document, paragraph 26. Cf. Paul Rajashekar and Satori Kishii, eds., *Theology in Dialogue: Theology in the Context of Religious and Cultural Plurality in Asia* (Geneva: Lutheran World Federation, 1987). Chung Hyun Kyung states this in very radical terms in *Struggle to Be the Sun Again: Introducing Asian Women's Theology* (Maryknoll, N.Y.: Orbis Books, 1990), 113, in indicating that she hopes Asian women's theology will "move away from the doctrinal purity of Christian theology and risk *the survival-liberation centered syncretism.*" Yet I take her to intend Christian continuity inasmuch as she links this hope with a critique of "traditional Western theologians'" *copyright* mentality. Emphasis hers.

22. That degree of discontinuity seems to be involved in Wilfred Cantwell Smith, *Toward a World Theology: Faith and the Comparative History of Religion* (Philadephia: Westminster Press, 1981), even though matters are stated in an evolutionary perspective.

23. See Paul Knitter's argument in "Toward a Liberation Theology of Religion," 178–202, in Hick and Knitter, *Myth of Christian Uniqueness*, 187. In *No Other Name? A Critical Survey of Christian Attitudes Toward the World Religions* (Maryknoll, N.Y.: Orbis Books, 1985), 231, Knitter specifies three sorts of criteria: "1) *Personally*, does the revelation of the religion or religious figure—the story, the myth, the message—move the human heart? Does it stir one's feelings, the depths of one's unconscious? 2) *Intellectually*, does the revelation also satisfy and expand the mind? Is it intellectually coherent? Does it broaden one's horizons of understanding? 3) *Practically*, does the message promote the psychological health of individuals, their sense of value, purpose, freedom? Especially, does it promote the welfare, the liberation, of all peoples, integrating individual persons and nations into a larger community?" Emphasis his.

24. Canberra document, 9.

25. Knitter writes in *No Other Name?* 188: "I am certainly not implying that there is only one way of understanding 'salvation' or that my Christian grasp of it is final or normative. . . . But one *does* have a starting point." Emphasis his. Cf. my discussion in chap. 5 above.

26. I take it this is what Chung Hyun Kyung may have in mind in stressing the need for (Asian women's, but presumably also all) theology to be "life centered" (*Struggle to Be the Sun Again*, 114). See also her critique (p. 107) of a "mystified" view of the Bible and her plea for "dialogical imagination" as a way of interpreting the biblical truth. Similarly, M. K. Taylor, *Remembering Esperanza,* 40ff., gives *independent* voice to the call to "resist domination" so that this creates the "postmodern trilemma" together with "acknowledging tradition" and "celebrating plurality."

27. Tillich, *Systematic Theology*, 1:111–14.

28. Darrell Jodock, in a review of David Chidester's *Salvation and Suicide: An Interpretation of Jim Jones, the Peoples Temple, and Jonestown* (Bloomington: Indiana University Press, 1988), in *dialog* 29, no. 2 (Spring 1990): 148–151.

29. Both the 1990 documents I have cited make this point: Baar, para. 10; Curitiba, para. 57. In his commentary on the WCC at Canberra, Jeffrey Gros notes that such broad hope is not very novel: "Both Eastern and Western church tradition have always recognized the salvific power of Jesus Christ beyond the borders of the explicit confession of the church, even when affirming that 'outside the church there is no salvation.'" See Jeffrey Gros, "Christian Confession in a Pluralistic World," *Christian Century* 108 (26 June-3 July 1991): 644–46. This could be supposed to be implied by Carl Braaten, when he speaks of "the final coming of the kingdom which will embrace universal historical forms beyond the separation between the church and the world and beyond the separation between Christianity and the religions." See Carl E. Braaten, "Lutheran Theology and Religious Pluralism," 105–28, in *Religious Pluralism and Lutheran Theology*, ed. Paul Rajashekar (Geneva: Lutheran World Federation, 1988), 124.

30. Baar document, para. 11. Emphasis mine.
31. Canberra document, 9. Emphasis mine.
32. See Knitter, *Towards a Protestant Theology of Religions*, chaps. 5 and 6. In Knitter, *No Other Name?* see especially the discussion of "Revelation-Yes! Salvation-No!" 98–107.
33. See pp. 96–98, 144 above, and my discussion in *God—The Question and the Quest,* chap. 7. In thus turning toward an "objective" element in atonement I am in sharp disagreement with John Hick and especially Stanley J. Samartha in Hick and Knitter, *Myth of Christian Uniqueness*, 33, 79.
34. Pannenberg commonly writes in such a vein, as in emphasizing that only the completion of history will show that God is God of all (*Systematische Theologie*, 1:269).
35. Pannenberg, "Religious Pluralism and Conflicting Truth Claims," in D'Costa, *Christian Uniqueness Reconsidered*, 104.
36. For Karl Rahner's famous phrase, see "Anonymous Christianity and the Missionary Task of the Church," in *Theological Investigations* (New York: Seabury Press, 1974), 12:161–78. As to the denial of genuine atheism, Schubert Ogden writes that "if we are human at all, we unavoidably *believe in God*." See his "Response," 45–57, in *Perkins School of Theology Journal* 26, no. 2 (Winter 1973): 55. Emphasis his. Ogden, in *The Reality of God, and Other Essays* (New York: Harper & Row, 1963), 42–43, speaks of this faith as "an original confidence in the ultimate significance of life." For a response to a quite different appeal to this slippery adjective, see Kaufmann's critique of Tillich's notion of "ultimate concern" in Walter Kaufmann, *The Faith of a Heretic* (Garden City, N.Y.: Doubleday & Co., 1961), 136–38.
37. Wingren, *Creation and Law*, 28–29, unmasks such arrogance: "To be surrounded by conditions and relations which have no connection with the relationship to God, and to conceive of this relationship as being non-existent among those who have not heard nor received the historically given word concerning Christ, is in itself a tremendous declaration of independence of God and of fellowship with Him, and this declaration cannot be modified or balanced by statements affirming Christ's lordship."
38. Max L. Stackhouse, *Creeds, Society, and Human Rights: A Study in Three Cultures* (Grand Rapids: Wm. B. Eerdmans Publishing Co., 1984), 16.
39. Augsburger, *Pastoral Counseling Across Cultures*, 52. Augsburger goes on to cite such studies as Malinowski's of "seven basic needs" (metabolism, reproduction, bodily comforts, safety, movement, growth, health) and "four global constants" (biological, psychological, spiritual, and sociocultural).
40. Morris Cohen, "The Dark Side of Religion," in *Religion from Tolstoy to Camus*, ed. Walter Kaufmann (New York: Harper & Row, 1961; Harper Torchbook, 1964), 289. Cf. the Canberra document on how "today in many parts of the world religion is used as a force of division and conflict."
41. I state this challenge rather fully in *God—The Question and the Quest*, chaps. 2–4.

42. Soelle, *Suffering,* 116.
43. Richardson, *Toward an American Theology,* chap. 1.
44. Cf. Chopp, *The Power to Speak,* 15–16: "The center is, in modernity, crack-
    ing, its fissures are widening, and in these fissures and cracks, discourses of
    emancipatory transformation may be formed."
45. See p. 102 above.
46. See my discussion in "The Divine Incognito: The Real, the Beautiful, and
    the Good," in Braaten and Jenson, *Christian Dogmatics,* 1:229–35.
47. Peter Berger, in *Rumor of Angels: Modern Society and the Rediscovery of
    the Supernatural* (Garden City, N.Y.: Doubleday & Co., 1969), considers
    such matters as human propensities for order, hope, judgment, play, and humor.
    On "safety," Norman Malcolm, *Ludwig Wittgenstein: A Memoir* (London:
    Oxford University Press, 1958), 70 n. 1, recounts: "Wittgenstein . . . said
    that he sometimes had a certain experience which could best be described by
    saying that 'when I have it *I wonder at the existence of the world.* And I am
    then inclined to use such phrases as "How extraordinary that anything should
    exist!" or "How extraordinary that the world should exist!" ' He went on to
    say . . . that he sometimes also had 'the experience of feeling *absolutely*
    safe.' I mean the state of mind in which one is inclined to say 'I am safe,
    nothing can injure me *whatever* happens.' " Emphasis his.
48. Augustine, *Confessions,* trans. Edward B. Pusey (New York: Pocket Books,
    1952), 1:1.1.
49. Blaise Pascal, *Pensées,* trans. W. F. Trotter (New York: Random House,
    1941), entry 554.
50. A classic discussion is that of William James in "The Will to Believe": "Were
    we scholastic absolutists, there might be more excuse. If we had an infallible
    intellect with its objective certitudes, we might feel ourselves disloyal to such
    a perfect organ of knowledge in not trusting to it exclusively, in not waiting
    for its releasing word. But if we are empiricists, if we believe that no bell in
    us tolls to let us know for certain when truth is in our grasp, then it seems
    a piece of idle fantasticality to preach so solemnly our duty of waiting for
    the bell" (Kaufmann, *Religion from Tolstoy to Camus,* 237).
51. Cf. Newbigin, *Gospel in a Pluralist Society,* 50, on "universal intent."
52. Cf. Pamela Dickey Young, *Feminist Theology/Christian Theology: In Search
    of Method* (Minneapolis: Augsburg Fortress, 1990), 76: "It is not necessary
    to choose one criterion or the other . . . appropriateness or credibility—for
    the two criteria work together."
53. Cobb, "Beyond 'Pluralism,' 83–95, in D'Costa, *Christian Uniqueness Re-
    considered,* 87. In developing this point, Cobb notes that all the great religious
    traditions "make some claim to the universal value of their particular insights
    and affirmations" and "teach a certain humility with regard to human un-
    derstanding of reality in its depth and fullness." He grants, of course, that
    "all traditions have fundamentalist subtraditions that reject all new learning,
    insisting on the total adequacy and accuracy of what has been received from
    the past" (p. 88).

54. Francis Schüssler Fiorenza, *Foundational Theology: Jesus and the Church* (New York: Crossroad, 1984), 305.
55. Chopp, *Power to Speak*, 15–16; cf. the discussion in chap. 3, note 57, above, of the analysis by Mary Douglas of "four kinds of social pollution."
56. Chopp, *Power to Speak*, 15–16, is citing Toril Moi, *Sexual/Textual Politics: Feminist Literary Theory* (London: Methuen, 1985), 167. Emphasis hers.
57. As to *what* is claimed the real enemy, analogously, could be said to be those who seek to tear apart what God has put together: the relationship between God and humankind. One can speak of the human person in such a way that with such a one there can be no room for a relationship with God. Or one can speak of God in such a way that God cannot be subjected to the flesh of human struggle and change. It is in reductive naturalism and rigidifying theism that faith finds its true enemies. Recognizing this, Jürgen Moltmann entitles a key section of *The Crucified God* "Beyond Theism and Atheism."
58. Canberra document, 9.
59. See John Milbank, "The End of Dialogue," 174–91 in D'Costa, *Christian Uniqueness Reconsidered*, 177. Milbank argues that this commitment to dialogue really regards the other "as valuable mainly in terms of their abstract possession of an autonomous freedom of spiritual outlook and an open commitment to the truth. In other words, . . . one takes them as liberal, Western subjects, images of oneself."
60. John Cobb, *Beyond Dialogue*, 39f., appropriately criticizes the World Council of Churches for resisting dealing "with religious traditions as such, and with people as representatives of these traditions."
61. Thus Richard Bernstein, "Incommensurability and Otherness Revisited" (Paper delivered at the Sixth East-West Philosophers' Conference, Hawaii, 1989), warns (pp. 12–13) against "a false essentialism where we are seduced into thinking there are essential determinate characteristics that distinguish the Western and Eastern 'mind.' This false essentialism violently distorts the sheer complexity of overlapping traditions that cut across these artificial simplistic global notions."
62. See, e.g., Juan Luis Segundo, *The Liberation of Theology*, trans. John Drury (Maryknoll, N.Y.: Orbis Books, 1976). Brian Erickson has particularly driven home this point for me. See his unpublished doctoral dissertation at Luther Northwestern Seminary in St. Paul, "Liberating Theology and Education for North Americans," 1990.
63. For a descriptive account of this issue, see Michael Welker, "Alfred North Whitehead's Basic Philosophical Problem: The Development of a Relativistic Cosmology," *Process Studies* 16, no. 1 (Spring 1987):1–25.
64. David Lochhead, *The Dialogical Imperative: A Christian Reflection on Interfaith Encounter* (Maryknoll, N.Y.: Orbis Books, 1988), 44.
65. See Rajashekar, *Religious Pluralism*, 187–88, for a proposal "that combines the two aspects—applying the theological principles *and* listening to the other—in an ongoing process of cross-reference and correlation. Experience

in dialogue *and* theological reflection on the basis of our theological principles move in a hermeneutical circle." Emphasis his.

66. John Dunne has written of "passing over" in *The Way of All the Earth* (New York: Macmillan Co, 1972). In an unpublished lecture ("Incommensurability, Truth and the Conversation Between Confucians and Aristotelians About the Virtues") at the Sixth East-West Philosophers' Conference, Hawaii, in 1989, Alasdair MacIntyre spoke of someone learning the language of a rival standpoint, inhabiting—as it were—both standpoints.

67. Martinson, "What Then Shall We Do?" 182.

68. See pp. 12–14 above.

69. Thomas Kuhn, *The Structure of Scientific Revolutions*, 2d ed. enl. (Chicago: University of Chicago Press, 1970), 148 and 150.

70. In addition to Richard Bernstein's much-cited (chap. 1, notes 30, 40, above) work *Beyond Objectivism and Relativism,* I am drawing on his paper cited in note 61 above. Ian Barbour was making the same point in philosophy of science (and then in philosophy of religion) as early as 1974 in *Myths, Models and Paradigms: A Comparative Study in Science and Religion* (New York: Harper & Row, 1974). The classic critique of the indefensibility of absolute incommensurability is Donald Davidson's "On the Very Idea of a Conceptual Scheme," *Proceedings and Addresses of the American Philosophical Association* 47 (1973–74): 5–20.

71. I am quoting Cobb, "Experience and Language" (Paper available from the Center for Process Studies, Claremont, Calif.), 12. See also Hilary Putnam, *The Many Faces of Realism* (LaSalle, Ill.: Open Court, 1987).

72. Mark S. Heim, "Mapping Globalization for Theological Education," 7–34, *Theological Education*, Supplement 1 (Spring 1990): 14. Mark Kline Taylor and Gary J. Bekker offer a comparable richness of reference in "Engaging the Other in the Global Village," 52–85, in the same issue.

73. Harrison, *Making the Connections.* See also Welch, *Feminist Ethic of Risk,* 128–9, who in developing this theme of "objectivity" incorporates Sandra Harding's emphasis (in *The Science Question in Feminism* [Ithaca, N.Y.: Cornell University Press, 1986]) on the "epistemological privilege of the oppressed." Cf. p. 190 n. 28.

74. In the lecture referred to in note 66 above MacIntyre speaks of two conditions needed in order for adherents of a particular tradition to come to see that an alternative tradition is superior. (1) The tradition should lead to irremediable failure in the light of its own standards in the face of some set of problems which its own goals require it to solve. (2) The alternative tradition must be able to provide the resources to explain why the first tradition failed by its own standard of achievement, and the resources for such explanation must not be available within the first tradition. It is to be noted that this process does *not* require common standards, not to mention neutral standards.

75. A good start for such work is represented by "The Decalogue Dialogue: Ground Rules for Interreligious, Interideological Dialogue," by Leonard Swidler in the *Journal of Ecumenical Studies* 29, no. 1 (Winter 1983): 1–4. I have

offered some suggestions about how the traditional Western truth theories might be employed in such conversation in "The Truth Will Make You Free," 139–73, in Klos, Nakamura, and Martensen, *Lutherans and the Challenge of Religious Pluralism.*

76. Cf. Rajashekar, *Religious Pluralism,* 181, on how dialogue is "deeply rooted in the nature of the Christian faith" and "is basic to the nature of being, for that is to be in relation to other humans."

77. Richard A. Schweder, *Thinking Through Cultures: Expeditions in Cultural Psychology* (Cambridge: Harvard University Press, 1991), 2. I have this reference from Curtis Thompson.

78. See the Pannenberg reference cited in note 34 above. It matters *how* such a hopeful claim for the future is presented. Thus Carl E. Braaten, who shares much of Pannenberg's eschatological emphasis, writes significantly in "The Problem of the Absoluteness of Christianity," 341–53: "The claim to absoluteness is more like a mission project to be worked out in the tension-field of history than a dogmatic postulate floating in the abstract" (p. 353). Elsewhere (Rajashekar, *Religious Pluralism,* 124–25), Braaten has spoken of "the final coming of the kingdom, which will embrace universal historical forms beyond the separation between the church and the world and beyond the separation between Christianity and the religions."

79. See pp. 135–145 above.

80. As a style fitting such a faith one might consider the sort of approach suggested by Theodor W. Adorno, as characterized by Wayne W. Floyd, *Theology and the Dialectics of Otherness: On Reading Bonhoeffer and Adorno* (Lanham, Md.: University Press of America, 1988), 284: "The style of Adorno drove particulars like wedges into the unintentional fissures of idealist totality. It hoped to disintegrate the monolithic presumptions of identity for the sake of the forgotten particular. . . . 'The result,' however, 'was not a relativistic chaos of unrelated factors, but a dialectical model of negations that simultaneously constructed and deconstructed patterns of fluid reality.' "

81. See Francis Schüssler Fiorenza, *Foundational Theology,* 307–11, for a discussion of "retroductive warrants" (Charles Pierce) in which an argument is accepted because "the hypothesis generates illuminative inferences," as well as the role of "background theories" about such matters as "human nature and human society."

82. The priority of "goals" over "positions" is well articulated in the practical wisdom of human negotiation as expressed in the writings of Roger Fisher. See Roger Fisher, *Getting to Yes: Negotiating Agreement Without Giving In,* with William Ury (New York: Penguin Books, 1981); and idem, *Getting Together: Building a Relationship That Gets to Yes,* with Scott Brown (Boston: Houghton Mifflin, 1988). Cf. the discussion of "Faith's Direction" on pp. 114–117 above.

INDEX

Aardahl, Wesley, 179 n.16
Abe, Masao, 214 n.72
Acosmic, 39, 192 n.45
Adler, Mortimer, 90, 211
    n.43
Adorno, Theodor, 237 n.80
Alcoholics Anonymous, 16
Allen, Charles W., 229 n.6
Althaus, Paul, 219 n.4, 230
    n.10
Altman, Walter, 116, 220
    n.9
Altruism, 42
Anderson, Bernard W., 221
    n.18
Animal rights, 39, 43–44,
    192 n.47
Anselm, 107 n.21
Anthropic principle, 31, 80
Appel, Karl-Otto, 183 n.49
Aquinas, Thomas, 231 n.17
Arendt, Hannah, 67–68, 72,
    202 n.58, 205 nn.75, 76
Arrow of irreversibility, 27–
    38, 40, 174, 186 n.3
Art, 2, 7–8, 11, 43
Asymmetry, 33
Augsburger, David, 161,
    204 n.67, 233 n.39
Augustine, 164, 234 n.48

Bacon, Francis, 18
Bailey, Derrick S., 195 n.73
Baldwin, James, 205 n.81
Baltazar, Eulalio, 139–42,
    159, 227 nn.93, 94
Barbour, Ian, 27, 30, 33,
    80–81, 187 n.5, 188
    nn.15, 20; 189 n.25, 190
    n.32, 193 nn.57, 59; 206
    nn.11, 14, 15; 207 n.16,
    217 n.98, 236 n.70
Barmen Declaration, 223
    n.43
Baar Document, 151, 154,
    157, 229–30 n.8, 231

nn.18, 21; 232 n.29, 233
    n.30
Barth, Karl, 85–86, 90, 209
    nn.29, 30; 211 n.45, 228
    n.105
Bayle, Pierre, 227 n.82
Baseball, 65
Bateson, Gregory, 199 n.35
Beardslee, Will A., 182
    n.35
Beaty, Michael D., 207 n.18
Behavior, 41, 61, 193 n.54
    See also Nature, vs.
    nurture
Behaviorist psychology, 43
Bekker, Gary J., 236 n.72
Bellah, Robert, 14, 183
    n.48
Benjamin, Jessica, 198 n.24
Benne, Robert, 220 n.9
Benson, Peter, 219 n.3
Berdyaev, Nicolai, 90
Berger, Peter, 186 n.2, 234
    n.47
Berger, Brigette, 186 n.2
Berkouwer, G. C., 198 n.30
Bernstein, Jeremy, 178 n.9
Bernstein, Richard, 172, 181
    n.30, 235 n.61, 236 n.70
Berry, Thomas, 192 n.45
Berry, Wanda W., 204 n.67
Berryman, John, 135, 140,
    227 n.79
Bertram, Robert W., 221
    n.15
Bettenhausen, Elizabeth,
    122, 223 nn.33, 35
Beyerlin, Walter, 206 n.9
Bible
    Genesis, 46–47
    1:2—156
    1:22, 28-30—37
    1:27—53, 63
    1:31—63
    2—37

2:7—37
2:9—37
2:18—63
2:23a—63
3:19—37
5—60
5:1-3—60
9:9-10—37
18—94
Exodus
    3:14—84
    19:9a—206 n.5
    20:3—83
    22:1—17
    23:9—17, 120
    33—196 n.4
Leviticus
    19:4-10—94
Numbers
    23:19—94
Deuteronomy
    4:32ff—83
    4:35—83
    7:7-8a—84
    14:28-29—17
    24:19-22—17
    26:10-13—17
1 Sam. 15:29—94
Job 38:4-7—79
Psalms
    10:14—63
    30:10—63
    33:11—84
    42:1—164
    54:4—63
    69:9—162
    90:1-2—83
    115:3-7—88
    135—88
    139:7-13—101
    139:13—102
Proverbs 31:8—133
Ecclesiastes
    4:9-12—169

Isaiah
  6:5—84
  28—137
  55:8—76
  65:17a—138
Jeremiah
  10:4-5—148
  22:16—164
  23:23-24—101
Hosea
  1:8-9—94
Amos
  9:7—164
Matthew
  22:39—71
  25—17, 120, 131
  25:21—137
  25:31ff—164
Mark
  9:24—162
  13:20—46
  14:16—86
Luke
  4:25-27—17
  10:35-37—117
  12:48—159
  14:16-24—17
  15:7—105
  16—139
  16:31—145
John
  4:23—141
  12:32—144
Romans
  1-2—157
  1:19-23—102
  5:8, 9—95
  8:18—32, 98
  8:22—117
  8:32—85
  8:39—85, 100
  8:33-35a—116
  11:36—39
  13—221 n.18
  13:10—32
1 Corinthians
  3:11—142
  3:13-15—141-42
  13—152-53
  13:12—137
  15:28—137
  15:49—48
  15:54—137

2 Corinthians
  3:8—144
  4:6—54, 117
  4:7—22, 81, 152
Galatians
  6:7—138
Ephesians
  4:24—113
Philippians
  2—130, 210 n.40
  2:12b-13—128
Colossians
  1—95
  2:10—113
1 Timothy
  2:4—17—151
2 Timothy
  2:13—84
1 Peter
  3:15—163, 168, 174
1 John 4
  4:1—18
  4:19—131
Revelation
  7:17—137
Big Bang, 30, 79-80, 206 n.12
Birch, Charles, 212 n.49
Birch, Bruce, 191 n.35
Blank, Josef, 209 n.34
Bloch, Ernst, 224 n.54
Body, 40-46, 54, 60, 131, 193 n.50, 195 n.82
Body/mind,
  problem, 40-46
  and religion, 42
Bonhoeffer, Dietrich, 16-17, 20, 85, 184 n.51, 185 n.62, 201 n.52, 209 n.30, 218 n.100, 224 n.45
Bonino, Jose M., 219 n.4
Bottomley, Frank, 46, 194 n.72, 195 n.74
Bouchard, Tom, 41
Boundary, 2-3, 21-23, 35, 41-46, 59, 76-79, 90-91, 101-2
  and being, 111-112
  malleable, permeable, 3, 64-65
  internal/external, 202 n.57
  See also Self, self/world distinction

Braaten, Carl, 105-6, 154, 183 n.59, 195 n.81, 207 n.18, 208 n.22, 213 n.60, 215 n.73, 217 nn.90, 92; 221 n.15, 231 n.20, 232 n.29, 237 n.78
Bright, John, 208 n.24
Brock, Rita Nakashima, 97, 126, 193 n.50, 194 n.69, 213 n.65, 214 n.68, 224 n.48, 224 n.48, 226 n.72
Brown, Delwin, 223 n.40
Brown, Peter, 195 n.73
Brown, Scott, 237 n.82
Buber, Martin, 57, 197 nn.15, 16
Burtness, James, 209 n.30
Cage, John, 7, 180 n.17
Cahoone, Lawrence, 11-12, 181 nn.32, 35; 182 n.36, 183 n.45, 202 n.54, 203 n.62
Caldecott, Leonie, 195 n.82
Calvin, John, 47, 184 n.54
Campbell, Joseph, 4, 178 n.7
Canberra (WCC), 114, 120, 151-2, 155, 157, 169, 222 n.22, 230 n.9, 232 n.24, 233 n.31, 233 n.40, 235 n.58
Capra, Fritjof, 9, 180 n.27, 188 n.19,
Carr, Anne, 114, 196 n.12, 220 n.6
Cassirer, Ernst, 179 n.12
Categorical difference, 75-94, 81-94, 115-16, 117, 152, 209 n.28, 217 n.98
Chaos, 29, 169, 187 n.13, 211 n.43
  theory, 29-30, 187 n.13
Chekov, Anton, 19
Chittister, Joan, 226 n.72
Chidester, David, 232 n.28
Christ. *See* Jesus Christ
Christ, Carol, 204 n.67
Chopp, Rebecca, 128, 169, 184 n.52, 225 n.59, 234 n.44, 235 nn.55, 56
Clayton, Philip, 215 n.73
Cobb, John, 114, 149, 167, 172-3, 182 n.35, 190

n.32, 194 n.63, 200–1
n.45, 212 n.49, 213 n.60,
218 n.99, 220 n.6, 229
n.5, 234 n.53, 235 n.60,
236 n.71
Cohen, Arthur, 92, 205
n.80, 212 n.51
Cohen, Morris, 162, 233
n.40
Collingwood, 185 n.56
Comings, David, 193 n.51
Community, 68–69, 114,
122–23, 129–30, 132,
134–137, 196 n.8, 196
n.8, 225 n.63, 226 n.77
Christa, 98
eschatalogical, 203 n.60
of believers, 114
of Christ, 192 n.46
Communicatio idiomata, 213
n.60, 217 n.89
Connection, 31, 33, 35, 37,
40, 45, 47, 51, 55, 87,
98, 111, 119, 121, 129,
148, 159–165
Conversation, 28–29, 149,
154–59
Cooke, Bernard, 85, 208
n.26
Covenant, 37, 84, 151, 157,
219 n.5
Covenoy, Peter, 186 n.3,
187 nn.4, 12
Cox, Harvey, 184 n.52
Creation, 19–21, 28, 29,
37, 53, 63, 79–81, 191
n.43, 221 nn.16, 18
abiding, 20
as opus proprium, 29, 91,
187 n.10
good not perfect, 63–64,
95
ground of moral claim,
71–72
orders of, 66, 201 n.52,
221 n.18
otherness there, 79–81
out of nothing, 80, 90,
177 n.2
spirituality, 188 n.17
Creator. See God, as creator
Creel, Richard, 85–86, 209
n.31, 217 n.95

Csikszentimihalyi, Mihalyi,
44, 48, 65, 192–93 n.49,
194 n.66, 195 n.83, 200
n.43, 222 n.26
Culture, 62, 71
Cupitt, Don, 216 n.83
Curitiba (LWF), 148, 154,
220 n.11, 229 n.2, 231
n.19, 232 n.29

Darwin, Charles, 14–15
Davaney, Sheila, 86–87,
209 n.33
Davidson, Donald, 236 n.70
Davis, Madeleine, 198
nn.23, 24; 199 n.32
Davis, Stephen T., 218
n.102
Dean, William, 13, 182
n.38
Death, 135–36, 183 n.49,
220 n.6
D'Costa, Gavin, 229 n.5,
231 n.20, 233 n.35
de Beauvoir, Simone, 5, 12,
182 n.37
Deconstruction, 11, 182
n.35
DeFries, John C., 193
nn.52, 56
DeMott, Benjamin, 203 n.62
Denbigh, Kenneth, 43
Derrida, Jacques, 11, 182
n.39, 225 n.63
Descartes, Rene, 6, 9, 10,
11, 47, 179 nn.13, 14;
225 n.63, 228–29 n.1
Difference, 30, 33, 35, 45,
51, 55–56, 62, 65, 77,
87, 98, 119, 129, 148–
153, 222 n.27
degree/kind, 36, 43, 73,
77–84
difference principle, 124
See also Categorical
difference
Dillenberger, John, 219 n.4
Dillistone, Frederick W.,
128, 214 n.68, 225 n.60
Disorder. See Order and
disorder
Distinction,
subject/object, 35, 67
See also Difference

Dominance, 2, 195 n.82
white male, 48
of social system, 121
Domination, 7, 29, 37–38,
124, 130, 134, 200 n.39,
226 n.72, 232 n.26
Dominion, 38, 200 n.39
Douglas, Mary, 67, 202
n.57, 235 n.55
Dostoevsky, Fyodor, 12, 19
Downward causation, 44–
45, 58
Dualism, 45–46
See also Body/mind
Duchrow, Ulrich, 221 n.18
Dunne, John, 236 n.66
Durkheim, Emil, 69
Eaves, Lindon, 41, 48, 195
n.84
Eck, Diana, 230 n.8
Ecofeminism, 192 n.48, 195
n.82
Ecology, 37–40
See also Nature,
destruction of
Edmundson, Mark, 11, 181
n.33
Efram, Jay, 182 n.41
Einstein, Albert, 14, 27, 77,
187 n.5
Eiseley, Loren, 18, 26, 33,
34, 37, 81, 185 n.57, 186
n.1, 189 n.24, 207 n.17
Eklin, Carolyn H., 219 n.3
Eliade, Mircea, 133, 185
n.63
Eliot, T. S., 59
Enlightenment, 6–12, 147,
172
See also Modernity
Entropy, 29, 36, 72, 80
Erickson, Brian, 235 n.62
Erikson, Erik, 61, 202–3
n.59
Eschatology, 11–14, 138,
140–43
Ethics, 12, 51-52, 68–69,
135–39, 183 n.49, 226
n.77, 231 n.17
Eternity, 77, 140–142
Evans, Donald, 188 n.18
Evil, 20, 36, 56, 69, 92–3,
109, 126, 205 n.80, 212
n.52

and finitude, 140
and sin, 63–64, 135–36
efficacy of, 92–93
natural, 136–37
Evolution, 30, 34–49, 66
biological, 37, 189 n.26
cultural, 37, 60–62
Exocentricity, 60–62, 200
n.39

Face, 54–55, 195 n.1
Faith, 3–5, 14–16, 28, 30–
33, 37, 75–79, 80–88,
103, 111–112, 185 n.61,
207 n.20, 219 n.3, 233
n.36, 235 n.57
and reason, 39, 80–82,
132
and salvation, 143, 158,
228 n.105
and unfaith, 4–5, 23,
160–165, 233 n.36
in community, 129–132
in a belief, 149
justification by, 114
nature of, 111
qua and quae, 14–15
telos of, 135–45, 159
witness of, 37, 76
See also Justification—
Sanctification
Falk, Richard, 8–9, 180
n.26, 183 n.49
Farley, Edward, 52, 56, 64,
67, 124, 185 n.66, 195
nn.1, 2; 196 n.11, 197
n.13; 200 nn.41, 44; 202
n.55, 227 n.86
Feminist thought, 4, 37, 70,
86–87, 97–98, 123, 128,
141
Fevold, Eugene, 221 n.15
Feyerabend, Paul, 10
Fiddes, Paul, 90, 144, 210
n.40, 211 nn.41, 42; 211
n.45, 228 n.109
Finitude, 56, 124, 153
Fiorenza, Francis Schüssler,
169, 235 n.54, 237 n.81
Fisher, Roger, 237 n.82
Floyd, Wayne W., 237 n.80
Forde, Gerhard, 220 n.6,
223 n.37

Forgiveness, 72–74, 96–97,
116, 128, 138
Foucault, Michael, 13, 121,
133, 182 n.39, 203 n.17,
222 n.27, 225 n.63
Fox, Matthew, 188 n.17
Frank, Elizabeth, 180 n.22
Frankenberry, Nancy, 207
n.20
Freedman, R. David, 200
n.39
Freedom, 41, 43–45, 58,
68, 70, 92, 112, 117,
123–24, 136, 144–45,
153, 218 nn.102, 104
free will defense, 92,
136–37
beyond freedom, 92
and ambiguity, 145, 158–
59, 174–75
Freeman, Walter, 187 n.13
Freud, Sigmund, 11, 14
Fretheim, Terrence, 94, 206
n.9, 209 n.35, 212 n.56,
216 n.85, 218 n.100, 221
n.16
Frost, Robert, 34, 189 n.23

Gadamer, Hans, 185 n.56
Gaia, 39–40, 192 n.48
Gallagher, William, 201
n.51
Gammie, John G., 206 n.5
Gauguin, Paulvico, 8
Gay, Peter, 179 n.12
Gay, Volney, 203 n.63
Geach, Peter, 197 n.19
Geertz, Clifford, 216 n.80
Gehlen, Arnold, 183 n.49
Gender, 2, 55–56, 196 n.12
Genes, 40–42, 49
Gerhard, John, 217 n.89
Gerrish, Brian, 184 n.54,
216 n.82
Gilkey, Langdon, 93–94,
180 n.24, 211 n.43, 212
nn.53, 54; 228 n.105, 229
nn.4, 6; 230 n.15
Gilligan, Carol, 202 n.58
Gleick, James, 187 n.13
God
action of, 93, 104–5, 217
n.99, 218 n.101

and world, 16–17, 20–21,
38, 211 n.43, 213 n.60,
215 n.74, 221– 22 n.20
as creator, 20–21, 28–30,
37, 47, 63, 72, 79, 82,
89–90, 104–5, 117–18,
123
aseity of, 83, 208 n.23
as first, 75
as object, 82
as Wholly Other, 209
n.29
attributes of, 77
commitment to humanity,
88–89, 213 n.63
doctrine of, 38
firstness, 88–93
for us, 87–100
forgiveness of, 73, 95–
97, 138
freedom of, 85, 87–93,
177 n.2, 207 n.23, 211
n.45
hiddenness of, 81, 184
n.54, 216 nn.81, 82
in relation, 91, 93–100,
103, 218 n.101
justice of, 184 n.54
knowledge of, 184 n.54;
214 n.71
love of, 90–92, 107, 110,
127, 151–52, 177 n.2
models of, 214 n.71
personal, 209–10 n.24
presence of, 102–3
proofs for, 81–82, 207
nn.18, 20, 21
repentance of, 94, 212
n.56
self-limitation of, 210
n.40
suffering of, 105–7, 211
n.48, 216 n.85, 217
n.89, 218 n.100
transcendence of, 39, 77,
88, 104, 113, 142,
152–53, 208 n.22
Trinity, viii, 47, 89, 90,
98, 177 n.2, 192 n.44,
217 n.89
will of, 83–96, 100, 103,
106, 114, 115–19, 121,
123, 136, 152, 208
n.25

unity of, 17, 115–17
work of, in Jesus Christ,
95–97, 113, 115–17,
128, 157–58, 220 n.11
See also Categorical
difference, Holy Spirit,
Image of God, Jesus
Christ
Gödel, Kurt, 139
Goldberger, Arnold, 187
n.13
Gould, Stephen Jay, 189
n.26
Griffin, David R., 182 n.35,
186 n.3, 188 n.19, 190
n.32, 193 nn. 50, 57; 197
n.17, 215 n.74, 228 n.100
Gros, Jeffrey, 232 n.29
Gunn, Giles, 185 n.56, 189
n.23, 216 n.80, 223 n.36
Gustafson, James, 81, 127,
194 n.63, 207 n.19, 209
n.34, 212 n.50, 220 n.6,
224 n.56
Guthrie, Shirley C., 130,
225 n.65
Gutierrez, Gustavo, 222
n.21

Habermas, Jurgen, 8, 180
n.25, 197 n.14
Haggmark, Steven, 220 n.6
Hall, Douglas John, 13, 38,
47–48, 106, 133, 181
n.31, 183 n.44, 189 n.25,
191 n.40, 195 nn.79, 80;
199 n.38, 217 n.90, 223
n.29, 225 n.58, 226 n.75
Halvorson, Neal, viii
Hammer, Margaret, 198
n.30
Harding, Sandra, 190 n.28,
236 n.73
Harmon, Willis, 42, 193
n.58
Harris, Errol, 189 n.27
Harrison, Beverly W., 222
n.21, 226 n.68, 236 n.73
Hartshorne, Charles, 77–78,
86, 201 n.51, 205 n.2,
207 n.21
Hasker, William, 208 n.25,
218 n.102
Hauerwas, Stanley, 225 n.63

Hawking, Stephen, 186 n.3
Hefner, Philip, 34, 47, 189
n.24, 193 n.59, 195 n.78,
208 n.22
Hegel, G. W. F., 7, 58, 180
n.19, 198 n.22
Heim, Mark S., 173, 236
n.72
Herder, Johann G., 185 n.56
Heschel, Abraham, 213 n.63
Hesse, Mary, 10, 181 n.30
Heidegger, Martin, 11, 196
n.11, 198 n.22
Herder, J. G., 185 n.56
Hermission, H. J., 221 n.18
Hick, John, 216 n.82, 223
n.42, 229 n.4, 231 n.17,
232 n.23, 233 n.33
Highfield, Roger, 186 n.3,
187 nn.4, 12
Hillerman, Tony, 177 n.2
Hillman, James, 65, 201
n.47
Hodgson, Peter, 10, 88, 98,
123, 138, 181 n.31, 210
n.36, 214 n.69, 217 n.98,
221 n.15, 223 n.38, 227
nn.87, 96
Hoeferkamp, Robert, 120,
223 n.29
Hoffman, Lynn, 182 n.41
Hofstadter, Douglas R., 190
n.29
Holland, Joe, 182 n.35
Holy Spirit, 98, 114, 143–5,
155–56, 214 n.67, 221
n.13
Hospitality, 17
Hoyle, Fred, 188 n.20
Hubbard, Ruth, 197 n.14
Hultgren, Arland, 95, 99,
142, 212 n.57, 213 n.66,
214 n.70, 228 n.105
Human,
as subject, 64
being 42, 117
and becoming, 63–64,
113, 117
complexity, 43
created in image of God.
See Image of God
destiny, 39, 48
development, 59–61, 71,
202–3 n.59

dignity, 212 n.59
distinctivenesss of, 43,
46–47
freedom, *See* Freedom
identity, 39, 60, 66–68,
119, 141
mentality, 44
nature, 43
responsibility of. *See*
Responsibility
spirit, 44–46
unity of, 45
well-being, 44
work, 117–18
See also Self
Hume, David, 6, 9, 43, 179
n.15
Husserl, Edmund, 196 n.11,
201 n.48
Huxley, Julian, 189 n.21

Ignatow, David, 21, 185
n.64
Image of God, 39, 46–49,
53, 54, 60, 63, 113, 195
n.79, 196 n.8
Jesus as, 210 n.35
Individuation, 45, 59, 122,
204 n.67
See also Self
Irreversibility, 27, 32, 124,
186 n.3
See also Arrow of
irreversibility
Irigaray, Luce, 125
Is/ought, 67, 122, 160

Jacoby, Russell, 183 n.46
James, William, 201 n.46,
234 n.50
Jauss, Hans R., 185 n.56
Jenson, Robert, 89, 183
n.50, 195 n.81, 207 n.18,
208 n.22, 210 n.39, 211
n.44, 213 n.60, 217
nn.90, 92
Jesus Christ, 17, 93, 95–98,
116, 157, 219 n.4,
and nature, 191 n.43
as stranger, 17
communication of
attributes, 213 n.60,
217 n.89
forgiveness of sin, 96–98,
116, 128

person of, 93–96, 213
n.60
resurrection of, 144, 205
n.79
today, 20
work of, 17, 20, 46, 93,
95, 214 n.66, 220 n.6
See also God, work of, in
Jesus Christ
Jodock, Darrell, 156, 232
n.28
Johnson, Elizabeth, vi, 177
n.2
Jonas, Hans, 183 n.49
Jones, Jim, 156
Joyce, James, 11
Julian, Lady, of Norwich,
90
Jüngel, Eberhard, 71, 87,
89, 91, 124, 127, 204
n.72, 209 nn.27, 34; 210
nn.37, 38; 211 n.46, 215
n.79, 219 n.4, 221–22
n.20, 223 n.39, 224 n.54
Justification, 87, 95, 113,
116, 122–23, 142–43,
219 n.4, 220 n.6, 221
n.15

Kant, Immanuel, 47, 194
n.67, 225 n.63
Kasper, Walter, 177 n.2
Kaufman, Stuart, 193 n.57
Kaufmann, Walter, 233
nn.36, 40; 234 n.50
Keeney, Bradford, 199 n.35
Keifert, Patrick, vii, 177
n.4, 184 n.53
Keillor, Garrison, 65, 200
n.42
Keller, Catherine, 65, 198
n.24, 200 n.45, 201 n.46
Kellner, Hansfried, 186 n.2
Kierkegaard, Søren, 28, 42,
45, 58, 73, 85, 89, 96–
97, 100, 102, 104, 117,
136, 144, 157, 162, 187
n.7, 194 n.69, 197 nn.18,
20; 198 n.22, 204 n.67,
205 n.77, 209 n.28, 213
nn. 60, 61, 64; 215 n.79,
216 nn.81, 85
King, Robert, 215 n.73
King, Ynestra, 195 n.82

Kishii, Satori, 231 n.21
Klein, Ann, 201 n.46
Klos, Frank W., 229 n.3
Kluckhohn, Clyde, 200 n.40
Knitter, Paul F., 155, 223
n.42, 229 n.4, 230 n.10,
231 n.17, 232 nn.23, 25;
233 nn.32, 33
Knutsen, Mary, 200 n.39
Kohlberg, Lawrence, 202
n.58
Kohn, Alfie, 126, 193 n.55,
224 nn.49, 50
Kohut, Heinz, 69, 126, 203
n.62, 63
Kolb, David, 59, 198 n.22
Kristeva, Julia, 70, 204
n.66, 226 n.77
Kuhn, Thomas, 10, 172,
236 n.69
Kundera, Milan, 13, 183
n.42
Küng, Hans, 180–81 n.28,
181 n.31, 209 n.34, 210
n.37, 225 n.58, 231 n.16
Kyung, Chung Hyung, 231
n.21, 232 n.26

Lacan, Jacques, 66, 133,
201 n.48
LaCugna, Catherine M., vi,
177 n.2
Lakeland, Paul, 186 n.69
Lakotos, Imre, 9
Language, 11, 37, 56–57,
62, 71, 172–73
inadequacy of, 78–79
Leibnitz, G. W., 7
Leland, Stephanie, 195 n.82
Levenson, Jon, 211 n.43
Levinas, Emmanuel, 18,
52–54, 69, 70, 184–85
n.55, 195 n.1, 196 nn.3–
6, 8; 197 n.16, 203 n.61
Lewis, C. S., 78, 206 n.7
Liberation, 87, 114, 118
liberation theology, 118,
170, 184 n.52
Likeness of God. *See* Image
of God
Limburg, James, 191 n.37
Liminality, 125–26, 132,
216 n.80
Little, David, 200 n.40

Lochhead, David, 171, 173,
235 n.64
Locke, John, 11, 47
Lofgren, David, 220 n.11
Logos, 46, 98
Lonergan, Bernard, 192
n.44
Loomer, Bernard, 215 n.74,
218 n.99, 226 n.73
Lorenz, Konrad, 183 n.49
Lorenzen, Paul, 202 n.59
Love, 71, 90, 121–22, 124,
126, 131
respect for otherness, 91–
92
selflessness/self–
relatedness, 131
Lovelock, James, 192 n.48
Lowe, Mary, viii
Ludwig, Theodore, 230 n.15
Lukens, Michael D., 182
n.41
Luther, Martin, 47, 106,
114, 184 n.54, 191 n.43,
215 n.79, 216 n.82, 219
n.4, 220 nn.6, 11—221
n.20, 223 n.39, 224 n.55
Lutheran World Federation.
See Curitiba
Lykken, David, 41

MacIntyre, Alasdair, 14,
173, 183 n.47, 236 nn.66,
74
Maclaine, Shirley, 85, 209
n.32
Malcolm, Norman, 234 n.47
Malinowski, Bronislaw, 233
n.39
Mapplethorp, Robert, 178
n.4
Marcel, Gabriel, 64, 67
Martensen, Daniel, 229 n.3
Martinson, Paul Varo, 149,
171, 188 n.19, 214 n.72,
229 n.3, 230 n.10, 236
n.67
Marturana, Humberto, 182
n.41
Marx, Karl, 11, 14
McCann, Dennis P., 220 n.9
McDaniel, Jay B., 223 n.42,
226 n.72

McFague, Sallie, 203 n.59, 214 n.71
McKibben, Bill, 180 n.28, 190–91 n.33
McMullin, Ernest, 80, 206 n.13
May, Rollo, 226 n.72
Mead, G. H., 62
Melanchthon, Philip, 220 n. 6
Merchant, Carolyn, 195 n.82
Merleau–Ponty, Maurice, 201 n.48
Mesle, Robert, 216 n.82
Mickelson, Kirsten, 205 n.78
Milbank, John, 169, 235 n.59
Mildenberger, Freidrich, 98, 213 n.66
Miles, Margaret, 5, 178 n.10, 195 n.82, 196 n.12, 197 n.14, 200 n.39, 202 n.57
Modernity, 56, 179 n.12, 181 n.30, 228–29 n.1
  post-modernity, 10, 12, 186 n.69
  self/world, subject/object, 6, 8, 9, 10, 181 n.30
Moi, Toril, 169, 235 n.56
Moltmann, Jürgen, 35, 47, 54, 77, 106, 113, 180–81 n.28, 186 n.67, 190 n.28, 191 nn.36, 43; 195 n.76, 196 nn.8, 9; 200 nn.39, 44; 205 n.1, 207 n.18, 209 n.27, 210 n.40, 217 n.95, 219 nn. 1, 2; 221 n.13, 225 n.62, 228 nn.106, 107; 235 n.57
Monet, Claud, 194 n.60, 198 n.24
Montaigne, Michel, 229 n.1
Moore, G. E., 202 n.53
Moore, Thomas, 201 n.47
Morgan, Robin, 204 n.67
Mother, 59–60
Muhlenberg, Ekehard, 221 n.15
Murray, Michael, 180 n.20

Nakamura, C. Lynn, 229 n.3

Narcissism, 69–71, 222 n.28
Nature, 26, 33–40, 190–91 n.33, 191 n.43
  destruction of, 36–38
  vs. nurture, 40
Neighbor, 70–71, 102, 119, 121–22
Nelson, E. Clifford, 221 n.15
Nelson, James B., 194 n.72
Neville, Robert, 201 n.51, 207 n.21, 211 n.43, 215 n.74
New Age, 3
Newbigin, Lesslie, 152, 230 n.11, 234 n.51
Newton, Isaac, 7, 9
Niebuhr, H. Richard, 91–92, 100, 212 n.50
Nielsen, Kai, 182 n.37
Nietzsche, Friedrich, 19
Nobel Conference 1989, 9, 180 n.28
Nygren, Anders, 217 n.87

Oakley, Francis, 191 n.42
O'Barr, Jean, 190 n.28
Object relations, 59, 199 n.32
O'Connor, Daniel, 191 n.42
Ogden, Schubert, 233 n.36
Ogletree, Thomas, 19, 70–71, 184 n.53, 185 n.60, 203 n.60, 204 n.69, 204–5 n.72, 227 n.88
Order and disorder, 29–30, 33, 36
  See also Chaos
Otto, Rudolph, 77, 206 n.5
Outka, Gene, 70, 200 n.40, 204 n.68
Owen, H. P., 208 n.23, 217 nn.88, 94

Page, Ruth, 101–2, 104, 215 nn.76, 77, 216 n.82, 217 n.99
Pailin, David, 217 n.99
Palmer, Parker, 120, 222 nn.23, 28
Panentheism, 143
Pannenberg, Wolfhart, 61, 140, 158, 199 nn.31–35,

37; 200 n.39, 201 n.52, 203 n.64, 215 nn.73, 79; 227 n.85, 228 n.104, 230 n.14, 231 n.20, 233 nn.34, 35; 237 n.78
Pantheism, 86, 143
Parsons, Kieth, 207 n.20
Pascal, Blaise, 234 n.49
Patripassionism, 105, 217 n.89
Peacocke, Arthur, 35, 36, 189 n.26, 190 nn.30–33; 206 n.13
Peck, M. Scott, 205 n.80
Peters, Ted, vi, 30, 177 n.3, 178 n.6, 188 n.16, 206 nn.10, 11, 13, 14, 15
Peukert, Helmut, 35, 68, 73, 135, 190 n.29, 202 n.59, 205 n.79, 227 n.80
Pierce, Charles, 237 n.81
Placher, William, 22, 181 n.30, 186 n.68
Plantinga, Alvin, 207 n.20
Plaskow, Judith, 204 n.67
Plato, 44, 106,
Plomin, Robert, 193 nn.52, 56
Pluralism, 15, 17, 152–157, 184 n.52
  internal/external, 153
Polk, David, 215 n.73
Polkinghorne, John, 188 n.16, 190 n.29
Pollock, Jackson, 8
Popper, Karl, 9
Porteous, Norman W., 194 n.71
Postmodern. *See* Modernity
Prayer, 127–28
Prestige, G. L., 106, 217 n.93
Prigogine, Ilya, 27, 30, 187 n.4
Providence, 93–94, 102, 109
Putnam, Hilary, 236 n.71

Rabi, Isaac I., 4, 178 n.9
Rabinow, Paul, 125, 224 n.51
Rahner, Karl, 211 n.44, 233 n.36

Rajashekar, Paul, 231 n.21, 232 n.29, 235 n.65, 237 nn.76, 78
Ramsey, Paul, 200 n.40
Rasmussen, Larry, 130, 191 n.35, 225 n.66
Rasolondraibe, Peri, 191–92 n.44
Rawls, John, 122
Reality, 11, 13, 14, 19, 30, 52, 55–56, 57, 141, 218 n.104, 237 n.80
  Enlightenment sense of, 147,
  experienced, 199 n.32
  human, 64
  of Jesus, 116
  of other faiths, 149
  of otherness, 112, 119
  self and, 68, 203 n.62
  ultimate, 42
Reason, 12, 47, 181–2 n.35
  as public, 132
  formal criteria, 155
Redemption, 20, 95, 117, 121, 212 n.59, 213 n.66
Reese, William L., 205 n.2
Relativity, 27–29
Religions, 3, 67, 148–159, 167–68, 216 n.80, 229 n.4, 231 n.17, 232 n.23, 234 n.53, 237 n.78
  Buddhism, 149, 153–155, 170–72, 229 n.5, 230–31 n.15
  Hindu, 3–4, 155, 160–61
  Islam, 3, 149, 153, 230 n.12
  Judaism, 4, 171
Responsibility, 12, 37, 38, 52, 67, 104, 116–19, 121–22, 145,
  ethical, 12, 52ff, 183 n.49, 222 n.21
  in telos, 142, 145, 158–59, 228 n.105
  to creation, 191 n.37
  See also Ethics
Resurrection, 140, 144
  See also Jesus Christ, resurrection of
Revelation, 102, 149, 152–53, 157, 216 n.82, 230

n.14, 230–31 n.15, 233 n.37
Richards, Caroline, 192 n.44
Richardson, Herbert, 95, 98, 162, 212 n.58, 213 n.60, 214 n.67, 234 n.43
Ricoeur, Paul, 138, 201 n.49, 205 n.80, 212 n.52, 227 n.88
Ritschl, Dietrich, 214 n.67
Roehlkepartain, Eugene C., 219 n.3
Rorty, Richard, 182 n.40, Robb, Carol S., 222 n.21
Rosenstock-Huessy, Eugen, 197 n.15
Rosenzweig, Franz, 197 n.15
Ross, Jeffrey M., 199 n.35
Ruether, Rosemary R., 192 n.48, 196 n.12, 227 n.96
Rupp, George, 128, 214 n.68, 225 n.61
Rushdie, Salman, 1, 23, 177 n.1, 186 n.70
Russell, Peter, 192 n.48
Russell, Robert J., 27, 80, 186 n.3, 188 n.20, 206 nn.10, 13

Sacks, Oliver, 42, 44, 58, 194 nn.60, 68
Samartha, Stanley, 233 n.33
Salvation, 17, 28, 29, 39, 116, 128, 143, 220 n.10, 232 n.29
  universal, 143, 232 n.29
  as criterion, 155–59
Sanctification, 113, 135, 214 n.67, 219 n.4
Sandel, Michael, 122, 134, 223 nn.32, 34, 41; 226 n.77, 227 n.78
Sanneh, Lamin, 230 n.12
Santmire, H. Paul, 37, 38, 191 nn.34, 41
Sartre, Jean-Paul, 201 n.48
Saunders, Will, 206 n.12
Saiving, Valerie, 204 n.67
Schell, Jonathan, 124, 203 n.59, 223–24 n.44
Schleiermacher, Friedrich, 220 n.6

Schmid, Heinrich, 198 n.30, 205 n.4, 212 n.55, 217 n.89
Schoenberg, Arnold, 7, 179 n.16
Schooneberg, Piet, 177 n.2
Schuon, Fritjof, 229 n.4
Schweder, Richard, 174, 237 n.77
Science, 9, 10, 30, 42, 182 n.41, 190 n.28
  and creation, 39
  end of, 9
  and scientism, 132
  See also Evolution
Segundo, Juan Luis, 205 n.74, 235 n.62
Self, 15, 29, 35–37, 44–45, 47, 64–65, 121–22, 124, 138, 141, 225 n.63, 226 n.72
  and mind, 47
  and other, 55–57, 64–65, 67–74, 203 n.62, 203 n.64
  and world, 29, 35
  consciousness, 43, 70
  development of, 59–60, 69, 204 n.70
  identity of. *See* Human, identity of
  intersubjective and intrasubjective, 134, 226 n.77
  myth of, 65
  sacrifice, 70–71
  unity of, 12
Self-psychology movement, 69–71
Sexuality, 46, 125, 200 n.50
Shaw, George Bernard, 116
Shaw, Marvin, 215 n.74
Sherburne, Donald, 193 n.50, 207 n.16,
Simon, Richard, 182 n.41
Simpson, Gary, 201 n.52, 205 n.79
Sin, 37, 63–64, 68, 70, 73, 92, 93, 95–99, 113–14, 116, 118, 123, 134–5, 153–4, 159, 185 n.185
  original sin, 64, 114
  as discontinuity, 96

as negation of self, 204
  n.67
and justification, 123
in religion, 154
  See also Evil
Singer, Peter, 43, 194 n.64
Smith, John, 102, 215 n.78
Smith, Steven, 70, 184
  n.55, 187 n.6, 196 nn.4–
  7, 12; 197 n.16, 203
  n.61, 204 n.65
Smith, Wilfred. C., 231
  n.22
Snook, Lee, 226 n.67
Sociobiology, 39, 41, 42,
  193 n.59
Soelle, Dorothee, 116, 132,
  162, 220 n.10, 226 n.71,
  234 n.42
Solomon, Robert, 200 n.44
Sontag, Frederich, 207 n.21
Spacetime continuum, 25,
  31–49, 114, 140, 187
  n.5, 198 n.23
  space, 57
  temporality, 31, 57–58,
    63, 140–141, 197 n.16
Sperry, Roger, 44, 45, 58,
  194 nn.67, 70
Spinoza, Benedict, 2
Spitz, Lewis, 221 n.15
Spirit, 98
  See also, Human, spirit
Sponheim, Paul, 195 n.81,
  207 n.20, 216 n.80, 227
  nn.84, 91, 99; 233 nn.33,
  41; 234 n.46
Starhawk, 4, 178 n.8
Stackhouse, Max, 160–61,
  220 n.9, 233 n.38
Stapp, Henry P., 197 n.17
Steck, Odil, 28, 38, 187
  n.8, 191 n.39
Steele, E. J., 193 n.57
Stengers, Isabelle, 187 n.4
Stevens, Wallace, 19, 185
  n.58
Strandjord, Jonathan, 186
  n.1, 225 n.57
Stranger, 17, 53, 70, 120–
  21
Stravinsky, Igor, 7, 180 n.20
Sturm, Douglas, 203 n.60

Suchocki, Marjorie, 141–42,
  159, 223 n.42, 228
  nn.100–102, 105
Suffering, 32, 105–7, 137
  See also God, suffering of
Sullivan, Lewis E., 188
  n.19
Swidler, Leonard, 236 n.75
Swift, Jonathan, 226 n.76
Swinburne, Richard, 207
  n.20

Takeda, Ryusei, 188 n.19
Taliaferro, Charles, 217 n.95
Tannenbaum, Rob, 180 n.17
Tanner, Kathryn, 216 n.84,
  217 n.97
Taylor, Daniel, 216 n.82
Taylor, Mark C., 12, 13,
  181 n.28, 182 n.37
Taylor, Mark Kline, 98,
  125, 185 nn.65, 66; 186
  n.69, 195 n.82, 196 n.12,
  214 n.68, 224 nn.46, 47,
  51, 52; 225 n.59, 232
  n.26, 236 n.72
Teilhard de Chardin, Pierre,
  139–40, 141, 207 n.18
Tellegen, Auke, 41, 193
  n.53
Telos, 135–37
  as discontinuous, 136–37
  as continuous, 137–39
  See also Faith, telos of
TeSelle, Eugene, 212 n.59
Theunissen, Michael, 196
  n.11, 197 nn.15, 16; 205
  n.73
Thermodynamics, 29–30,
  36, 43
Thomas, Lewis, 66, 201
  n.50
Thompson, Curtis, 181
  n.32, 197 n.14, 237 n.77
Tillich, Paul, 156, 217 n.96,
  232 n.27, 233 n.36
Time. *See* Spacetime
  continuum
Tipler, Frank, 140, 227 n.95
Torrance, Thomas, 139, 227
  n.92, 228 n.108
Toulmin, Stephen, 6, 10,
  11, 13, 26, 29, 179

nn.12, 14; 180 nn.18, 21;
  181 nn.29, 34; 183 n.43,
  186 n.2, 187 n.11, 206
  n.10, 226 n.76, 228 n.1,
  231 n.16
Tracy, David, 128, 133,
  180–1 n.28, 186 n.67,
  209 n.34, 210 n.37, 225
  n.58, 226 n.74, 231 n.16
Traducianism, 198–99 n.30
Trible, Phyllis, 200 n.39
Turner, Victor, 19, 55, 67,
  69, 185 n.59, 196 n.10,
  203 n.60
Twain, Mark, 19
Twins' study, 41, 45, 55,
  193 n.53
Two kingdoms doctrine,
  116, 220 n.9

Ulanov, Ann B., 224 n.57
Ulanov, Ann and Barry,
  127, 205 n.6
Unfaith, 3, 76
Ury, William, 237 n.82

van Huyssteen, Wenzel, 181
  n.30
Vico, Giambattista, 18, 185
  n.56
von Weizacker, Carl F., 189
  n.25

Wallum, Mary, viii
Ward, Keith, 90, 104, 136,
  142, 208 n.23, 210 n.40,
  211 n.47, 216 n.85, 217
  n.86, 218 nn.101, 104,
  227 n.81, 228 n.103
Wattenberg, Ben, 178 n.3
Watzlawick, Paul, 181 n.41
Welch, Sharon, 118, 221
  n.19, 223 n.36, 225 n.64,
  226 n.76, 236 n.73
Welker, Michael, 222 n.24,
  235 n.63
Wentz, Richard, 34, 55–56,
  189 n.22, 196 n.11
West, Cornel, 195 n.82
Westermann, Claus, 29, 47–
  48, 137, 187 n.9, 195
  n.77, 227 n.84
Westhelle, Vitor, 191 n.43
Wheeler, John, 26

White, Lynn, 191 n.38

Whitehead, Alfred North, 40, 65, 90, 141, 190 n.32, 193 n.50, 201 n.51, 207 n.16, 211 n.43, 216 n.81, 225 n.57, 227 nn.97, 98; 235 n.63

Wicken, Jeffrey, 30, 36, 44, 58, 187 n.14, 187 n. 14, 190 n.31, 192 n.49. 194 n.65

Wiersma, Jan, viii

Wilden, Anthony, 201 n.48

Wilken, Robert, 222 n.21, 229 n.5

Willey, Basil, 179 n.12

Williams, Daniel D., 212 n.50, 217 n.87

Williams, Rowan, 218 n.103

Wilmore, Gayraud, 178 n.11

Wilson, August, 71, 204 n.71

Wilson, Edward O., 192 n.47

Wingren, Gustaf, 29, 91, 185 n.61, 198 n.10, 201 n.52, 233 n.37

Winnicott, Donald W., 59, 125, 198 nn.23, 25, 26, 27, 28, 29; 199 nn.32, 36

Winquist, Charles, 132, 226 n.70

Wittgenstein, Ludwig, 11, 77, 205 n.3, 234 n.47

Wolff, Hans W., 227 n.85

World, 16–17, 57

Worldview, 6–17, 56–57, 161, 197 n.14

World Council of Churches. Seventh Assembly, 220 n.7
See also Canberra

Yonker, Nicholas, 180 n.27

Young, Pamela Dickey, 234 n.52

CREDITS